T0308421

YPRES

GREAT BATTLES

YPRES

MARK CONNELLY
AND
STEFAN GOEBEL

UNIVERSITY PRESS

Great Clarendon Street, Oxford, OX2 6DP,
United Kingdom

Oxford University Press is a department of the University of Oxford. It furthers the University's objective of excellence in research, scholarship, and education by publishing worldwide. Oxford is a registered trade mark of Oxford University Press in the UK and in certain other countries

First Edition published in 2018

Impression: 1

Published in the United States of America by Oxford University Press
198 Madison Avenue, New York, NY 10016, United States of America

British Library Cataloguing in Publication Data
Data available

Library of Congress Control Number: 2018944181

ISBN 978–0–19–871337–1

Printed and bound in Great Britain by
Clays Ltd, Elcograf S.p.A.

FOREWORD

For those who practise war in the twenty-first century the idea of a 'great battle' can seem no more than the echo of a remote past. The names on regimental colours or the events commemorated at mess dinners bear little relationship to patrolling in dusty villages or waging 'wars amongst the people'. Contemporary military doctrine downplays the idea of victory, arguing that wars end by negotiation not by the smashing of an enemy army or navy. Indeed it erodes the very division between war and peace, and with it the aspiration to fight a culminating 'great battle'.

And yet to take battle out of war is to redefine war, possibly to the point where some would argue that it ceases to be war. Carl von Clausewitz, who experienced two 'great battles' at first hand—Jena in 1806 and Borodino in 1812—wrote in *On War* that major battle is 'concentrated war', and 'the centre of gravity of the entire campaign'. Clausewitz's remarks related to the theory of strategy. He recognized that in practice armies might avoid battles, but even then the efficacy of their actions relied on the latent threat of fighting. Winston Churchill saw the importance of battles in different terms, not for their place within war but for their impact on historical and national narratives. His forebear, the Duke of Marlborough, commanded in four major battles and named his palace after the most famous of them, Blenheim, fought in 1704. Battles, Churchill wrote in his biography of Marlborough, are 'the principal milestones in secular history'. For him 'Great battles, won or lost, change the entire course of events, create new standards of values, new moods, new atmospheres, in armies and nations, to which all must conform'.

Clausewitz's experience of war was shaped by Napoleon. Like Marlborough, the French emperor sought to bring his enemies to battle. However, each lived within a century of the other, and they fought their wars in the same continent and even on occasion on adjacent ground. Winston Churchill's own experience of war, which spanned the late nineteenth-century colonial conflicts of the British Empire as well as two world wars, became increasingly distanced from the sorts of battle he and Clausewitz described. In 1898 Churchill rode in a cavalry charge in a battle which crushed the Madhist forces of the Sudan in a single day. Four years later the British commander at Omdurman, Lord Kitchener, brought the South African War to a conclusion after a two-year guerrilla conflict in which no climactic battle occurred. Both Churchill and Kitchener served as British Cabinet ministers in the First World War, a conflict in which battles lasted weeks, and even months, and which, despite their scale and duration, did not produce clear-cut outcomes. The 'Battle' of Verdun ran for all but one month of 1916 and that of the Somme for five months. The potentially decisive naval action at Jutland spanned a more traditional twenty-four-hour timetable but was not conclusive and was not replicated during the war. In the Second World War, the major struggle in waters adjacent to Europe, the 'Battle' of the Atlantic, was fought from 1940 to early 1944.

Clausewitz would have called these twentieth-century 'battles' campaigns, or even seen them as wars in their own right. The determination to seek battle and to venerate its effects may therefore be culturally determined, the product of time and place, rather than an inherent attribute of war. The ancient historian Victor Davis Hanson has argued that seeking battle is a 'western way of war' derived from classical Greece. Seemingly supportive of his argument are the writings of Sun Tzu, who flourished in warring states in China between two and five centuries before the birth of Christ, and who pointed out that the most effective way of waging war was to avoid the risks and dangers of actual fighting. Hanson has provoked strong criticism: those who argue that wars can be won without battles are not only to be found in Asia. Eighteenth-century European commanders, deploying armies in close-order formations in order to deliver concentrated fires, realized that the destructive consequences of battle for their own troops could be self-defeating. After the First World War, Basil Liddell Hart developed a theory of strategy which he called 'the indirect approach', and suggested that manoeuvre might substitute for hard fighting, even if its success still relied on the inherent threat of battle.

The winners of battles have been celebrated as heroes, and nations have used their triumphs to establish their founding myths. It is precisely for these reasons that their legacies have outlived their direct political consequences. Commemorated in painting, verse, and music, marked by monumental memorials, and used as the way points for the periodization of history, they have enjoyed cultural afterlives. These are evident in many capitals, in place names and statues, not least in Paris and London. The French tourist who finds himself in a London taxi travelling from Trafalgar Square to Waterloo Station should reflect on his or her own domestic peregrinations from the Rue de Rivoli to the Gare d'Austerlitz. Today's Mongolia venerates the memory of Genghis Khan while Greece and Macedonia scrap over the rights to Alexander the Great.

This series of books on 'great battles' tips its hat to both Clausewitz and Churchill. Each of its volumes situates the battle which it discusses in the context of the war in which it occurred, but each then goes on to discuss its legacy, its historical interpretation and reinterpretation, its place in national memory and commemoration, and its manifestations in art and culture. These are not easy books to write. The victors were more often celebrated than the defeated; the effect of loss on the battlefield could be cultural oblivion. However, that point is not universally true: the British have done more over time to mark their defeats at Gallipoli in 1915 and Dunkirk in 1940 than their conquerors on both occasions. For the history of war to thrive and be productive it needs to embrace the view from 'the other side of the hill', to use the Duke of Wellington's words. The battle the British call Omdurman is for the Sudanese the Battle of Kerreri; the Germans called Waterloo 'la Belle Alliance' and Jutland Skagerrak. Indeed the naming of battles could itself be a sign not only of geographical precision or imprecision (Kerreri is more accurate but as a hill rather than a town is harder to find on a small-scale map), but also of cultural choice. In 1914 the German general staff opted to name their defeat of the Russians in East Prussia not Allenstein (as geography suggested) but Tannenberg, in order to claim revenge for the defeat of the Teutonic Knights in 1410.

Military history, more than many other forms of history, is bound up with national stories. All too frequently it fails to be comparative, to recognize that war is a 'clash of wills' (to quote Clausewitz once more), and so omits to address both parties to the fight. Cultural difference and, even more, linguistic ignorance can prevent the historian considering a battle in the round; so too can the availability of sources. Levels of literacy matter here, but so does cultural survival. Often these pressures can be congruent but they can also be divergent. Britain enjoys much higher levels of literacy than Afghanistan, but in 2002 the memory of the two countries' three wars flourished in the latter, thanks to an oral tradition, much more robustly than in the former, for whom literacy had created distance. And the historian who addresses cultural legacy is likely to face a much more challenging task the further in the past the battle occurred. The opportunity for invention and reinvention is simply greater the longer the lapse of time since the key event.

All historians of war must, nonetheless, never forget that, however rich and splendid the cultural legacy of a great battle, it was won and lost by fighting, by killing and being killed. The Battle of Waterloo has left as abundant a footprint as any, but the general who harvested most of its glory reflected on it in terms which have general applicability, and carry across time in their capacity to capture a universal truth. Wellington wrote to Lady Shelley in its immediate aftermath: 'I hope to God I have fought my last battle. It is a bad thing to be always fighting. While in the thick of it I am much too occupied to feel anything; but it is wretched just after. It is quite impossible to think of glory. Both mind and feelings are exhausted. I am wretched even at the moment of victory, and I always say that, next to a battle lost, the greatest misery is a battle gained.' Readers of this series should never forget the immediate suffering caused by battle, as well as the courage required to engage in it: the physical courage of the soldier, sailor, or warrior, and the moral courage of the commander, ready to hazard all on its uncertain outcomes.

HEW STRACHAN

PREFACE

In August 1914 Ypres was a sleepy Belgian city admired by many for its remarkable Gothic architecture. By that point it was already a palimpsest on which writers and artists had inscribed their own messages and meanings. A few months later the armies arrived, and the destruction of its fabric commenced. At the same time, each combatant nation present in and around the city began to construct its own particular definition of the meaning of the place. Many sites along the Western Front achieved greatness, or notoriety, between 1914 and 1918, but in no other place did the combatants overlap each other so closely and thus no other place gathered such a disparate range of competing visions. Interpretations of Ypres, its landscape and its hinterland, by Belgium, Britain and its Empire, France, and Germany soon developed a rich vocabulary of symbolism and iconography. In fact, the battle for the spiritual meaning of Ypres was every bit as intense and vigorous as the fighting at the front, and started a public discourse that has continued ever since that First Battle.

This book is the first truly transnational interpretation of the meaning of Ypres and, by extension, the Western Front, placing competing visions of its meaning and significance side by side throughout. Transnational approaches to the First and Second World Wars have proliferated over the last two decades, but this laudable trend has often resulted in studies which still compartmentalize differing national standpoints in discrete chapters or sections. Although much of this comparative work is of excellent quality and provides many valuable insights through its multinational approach, it falls short of full integration. In this study we have deliberately juxtaposed the variations and nuances of interpretation created by different national perspectives continually.[1] This is not something a lone scholar could accomplish. The research for this book itself has been a project in transnational history: all chapters in this 'duo-graph' are the result of collaboration between a British and a German historian.

A highly important practical, historical problem was a major driver of this transnational, multivocal approach: determining what each combatant nation defined, or perhaps more properly failed to define, as its Ypres front, sector, or salient revealed the extreme haziness of terms. Often used interchangeably with the equally hazy term of 'Flanders', Ypres as an imagined geography differed from nation to nation. For the French, after the First Battle in 1914, Ypres was a component of a front running from Dixmude in the north through Steenstraat down to about Pilckem. For the Belgians, to whom the city meant so much, Ypres was part of the last line of national defence, in which its army held the northernmost sector from Dixmude to the coast. The Germans often used the term *Flandern* to mean the whole sector from the Franco-Belgian border to the sea, but it was also used to describe the line running from the salient itself northwards to the sea. Britain and its imperial contingents were equally idiosyncratic in definitions. Depending on context, 'Flanders' meant either the entire line in Belgium, or a sector running from Ploegsteert–Le Gheer at the border to roughly Pilckem. This geographical categorization could also be labelled 'Ypres', whereas 'the salient' was the line arcing out from roughly Saint-Éloi in the south through a central apex around Hooge before bending back to a hinge point in the Pilckem–Boesinghe district. The thick Flanders fog enveloping the 'naming of parts', to use Henry Reed's poetry from the later world war, resulted in the disaggregation of histories, visions, and interpretations, and made assignment of a simple geographical definition of Ypres impossible.[2] At one and the same time, it made an exploration of the meaning of Ypres much more complicated and much more interesting. Ypres proved bigger than we had imagined at the start of the research.

In considering the geography, the global perspective came into play. Over recent years much First World War historiography has, quite rightly, emphasized the way in which the war stretched beyond Europe, affecting people across the globe. Moving to centre stage what were once conceived as histories subordinate to the truly important narratives has provided a valuable corrective, and has considerably deepened understandings of the conflict.[3] Here, the focus is very much back on the Western Front, and a very small section of that front. However, it shares the vision of the In Flanders Fields Museum in Ieper (Ypres), encapsulated in its 2008 exhibition and accompanying book, *Five Continents in Flanders*.[4] The world came to Ypres between 1914 and 1918, and many people from across the globe have been coming ever since.

Elasticity of place and space was driven by two elements. First, there is the question of the sheer number of battles around Ypres. Technically, there were five great engagements, which makes Ypres very different to other major battlefields such as the Somme, which was fought over in 1916, had a brief flurry of activity in the spring of 1918, and then—in its southern section—became a focal point for an equally brief period in the summer of 1918. Ypres and the region around it was fought for, and over, in every year of the war, making it a spreading, molten slick of violence. Secondly, the elasticity was driven by the practical realities of commemoration and remembrance, which are a very important part of this study. A man could be killed and buried in one place, but be exhumed and reburied somewhere quite different. Alternatively, if his body was lost, he might be formally commemorated on a memorial a long way from where he actually met his death. Such factors influenced the way veterans and bereaved interpreted the spaces and visited and revisited them after the war. This has made the 'spatial turn'—meaning an understanding of the way space is socially constructed and reconstructed, used and reused—an implicit approach in this book.[5] Building on the ideas and research of Pierre Nora, concepts of memory inscription and reinscription on places—and occasionally things (although a full cultural history of the material culture relating to Ypres requires a book-length study in its own right)—are important because they take the study away from too narrow a focus on memorials and cemeteries.[6]

In this study the emphasis has been on producing a 'media' history, or perhaps 'mediation' history is a better term. By that, we mean a study of many different types of evidence from official documents through books and journals to photographs, films, and music with the intention of revealing that remembrance of the Great War stretched way beyond formal commemorative activity. It also reveals that the 'war touch', to use Michael Williams's highly useful and insightful phrase, could be discerned across cultural expressions, particularly in the 1920s and 1930s.[7] As our study shows, this 'touch' meant that although Ypres may have been reified, it existed in a number of different registers in popular culture and was quotidian as well as ethereal. Ypres was the home of the Menin Gate memorial *and* provided the name for a greyhound, 'Ypres Mist', as well as a West London garage, just as Langemarck was a 'sacred site' *and* the name of streets and bus stops across Germany.

Realizing this quotidian aspect also made clear the multivocal element of the memory of Ypres: many tried to 'own' Ypres outright and some were more successful than others at putting their own stamp on the place—notably the Imperial War Graves Commission (IWGC)—but it was no one's sole possession. The sheer breadth of meanings and interpretations reveals much about agency and authority over Ypres. Vast numbers of individuals and groups felt that they had a special claim over Ypres (indeed this can still be detected today). This created a situation in which groups and people jostled for space and influence, working hard to enlist others in their cause and to gain the right to act as spokesperson for that cause. Some groupings proved influential over a considerable span, others had gadfly-like existences, but the crucial thing was their common agreement that Ypres was special and needed remembering and commemorating. What precisely needed remembering and commemorating was, of course, a matter keenly contested.[8] Historiographically, this is significant for its complicating of the story. Much of the literature on

Germany's relationship with Ypres and Flanders has focused on the right wing's domination of war memory.[9] But our research led us to the conclusion that war commemoration was not simply a rehearsal for fascism in Germany. And even when the Nazis appropriated Langemarck they often contradicted themselves. There is not a simple German metanarrative as some historians have suggested.[10] By the same token, the work of the IWGC may have lauded the efforts of the British Empire, but for men like Sir Fabian Ware, its vice chairman and guiding light, the Menin Gate could also be a site of reconciliation for the veterans of the opposing armies. Much of the literature on commemoration is, naturally enough, centred on the key expressions of corporate remembrance and individual memory in the form of studies of war memorials. Moreover, the vast majority of this literature concentrates on memorials erected on the home front and how people sought to deal with mass death a long way from the fighting zone.[11] Here, the focus is on the fields of battle and the extent to which public attention remained fixated on the sites of combat.

However, the memorial landscape of Ypres was much more than the consciously-constructed. Indeed, the chain of events and causality need to be emphasized: a place has things built on it because the place itself is deemed significant. This may sound an extremely obvious point, but it needs to be stated nonetheless. Ypres, and its hinterland, is a landscape saturated with discrete locations which have been invested with special significance. This makes Ypres a world of 'micro-geographies' and circuits of remembrance criss-crossed with ley lines, of which some remain easily traceable in the landscape, some have disappeared, while others are emerging as new interests and preoccupations enter the scene of public and private commemoration.[12]

As many historians and commentators on commemoration and memory have noted, seemingly well-established traditions and modes of expression are in fact constantly being reoriented and reworked. By the same token, much of the literature on First World War commemoration adopts relatively narrow time frames and inserts convenient and justifiable start and stop dates with 1919–39 a very common period of study. Thanks to the ability to concentrate on a particular aspect and site, we have had the opportunity to cover a much broader chronological sweep including the 'prehistory' of Ypres, which needs to be explored if its subsequent reification is to be fully understood. At the same time, the research revealed to us that in the case of Ypres the footprint of the First World War can be detected in the second global conflict. The imagined Ypres loomed large especially in 1940 and 1944. There was no forgetting in the Second World War; rather Ypres was incorporated into a new (hi)story.

Investigating this richly detailed Flemish tapestry of a history has required a great deal of research in an extensive range of archives. Material has been accessed from the state archives of Australia, Britain, Canada, France, Germany, and New Zealand; local and regional archives have been explored across the United Kingdom and Northern Ireland, in Belgium and Germany, as well as museum archives and collections in Britain and Belgium, and we are particularly grateful to the assistance we have received from the staff of the In Flanders Fields Museum. Yet the spatial turn requires historians to rethink and enhance their research methods. Thus, in addition to classical historical research in archives and libraries, we have undertaken fieldwork in and around Ypres, walking the former battlefields and visiting the war cemeteries. All this helped us to understand the fascinating history of Ypres and its looming presence in the remembrance of the Great War.

Note on Place Names

The spelling of place names has altered greatly over the years. As a general rule, we have used the common spellings in each time period and the modern Dutch/Flemish only where semantics became important to the debate over the meaning and ownership of war memories and commemorative practices.

ACKNOWLEDGEMENTS

There are many people and institutions to which we owe thanks for assistance, encouragement, and support. Sir Hew Strachan invited us to write this book for the Great Battles series, and he also offered perceptive comments on the manuscript. Sophie De Schaepdrijver, selflessly generous with her expertise and time, undertook to read the entire first draft. For valuable suggestions on earlier drafts of chapters, we are also grateful to members of the reading group of the Centre for the History of War, Media and Society at the University of Kent, notably William Butler and Mark Lawrence. For advice on specific points, we wish to thank warmly Dominiek Dendooven, Serge Durflinger, Malcolm Gaskill, Tim Godden, Markus Köster, Ulf Schmidt, Gerhard Schneider, Bernd Thier, Bruno De Wever, and Nico Wouters.

The British Academy and the Leverhulme Trust facilitated the research for this book through a Small Research Grant which made a big difference. Additional support was provided by the School of History at Kent and the AHRC-funded 'Gateways to the First World War' project. We are grateful to our research assistants Aoife O'Gorman, Philippa Gregory, Katia Günther, Janine Rischke-Neß, Femke Soetaert, and Christina Theodosiou. We should like to record our appreciation to the staff of the archives, libraries, and museums that we visited in the course of our research, especially Piet Chielens and his colleagues at the In Flanders Fields Museum, Andrew Fetherston and the archives team at the Commonwealth War Graves Commission, Debbie Manhaeve at the Passchendaele Memorial Museum, and Peter Päßler of the Volksbund Deutsche Kriegsgräberfürsorge. Finally, we are indebted to two children of IWGC gardeners, George

Godden and Mary Setchfield, for sharing their memories and photographs of Ypres.

At Oxford University Press, Luciana O'Flaherty, Matthew Cotton, and Martha Cunneen provided expert guidance. Every effort has been made to secure necessary permissions to reproduce copyright material in this book, though in some cases it has proved impossible to trace copyright holders. If any omissions are brought to our attention, we shall be happy to include appropriate acknowledgements on reprinting.

This book is an exercise in comparative and transnational history, and a product of collective research. All chapters in this book were jointly written by the authors.

MARK CONNELLY and STEFAN GOEBEL
Canterbury, October 2017

CONTENTS

LIST OF FIGURES

LIST OF MAPS

LIST OF ABBREVIATIONS

BArch	Bundesarchiv
BArch-MA	Bundesarchiv–Militärarchiv
BArch-SAPMO	Bundesarchiv–Stiftung Archiv der Parteien und Massenorganisationen der DDR
BayHStA	Bayerisches Hauptstaatsarchiv
BBC	British Broadcasting Corporation
BEF	British Expeditionary Force
BRT	Belgisch Radio- en Televisieomroep
CWGC	Commonwealth War Graves Commission (since 1960)
GHQ	General Headquarters
HStAS	Hauptstaatsarchiv Stuttgart
IRA	Irish Republican Army
IWGC	Imperial War Graves Commission (1917–60)
LAC	Library and Archives Canada
NCO	non-commissioned officer
PA AA	Politisches Archiv des Auswärtigen Amts
RTB	Radio-Télévision Belge
StdA	Stadtarchiv
TLS	*Times Literary Supplement*
TNA	The National Archives
VAD	Voluntary Aid Detachment
VDK	Volksbund Deutsche Kriegsgräberfürsorge
YMCA	Young Men's Christian Association

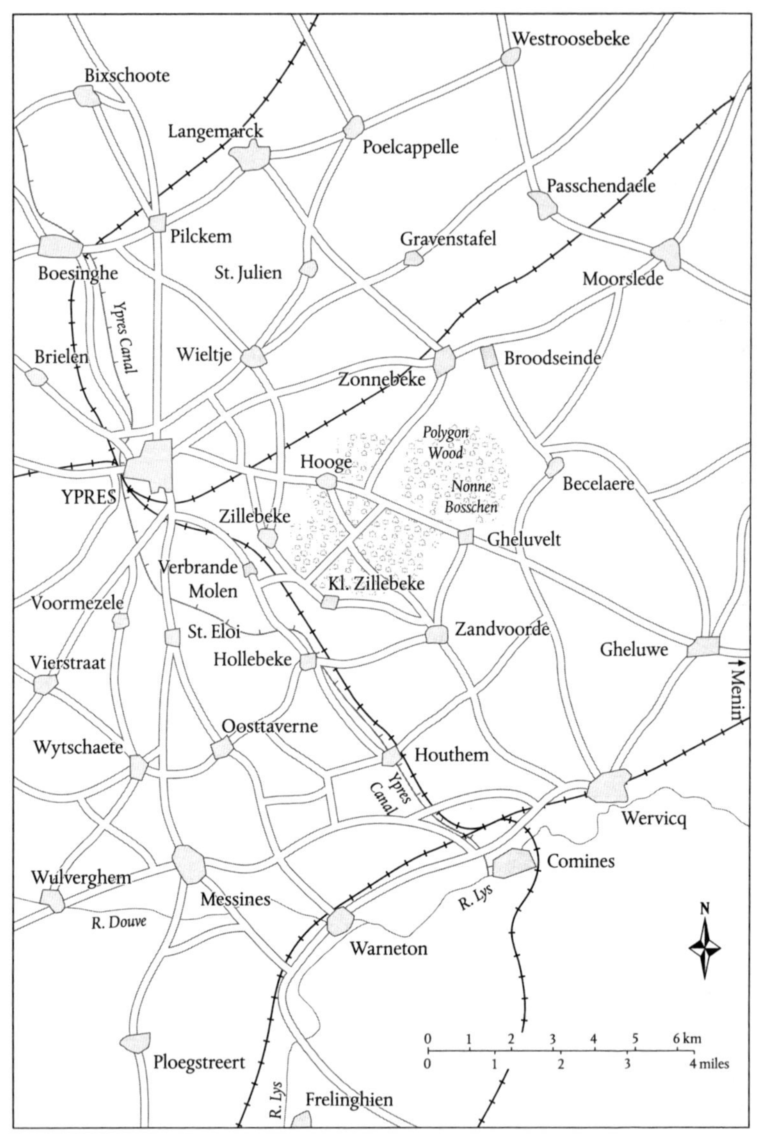

Map 1. Ypres and its surrounding battlefields, 1914–1918.

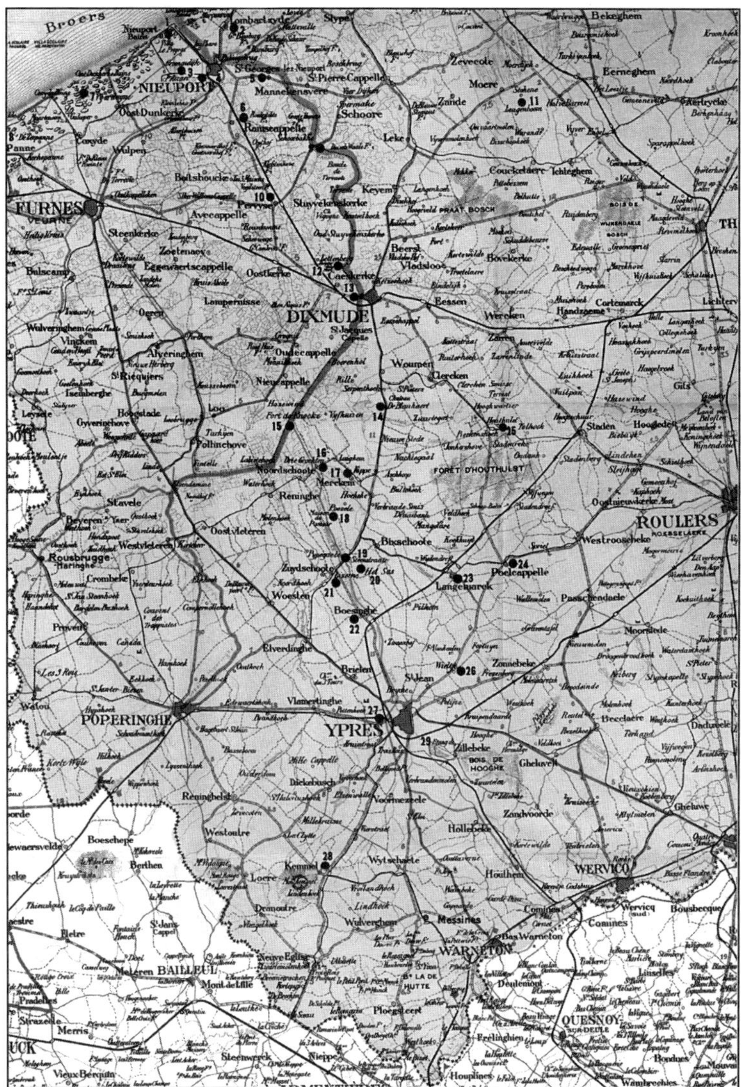

Map 2. The Flanders Front, 1914–1918. Portion of a map produced by C.A.T.A. Tours, Brussels, *c*.1926.

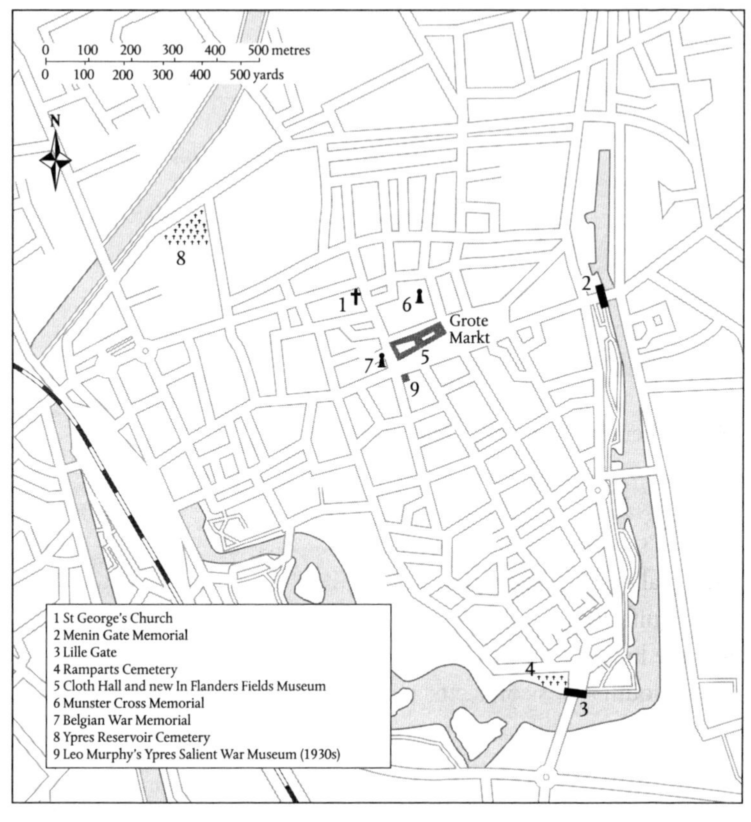
0 100 200 300 400 500 metres
0 100 200 300 400 500 yards
N
1
2
3
4
5
6
7
8
9
Grote
Markt
1 St George's Church
2 Menin Gate Memorial
3 Lille Gate
4 Ramparts Cemetery
5 Cloth Hall and new In Flanders Fields Museum
6 Munster Cross Memorial
7 Belgian War Memorial
8 Ypres Reservoir Cemetery
9 Leo Murphy's Ypres Salient War Museum (1930s)

Map 3. Ieper, 2017.

1

Prologue

The Salient Facts

When the first bullets were fired around Ypres in 1914, it was by no means a new experience, for this placid Belgian city had found itself prized by warring forces over many centuries. Although the city's economic fortunes had gone into steep decline since its medieval peak, its geography, a crucial element in its earlier expansion and significance, remained. Sitting in the middle of West Flanders, it was the hub of a series of road spokes radiating out in all directions. To the south it was connected to the French industrial towns and cities of Armentières, Lille, and thence on to Arras, as well as the coalfields of Bethune-Lens. From its eastern face, it was connected to Bruges, Courtrai, and Ghent; to the north lay the coast and Nieuport. Most crucially, in 1914, it was the route to the French coast and the ports of Dunkirk, Calais, and Boulogne. Sitting in a shallow bowl, from the east of Ypres a series of rippling ridges radiated outwards, forming a rough semicircle around it. To its west and south-west lay a string of humps and creases in the landscape, highly visible in this otherwise flat country, and given the picturesque name of 'la petite Suisse Flamande' in many late nineteenth-century guidebooks: Mount Kemmel, Scherpenberg, Mont Noir, and Mont Rouge terminating at Cassel in France.

The road links connecting Ypres to its neighbours had grown and improved considerably since the sixteenth century, and the railway had, of course, come in the nineteenth century. Alongside that, Ypres was, like all major Flemish towns and cities, a place of waterborne communications. Sitting on the Yperlee, a tributary of the Yser, Ypres had easy access to the sea, and by the 1860s the Ypres–Comines Canal had provided a modern through navigation to the Lys. Using the Yperlee connection, and with the encouragement of the early Counts of Flanders, the city grew rapidly as a centre of the weaving and cloth trade. By 1276 Ypres was home to 200,000 people, and its immense wealth and status was reflected in the building of Europe's largest secular Gothic building, the Cloth Hall, which stood next to the equally splendid church of St Martin (it became a cathedral in 1561 when the diocese of Ypres was created). Problems came with this great success as intense rivalries grew with other Flemish trading cities, particularly Bruges and Ghent. The burghers of Ghent formed an alliance with English traders, and in 1383 Ypres was besieged by a force commanded by the Bishop of Norwich.

Although unsuccessful, two years of siege seriously disrupted trade and this was the start of a long decline. Appalling violence was once again unleashed in the sixteenth- and seventeenth-century wars of religion. In 1583–4 Ypres was besieged for eight months. This took an appalling toll on its population which had shrunk to 5,000 by the time it was formally annexed to the Spanish Netherlands in 1584. The armies of France, Austria, and Spain then caused immense misery in the region, and the city changed hands in 1645, 1649, 1658, and 1678. On the final occasion in 1678 it fell to Louis XIV, and was occupied by the French for the next twenty years. It was during this period that an extensive fortification scheme was designed and overseen by the military engineer Sébastien Vauban. His trademark bastion ramparts surrounded much of the town and the moat was improved to provide greater protection along with a new gate opening on to the road to the town of Menin.

Reverting to Spanish control as a result of the 1697 Treaty of Ryswick, Ypres became a potential target of the Duke of Marlborough in his Flanders campaign of 1709, but fearful of a prolonged siege in the boggy, unhealthy country, he abandoned the plan. In 1713, as part of the Treaty of Utrecht ending the War of the Spanish Succession,

Ypres passed into the Austrian Netherlands. Emperor Joseph II ordered the dismantling of some of its fortifications, which, ironically enough, helped French Revolutionary forces capture the city in 1794. At the end of the Revolutionary Wars in 1815, Ypres found itself within the frontiers of an expanded Netherlands, but the Southern Netherlands with its Roman Catholic population was never a particularly happy part of this wider Dutch state. Revolution came in 1830 and with it the establishment of a new Kingdom of Belgium under the rule of the German princely family of Saxe-Coburg-Gotha.

Thus, although over the centuries the economic fortunes of Ypres had declined, its pivotal position as the guardhouse between French and Flemish Flanders, gateway to the Channel coast on one side and the heartland of central Belgium on the other, had remained constant in the power games of European politics and strategy. A new era of peace in the region was ushered in by Waterloo, the establishment of an independent Belgium, and the confirmation of its neutral status through the Treaty of London signed in 1839 by Britain, Russia, France, and Prussia. A shadow of its former self, Ypres was nonetheless an important market town serving as an entrepôt for its immediate hinterland. Now a sleepy backwater of West Flanders, its peaceful present was symbolized in 1855 by the dismantling of more sections of the city fortifications and the widening of its principal streets. By 1914 it was a quaint wonder of the medieval age, amazing tourists with its stunning architectural and artistic heritage. But this remnant of a seemingly long dead past was about to become the focal point of a European struggle for precisely the same reasons as in centuries past.

* * * * *

During the course of the First World War, five great battles were fought around Ypres. The intensity of the fighting on the Flanders front, in which Ypres was the linchpin, transformed the whole region into a place of legend and myth understood by both front-line combatants and home-front populations.

The First Battle was fought in the autumn of 1914 (19 October–22 November[1]) and consisted of a series of desperate engagements in which the Germans threw huge numbers of men and four newly formed army corps (supposedly consisting of young volunteers) at Belgian, French, and British defenders—an episode which inspired a rich mythology in Germany. For the Germans, initial war plans having been blunted along the rivers Marne and Aisne, West Flanders seemed to offer the space in which it could rescue the situation and break through to the coast with the intention of sundering Anglo-French unity. Fighting raged across the Flanders front in a series of attacks and counter-attacks, which made household names of places like Dixmude, Gheluvelt, and Langemarck in Britain, France, and Germany. This started the process of mythologizing the Flanders front, and the creation of a mosaic of microgeographies with particular associations for each combatant. Both sides exhausted themselves in these desperate struggles, and as a result the front slipped into stasis, aided by the grip of winter weather. Trenches and field fortifications now sprung up to create the battle lines of the Western Front. In low-lying Flanders, with its high water table, winter combined with artillery action to turn the region into a claggy mess. North of Ypres, where King Albert of the Belgians had ordered the opening of the sluices and the inundation of the land by the sea, the scene teetered on surrealism as vast lakes were created, forcing both sides to cling to outcrops of high ground and manmade features such as the railway embankment. The fighting in this region created a front along the River Yser, which in turn became a key part of Belgian–Flemish memory of the war, and gave the French a particular commemorative foothold in the area around Dixmude.

At the conclusion of the 1914 fighting, defining principles of life on this particular stretch of front were established which would last until the end of the war. At its northernmost end, along the Belgian section, life was relatively quiet. The flooding made large-scale operations impossible and King Albert committed his army strictly to the defensive, not wishing to fritter it away through offensive gambles. At

Ypres, the Germans held on to the most imposing high ground arcing around the city, before the line tapered away to the French frontier. For the Franco-British defenders, this meant a salient in which the enemy could see them and bombard them almost with ease: Ypres rapidly became known as a place of constant tension and activity.

The sense of being overlooked and hemmed in was intensified greatly by the second great German assault in the area between 22 April and 25 May 1915. Although German strategy was most intensively focused on the Eastern Front during 1915, the German commander-in-chief, Erich von Falkenhayn, was determined not to give up the initiative in the west entirely. For this blow, the Germans gave a full debut to asphyxiating gas developed with the help of Nobel Laureate Fritz Haber; this allowed the Second Battle of Ypres to be categorized as yet more evidence of German wickedness and depravity. The panic and confusion created by the initial use of this gas on 22 April almost threw open the door to a wholesale German advance, but once again a dogged defence did just enough to halt the onslaught. However, the pressure it put on the Anglo-French positions was enormous and significant high ground was conceded, tightening the German grip on the salient.

In 1916 attention switched away from Flanders with the German assault on Verdun, followed by an Anglo-French offensive on the Somme front. However, this did not mean a quiet year for Ypres. Following on from their debut in action in the Second Battle, Canadian forces engaged in a series of nasty struggles for the craters around Saint-Éloi, forming a ragged curve from the Ypres–Ploegsteert–Le Bizet road towards the Menin Road (see Map 1).

It was not until the following year that the British made Ypres the site of their main offensive effort. Emerging from the shadow of France, Britain was becoming the senior partner on the Western Front by early 1917, thanks to the massive expansion of its forces and its economic and industrial support of the war effort. The transition was aided by the breakdown of discipline in the French army as a result of the failed Chemin des Dames offensive on the Aisne front in April 1917. Fearful of a repeat of the Somme, the British prime minister, David Lloyd George, had eagerly embraced the idea of a French-led offensive, and, much to the disgust of Field Marshal Sir Douglas Haig, temporarily subordinated the British Expeditionary Force (BEF) to the French commander, Robert Nivelle. Power swung back to Haig with the failure of the offensive, for it was now obvious that, for the foreseeable future, the BEF was the only active and effective opponent of Germany on the Western Front.

Deeply aware of the vital significance of Flanders and the Channel coast to British security, Haig had long wished to force the enemy back in this region. He now gained a vital ally in the form of the Admiralty where there was mounting concern at the scale of shipping losses through submarines operating from the Belgian ports. Backed by supporters in the War Cabinet, Haig was given permission to launch an offensive at Ypres, but the government demanded the right to review its progress and, if necessary, suspend operations. The 'curtain-raiser' for this new engagement was the Battle of Messines (7–14 June). Lieutenant General Sir Herbert Plumer, commander of British Second Army, had been evolving plans for an assault in the region for a year and was particularly engaged in mining activity. At 3.10 a.m. on 7 June, nineteen enormous mines containing a million pounds of high explosives were detonated. The infantry assault was almost entirely successful, but by no means bloodless, and it secured the BEF's lines in the southern arc of the salient.

Attention now switched to the sector from the Menin Road round to the canal line near Pilckem, which was under the command of Lieutenant General Sir Hubert Gough and his Fifth Army. The operations subsequently overseen by Gough as part of the Third Battle of Ypres (31 July–10 November) have come to symbolize the entire conflict in British Commonwealth popular culture. Launched just as unseasonably wet weather descended, the battle failed to achieve breakthrough—if that indeed was its main aim—and became a bloody slogging match in which forces from across the Empire doggedly pushed the line forward. The battle ended in November when soldiers of the Canadian Expeditionary Force finally captured the village of Passchendaele.

German soldiers had undoubtedly been tried just as hard as the British during this dreadful contest, and its commanders had been severely unnerved by the experience, but the line had not disintegrated and there was still just enough of a coherent German defensive system. Further, during the course of the winter of 1917–18, German forces were swollen by the transfer of troops from the Eastern Front where victory had been gained over the Russians. With the German commanders Paul von Hindenburg and Erich Ludendorff determined to force a decision in the west through one last great offensive, the British and French began preparations to meet the looming threat. Around Ypres the pyrrhic victory of the autumn was fully realized when most of the gains were voluntarily given up in mid-April 1918 for a more effective defensive line. Radiating out from the German offensive launched in the sector of the La Bassée–Lys canals, assaults fell on the Franco-British positions in the southern arc of the salient in this Fourth Battle of Ypres (officially the Battle of the Lys, 9–29 April 1918). When Mount Kemmel fell on 25 April, the situation looked extremely threatening, and the British withdrew their line into a still tighter cordon immediately around Ypres. Fortunately, as with every other German operation in the spring of 1918, its high-water mark had been reached and the position stabilized.

By the early summer, the Allies, now backed by considerably larger US forces, began serious planning for a counter-offensive and a series of successful assaults were launched across July and August. Advancing continually across a broader and broader front, the offensives radiated out along the line from their original starting point on the Somme until the Allies, led by the BEF, were throwing multiple punches against German forces. In September the fighting reached the Ypres sector. In an important gesture—both symbolic and practical—King Albert was made commander of all forces in the area, and committed the Belgian army to its first major offensive actions since the start of the war. Commencing on 28 September, ten British, three French, and the combined forces of the Belgian army went into action (unofficially referred to as the Fifth Battle of Ypres, 28 September–2 October 1918). By the end of that day, British Second Army had recaptured, and gone beyond, the ground won in 1917. Given the early strategic importance attached to this area by the British, it was now regarded, somewhat ironically, as something of a supporting operation due to the great advances being made elsewhere. As a consequence, the forces in this area were not accorded top priority in terms of logistics support, and, when combined with communication difficulties across the shattered landscapes, it made the advance a steady process rather than an exhilarating spring. Nonetheless, there were moments of glory. A particular highlight occurred on 21 October when King Albert entered Bruges to a rapturous reception: Ypres's mirror-image twin, the surviving gem of West Flanders, had been liberated. Bruges was everything that Ypres had once been. The question now arose as to whether Ypres could, or even should, be like that ever again.

2

Ypres before Ypres, 1900–1913

Although it was the fortunes of war that thrust Ypres on to the world stage, the city was by no means unknown before 1914. Indeed, its profile in Western European, and more particularly British, culture contained a significant number of elements that were to become an essential part of its wartime image and post-1918 legacy. Intimately connected with the pre-1914 image of Ypres was the growing significance of tourism combined with the Victorian interest in medieval history and Gothic art and architecture. During the late nineteenth century the modern concept of the holiday began to emerge as a pleasure pursuit for a much wider social and economic demographic. As more and more groups of workers were granted guaranteed leisure time across ever extending periods, the potential for travel was enhanced. For many this meant little more than a day trip, but others were gaining the opportunity for longer excursions. Although a holiday was conceived as a complete break from the usual routine, the concept of leisure included a sense of spiritual and cultural enrichment through travel, which was partly inherited from the older aristocratic tradition of the 'Grand Tour'. In Germany the phenomenon was called the *Bildungsreise* (educational trip) and its elements were well enough established in European culture by the Edwardian period for E. M. Forster to very gently lampoon them in his novels *Where Angels Fear to Tread* (1905) and *A Room with a View* (1908). It was in this milieu that visions of Ypres were distilled.[1]

* * * * *

The rapid growth of railway transport, combined in the British case with the equally rapid expansion of cross-Channel steam shipping, opened up Europe to tourism with Belgium and France suddenly made accessible for day trips to people in south-east England.[2] Belgium became a favoured tourist destination, although the evidence suggests that the British and Germans found it more attractive than the French. If the number of guidebook editions is taken as an indicator of popularity, by 1906 the Low Countries (Belgium and Holland, often combined into one tour) were the third most sought-after destination (outside the homeland) for German tourists, eclipsing the wonders of Paris and northern Italy.[3] For the British, the increase of logistics infrastructure in terms of piers, sheds, quays, and track at ports such as Dover, Harwich, and Ramsgate allowed much easier access to the Channel ports of Belgium and France. In 1893 95,000 people travelled between Harwich and the Belgian ports, and just four years later this had risen to 130,000.[4]

With the expansion of transport networks encouraging tourism, Belgian entrepreneurs responded by increasing the number and quality of facilities available to the traveller. Of particular importance were the scenic delights of the Belgian coast. Capitalizing on the existing taste for seaside holidays, it was easy to exploit the geographical advantage of a very long, flat sandy coast ideal for sea bathing and promenading. By the late 1890s Belgian resorts were firm favourites for British, Dutch, and Germans, as well as domestic tourists. In August 1899 the *Daily Mail* carried two articles praising 'Simple Blankenberghe' and 'The Charms and Cheapness of Blankenberghe'. The latter stated that 'The British visitor will not find himself among strangers. At the moment the town is very full, and the English and Americans seem to have taken absolute possession of it.'[5] In 1906 the Lancashire and Yorkshire Railway, anxious to cash in on the lucrative market, launched a bi-weekly summer service to Zeebrugge from Hull which offered 'considerable inducements to tourists and excursionists from the North of England to visit the attractive Belgian seaside resorts of Ostend, Blankenberghe, Heyst, etc.'.[6]

The coast was soon linked into a host of road and rail networks which opened up the littoral to visitors, bringing Ypres into the tourist ambit. This was noted by a *Manchester Guardian* correspondent in 1906 who highlighted the attraction of being in 'the vicinity of the ancient cities Ypres, Bruges, and Ghent'.[7] In 1898 British newspapers made their readers aware of the opening of a new cycle path linking Ypres to Brussels in articles designed to appeal to cycling enthusiasts.[8] Further insights were to be gleaned from the 1899 *Cyclists' Continental Companion*. Route seven in the Belgian border section provided a guide from Dunkirk to Liège via places that later became synonymous with the salient—Poperinghe, Vlamertinghe, and then Ypres itself, which was recommended as a stopping point due to its hotels.[9] These innovations of the 1890s significantly increased the profile of Ypres as a tourist attraction in its own right. On 3 August 1897 the London *Morning Post* noted that a new railway had opened, linking the coast to Ypres. 'The vegetation is superb', it stated, adding that 'the small towns such as Nieuport, Furnes, Dixmude, and Ypres were picturesque, and bathing excellent', before going on to praise the facilities for cycling, sailing, and fishing in the region.[10] Such was its reputation that when the *Manchester Guardian* reviewed Grant Allen's 1897 *Cities of Belgium*, the correspondent bemoaned the fact that Ypres had been omitted from the selection: 'No doubt these [Antwerp, Bruges, Brussels, and Ghent] are the most important for the point of view of the author and the presumable requirements of those for whom the guide is intended, but one cannot help expressing a regret that space should not also have been found for Ypres.'[11]

Ypres had become a tourist destination not only on account of its much vaunted architecture and history, but also because it had finally started to marry its heritage with tourist facilities. Percy Fitzgerald, a British tourist who travelled across West Flanders in the 1880s, recorded his enchantment with the town, but bemoaned its lack of bars and restaurants.[12] However, the environment was beginning to change. Moreover, this was happening at precisely the same moment that tourist guidebooks began to mature and proliferate, and by the turn of the century had become an integral part of the tourism infrastructure. In particular, the brand name 'Baedeker' had established itself as a synonym for travel guide. The 'little red books' channelled the tourist's gaze: they outlined itineraries, ranked the various sights according to historical significance, and were packed with useful travel information. Baedeker's sparse style, adherence to precise description, and practical format established it as the most trusted series of travel guides in Europe. The supposedly 'methodical German mind' behind the Baedeker was appreciated not only by Germans themselves but also by travellers of many nationalities.[13]

The original German-language Baedeker to Belgium was published in 1839; by 1914 it had gone through twenty-five editions (and now included Holland and Luxembourg). The guidebook took the tourist on a two-and-a-half-hour train journey from Ostend to Ypres, passing through a number of unremarkable villages—Poelcapelle, Langemarck, and Boesinghe—places that were soon to acquire a special resonance.[14] The first English edition appeared in 1869, and the French-language version had reached seventeen editions by 1901.[15] Ypres featured in all three national editions, yet not as prominently as the larger Flemish cities of Antwerp, Bruges, and Ghent, mainly because, at this stage, it was still not particularly well connected to the main tourist nodal points. But the later editions reveal the increasing facilities, suggesting a destination that could be viewed as more than a brief stopping point. The British 1894 edition of Baedeker lists five hotels and a number of public houses and hostelries offering accommodation.[16] Other guides joined Baedeker in listing Ypres as a place worth visiting. In 1896 it was added to Thomas Cook's *Tourists' Handbook for Belgium,* and Ward, Lock and Company began including the town in its guide to Belgium from 1906.[17] Such guides were usually far more succinct and significantly cheaper than Baedeker, and reveal the growing importance of the 'white collar class' to the travel industry. In Germany this market was catered for by Grieben's 1891 'practical guidebook', which covered Ypres in less than one page. Nonetheless, it reflected a growing sense that Ypres had to be included in any tourist guide to Belgium claiming to be comprehensive and valuable to its owner.[18]

Revealing a local determination to promote the town, the Ypres publishing firm Callewaert-De Meulenaere produced a French-language guide in 1897 and a revised edition in 1909.[19] It reflected a wider strategy on the part of regional and national authorities to promote travel to Belgium, and in particular Flanders, usually as part of a package which included the coast. In 1902 the *Manchester Guardian* noted the importance of Belgian railway companies in reviving the fortunes of the Flanders towns, and by the turn of the decade the Belgian Information Bureau in Regent Street was regularly taking out advertising space in British newspapers. The summers of 1910, 1911, 1913, and 1914 saw adverts featuring the coastal resorts as the main attractions alongside supplementary tours of towns including the circuit 'Bruges, Ypres, Mons, Courtrai, Malines and Furnes'.[20] However, there remained a great weakness commented upon by virtually every guide; namely, the lack of a fast rail link to Ypres.[21] A correspondent for the *Hull Daily Mail,* providing a series of essays on his 1912 holiday in Flanders, warned his readers: 'I cannot recommend the railways of Western Flanders. The trains are slow, the stations and trains dirty, the permanent way very shaky. Third class is practically impossible... Ypres, however, is worth a great deal of discomfort.'[22]

For both those willing to face the vagaries of the local railway system and those who declined the opportunity, the guidebooks set an agenda and, along with a proliferation of other sources, shaped an Ypres in the imagination which was to have a significant influence on its wartime and post-war interpretation.[23] Unsurprisingly, every tourist guide commented on the Cloth Hall (Europe's largest Gothic civic building) and cathedral, usually in that order of precedence.[24] Most other commentators identified these two buildings as the iconic sights and sites of Ypres. For the French geographer Paul Vidal de la Blache, the 'gigantic edifice' of the Cloth Hall encapsulated the history of the city and the region, a point echoed by many.[25] The sheer size and scale of the building also struck Percy Fitzgerald who wrote:

> Now, of all the sights that I have ever seen, it must be confessed that this offered the greatest surprise and astonishment. It was bewildering. On the left spread away, almost a city itself, the vast town-hall… In the centre rose the enormous square tower—massive—rock-like—launching itself aloft into Gothic spires and towers… It is really a wonder of the world, and, in a phrase applied to more ordinary things, 'seemed to take your breath away.' It is the largest, longest, most massive, solid, and enduring thing that can be conceived.[26]

He added that 'this astonishing work would take some minutes of brisk motion to walk down from end to end', which was echoed by an article in the *Western Times* nearly twenty years later in declaring that the vast building 'will take at least five minutes to briskly walk round'.[27] T. Francis Bumpus was equally enthusiastic about the building in his 1909 *The Cathedrals and Churches of Belgium,* describing the Cloth Hall as 'this great pile of building… perhaps the noblest example of civic architecture in the Low Countries'.[28]

* * * * *

Visualizing these wonders of Ypres was made much easier by the proliferation of images by the late nineteenth century and their presentation in various formats, although most were aimed firmly at a middle- and upper-class market. British artists were particularly inspired by Ypres. In 1898 Ella Du Cane exhibited her watercolours at the Graves Galleries in London which included several Ypres scenes.[29] A year later the Scottish artist William Strang displayed his series on the Flemish Gothic towers of Bruges, Furnes, Ypres, and Courtrai as part of the Royal Society of Painter-Etchers and Engravers' annual exhibition at the Pall Mall Galleries.[30] Possibly as a result of this exhibition, Laurence Binyon, poet, writer, and curator at the British Museum, and later famous for his wartime poems including 'For the Fallen' (1914), collaborated with Strang to compile a series of textual and visual reflections on Flanders. The images Strang produced for the publication then appear to have formed the centrepiece of his contribution to the exhibition of the Society of Twelve (a guild of Scottish artists) at Obach's Gallery, New Bond Street, in the autumn of 1906.[31]

Figure 1. 'The Ramparts of Ypres' by William Strang. Engraving, 1898.

Also in 1906, the Anglo-French artist famous for his historical scenes, Amédée Forestier, produced a book of his studies of Flanders supplemented with commentary by G. W. T. Omond.[32] In 1908 the *Illustrated London News* included a photograph of Ypres to adorn its Christmas edition, which was always a highlight of its year.

The 1884 exhibition of the Société nationale des Beaux-Arts saw crowds particularly drawn to Gustave Grau's *Les Halles à Ypres*, and in 1913 the society travelled to Ghent for its conference, making special arrangements for an excursion to Ypres.[33] Others got the chance to experience the sights of Ypres through illustrated talks—a firm favourite of late nineteenth- and early twentieth-century culture. The people of Gloucester were treated to a 'most interesting lecture on "A Tour of Belgium"', which included slides of Ypres.[34] Similarly, T. W. G. Borthwick, vice president of the Berwick Arts Club, addressed the members on 'Western Flanders', outlining the history of the region and providing 'graphic accounts of Dunkirk, Lille and Ypres'.[35] Detailed illustrated histories of Ypres were also available. Henri d'Ideville's 1876 *Lettres flamandes* provided five dense pages on the town's decline and fall in his overview of Flemish history and culture; Omond did the same in his 1906 study of Bruges and West Flanders, as did the American George Wharton Edwards in *Some Old Flemish Towns* of 1913, which contained sections plagiarized almost word for word from Omond.[36]

A running theme for all discourses on Ypres was the contrast between its medieval heyday and its extremely mundane present. The 1894 English-language Baedeker stated: 'These days of prosperity, however, have long since passed away... Ypres thus possesses now but a shadow of its former greatness', and similar points were made in the French 1901 edition, as well as the German edition of—ironically enough—1914.[37] Examples of such sentiments abound in a host of other media. The *Western Times* noted that 'Ypres [was] once the pride of Flanders. It has barely 20,000 to-day. But monuments of its thriving past are maintained.'[38] Borthwick made an almost identical point to the Berwick Arts Club, describing how West Flanders cities like Ypres, 'which formerly had populations of 200,000 have now become almost deserted'.[39] This tended to make Ypres feel abandoned and somewhat melancholy. Henri d'Ideville referred to the monotony and depressing sensation induced by the countryside around Ypres and commented on how far it had fallen since its days of medieval glory.[40] According to *Le Figaro* it was a place of melancholy, like all West Flanders' once great cities.[41] The first German guidebook to Bruges and Ypres described the surviving art and architecture of the city on forty-three pages in great detail, but gave the impression that Ypres was a perfect time capsule, and the overall impression gained is of a shell of a city devoid of people. Unsurprisingly, given this sensation, many commentators identified Ypres as a city of the dead. Fitzgerald stated that 'It was all dead!' and questioned, 'Who could live in a Dead City, even for a day?' To him the strangest sight was the desolation of the central square where he expected to see bustle and activity.[42] The great magpie George Wharton Edwards stole the idea, telling his readers that 'it is to the Grand' Place that one instinctively turns, one of the finest and largest in all Flanders, and nearly always empty and deserted'.[43] The Grieben guidebook reminded the visitor of an older German and Netherlandish proverb—'He looks like the death of Ypres'—which could refer to any pale-looking person but, apparently, had its origin in the city's polluted moats and the nearby swamps and the miasma they exhaled.[44]

These reflections on Ypres seem uncannily prescient. Fitzgerald wrote of the Cloth Hall swallowing armies and made constant references to the atmosphere of death and the sense of the city being inhabited by fleeting spectres. This strange sensation of unsuspecting prophecy is most strongly perceived in Laurence Binyon's *Western Flanders: A Medley of Things Seen, Considered and Imagined.* A beautifully produced large folio publication limited to 250 copies, it was clearly not designed for the mass market, although it was favourably reviewed by the *Manchester Guardian,* which praised it for its perfect combination of text and images, particularly those concerning Ypres.[45] Like many other pre-1914 writers on Flanders, the stoic, reserved, stolid nature of the Flemings is stressed by Binyon, and like those other commentators, the weight of history in Flanders is also given great emphasis. Perhaps slightly different is Binyon's understanding of the Spanish role in the region in the early modern period which pre-empts R. H. Mottram's focus on this aspect of Flemish culture. It is interesting to speculate as to whether Mottram was aware of these other works, and Binyon's work in particular, when he came to write his famous post-war series *The Spanish Farm Trilogy*.[46] *Western Flanders* opens with a statement on the landscape and its people who are compared to the English in their love of individual liberties, which they defended stoutly in the Middle Ages to avoid being placed under a feudal yoke. The comparison with England had already been made by Fitzgerald, who, when glimpsing Ypres from afar, believed it 'suggested forcibly the view of an English cathedral town seen from the railway'.[47] A similar point was made by Omond in comparing Ypres to 'a quiet country town in an out-of-the-way corner of England. That is what the Ypres of to-day is like—a sleepy country town, with clean, well-kept streets, dull and uninteresting save for the stately Cloth Hall, which stands there a silent memorial of the past.'[48]

For Binyon, arriving in Ypres brought about the impression of an ancient city gradually melding into the landscape symbolized by its 'ramparts, once a masterpiece of Vauban... [now] an exquisite fabric of Nature's handiwork'.[49] It was a place that time had forgotten, indeed that was now outside time itself, residing in almost total silence. He believed that Ypres was a state in which men might live for centuries because it was governed by a different set of cosmic rules. This was confirmed by a stroll on the ramparts where his companion meets an old man who tells them how fortunate they are to have come in October as 'the beauty of this city is autumnal'. This comment throws up a number of intriguing possibilities. Binyon may have been aware of Armand Heins and Georges Meunier's *En pays flamand* (1892). According to Heins and Meunier, the best time to view Flanders was on autumn afternoons, as it was the moment when the spirit of the region could be most fully perceived.[50] Binyon was possibly drawing on this source and conjuring it up by embedding it in a supposed dialogue with a Flemish visitor. Alternatively, perhaps the old man was Heins or Meunier unknowingly stumbled upon. The old man went on to say that the antiquity of Ypres contained the very essence of life and in looking on this quiet city he perceived a vital force everywhere. Ypres is eternal because it seems so dead; it is beyond the fetters of temporal forces. As Binyon wanders on, he is stunned by its buildings—'the architectural glories of the Middle Ages'. Once again precise timing and environmental conditions enhance the experience, for his first glimpse of the Cloth Hall is on a moonlit night when the square is deserted, making the Cloth Hall and cathedral brood like 'phantasms'. The contemplation of the architecture leads to a deep meditation on art, the intellect, and the spirit inspired by the famous cavernous trading chambers of the building known as Les Halles. Binyon's text makes it clear that such thoughts could only be distilled in Ypres and not the other Flanders towns because 'At Ypres the past quite overcomes the present. The thoughts and the aims of modern life seem idle there and unreal.'

The book ends with Binyon's 'Ode' to Flanders which ostensibly plays upon the English link with the region, particularly Sir Philip Sidney's expedition to the Low Countries in the 1580s, but again is uncanny in its prescience and mood. He established the registers of

John McCrae's 'In Flanders Fields', which we will discuss in Chapter 3. Binyon's poem includes the stanzas:

Now mine eye wanders wide,
And my thoughts quickens keen.
O Cities, far descried,
What ravage have you seen.

Of an enkindled world,
Homes blazing, and hearths bare;
Of hosts tyrannic hurled
On pale ranks of despair,

Who fed with priceless blood
The cause unquenchable,
For which your heroes stood,
For which our Sidney fell...

Prove if the sap of old
Shoots yet from the old seed,
If faith still be unsold,
If truth be truth indeed?[51]

Binyon's musings on Ypres have an almost chilling quality for anyone approaching them after 1914. At one and the same time he appeared to encapsulate the seeming solidity of the antediluvian world utterly wrecked by the disaster of the war claimed by Paul Fussell to be the predominant note of modern memory *and* to foreshadow it unwittingly. Oddly, Binyon is the proof of Fussell's age of irony, but ten years too soon; he is blissfully unaware of his own irony. If the writer Geoff Dyer is right that the Great War was fought in order that it might be remembered, Binyon slipped in an advance secret mnemonic. The weird beguiling presence of this foretelling is made even stranger when Binyon's 'For the Fallen' is taken into account. Written in September 1914, this celebrated poem has become an icon of anglophone remembrance, and yet it was an anthem for doomed youth long before anyone could have guessed they were indeed doomed. As Dyer has brilliantly noted: '"For the Fallen", in other words, is a work not of remembrance but of anticipation, or more accurately, the *anticipation of remembrance*: a foreseeing that is also a determining.'[52] In their studies of English literature and the Great War, Samuel Hynes and Paul Fussell have created a checklist of the elements that make up the myth of the conflict, but here Binyon is the unheralded writer of the blueprint for Ypres: it is a city of the dead, it is a city of silence, it is a city that regenerates and sanctifies itself through its very communion with the past.[53]

Coming from a completely different angle, but making the same impression of uncanny prescience, is the 1914 revised German edition of Baedeker. Innocuous though it was, the 1914 edition appeared to the enemy like a plan for history's very first Baedeker raid: 'The book on Belgium and Holland is a wonderful survey of every inch of these countries ... Not a detail is overlooked that could have been regarded as of military importance', claimed the *Scientific American* in 1918. The magazine suggested that Baedeker was nothing less than a de facto 'office of military intelligence' for the German aggressor.[54] Before the war Baedeker's thoroughness and reliability had been a chief selling point with anglophone readers. Yet, in the era of the Great War, the publisher's quasi-scientific approach to travel backfired and foreign travellers began to turn against this quintessentially German product.

Ypres was, of course, made truly famous and truly memorable by the Great War. But during the war many commentators made reference to the stock of concepts relating to Ypres and consciously played on the images already present in popular culture. These pre-war works built upon longer traditions of an imagined Flanders in British, French, and German culture and were part of a continuum handed on to the world of 1914–18. By 1914 the world of the imagined Flanders and Ypres had by osmosis seeped deep into public culture, more especially perhaps that of the British, which in turn helped influence the way Ypres was interpreted in wartime discourses and has been ever since.

3

Ypres during Ypres, 1914–1918

Between 1914 and 1918 Ypres had a significant profile in British and German public discourse on the war. A rich rhetorical language was forged, which both built on the more reflective and discursive pre-war literature about the city and foreshadowed the cult of remembrance to come. A notable facet of the representation was the growth of microgeographies in which specific places within the salient, and across the extended battlefield to the north, were identified and referred to repeatedly, hammering them into the public consciousness. These sites were then often associated with particular nations, regions, colonies, and dominions as their troops fought over them. In turn, this ensured that the Ypres salient rapidly became something far more than simply a site of strategic military interest, being invested with a spiritual significance. In this process of heightened meaning, precise topography took on a self-reflexive status. Not only did it shape the experience of fighting, but it seemed to have been designated for fighting by its very nature. Ypres was the point where the war's ley lines converged. Although this phenomenon was less well marked for the French—as Verdun became the spiritual and military focus of France's war—the particular landscapes of the Yser front were associated with distinctive characteristics and qualities. For unoccupied Belgium and Belgian refugees, the Yser/IJzer river was the focus of the war; this tiny fragment of the nation was transformed into a crucible in which the very meaning of Belgium was tested. Soldiers and auxiliaries from across the globe came to Ypres during the course of the conflict, making it what many believed to be an essential experience of the Great War, and the public process of exploring this phenomenon played an important part in shaping post-war representation.

* * * * *

Fighting around Ypres commenced in October 1914 in what became known as the First Battle of Ypres. In a series of high-intensity actions the Germans attempted to break through the cordon of Belgian, British, and French defenders with the intention of sweeping round their enemies' flanks and potentially forcing the British to break contact with their allies and flee for the coast. British public knowledge of the First Battle was crystallized in the spring of 1915 when the *Daily Mail* published an extensive report by the American journalist Will Irwin, which brought together all of the fragments about the battle in one overarching narrative.[1] This dramatic and colourful account gained much attention with, unsurprisingly, the *Daily Mail* leading its own plaudits, as it announced on the day following publication that the entire print run had been sold out due to the story. The claim was reinforced by the inclusion of a testimonial from 'A Parent of an Officer Who Took Part in It', giving sincere thanks for publishing the article. Over the next few days other letters were printed, including one from Private H. Polley who stated: 'Having read the splendid story of the battle of Ypres in the *Daily Mail*, I think it most exact. I am speaking from experience, because I took part in it and am now home wounded.' Able to mix patriotism with profit, the *Daily Mail* reprinted the article as a pamphlet and requested that lord lieutenants, teachers, commanding officers of training camps, and others in authority obtain supplies and distribute them as widely as possible.[2]

Whilst discussing the ebb and flow of the engagements, the newspapers also emphasized the destruction of Ypres itself. A striking aspect of the coverage is the deployment of a 'tourist gaze', with the loss of the city's historical fabric foregrounded as one of the most important effects of the battle. Whilst the strategic significance of

Figure 2. The Cloth Hall around the turn of the twentieth century, and immediately after the conflict. The Cloth Hall was not completely restored until after the Second World War.

Ypres was therefore both implicit and explicit in the reportage of military activity, the cultural and spiritual components were emphasized from the start. With the German destruction of Louvain in August and the bombardment of Rheims in September having already achieved notoriety, in October Ypres became the next site in the 1914–18 'Baedeker raids'. Whilst admitting that some of the damage was justifiable due to its military significance, *The Times* nonetheless entitled an article about the bombardment of the city, 'Wanton Destruction at Ypres'.[3] In quoting a French staff officer, the *Daily Mail* drew attention to 'the pointed arches of the Cloth Hall [turned] into a glowing brazier of fire... Among the thousand horrors that I have witnessed during this war, as the Germans wage it, I knew none more poignant than the spectacle of devastation and sacrilege which I then beheld.'[4] G. Valentine Williams, the *Daily Mail*'s correspondent attached to British General Headquarters (GHQ), added a powerful sketch in the spring of 1915 just as the Second Battle was petering out. Explicit in his commentary was the juxtaposition between what had been and what now remained: 'Then I came to the Grande Place, where once stood the Cloth Hall and the Basilica of St Martin, the glory of Ypres and Western Flanders. The great square was a sight to haunt the memory for ever.' His account contained the arresting subheadings 'Awful Silence', 'Broken Angels', 'Of Human Life No Trace', leaving his readers in no doubt about the scale of devastation.[5]

Rich in descriptions of Ypres's architectural glories now obliterated, Williams created a kind of nightmare tourists' guide in its shocking, yet elegiac, descriptions of the ruins. Such accounts provoked 'Louise' to muse on her pre-war visit to Ypres in which she used all the standard reference points of the pre-1914 tourist literature: 'Several hours were once spent by me in this peaceful and delightfully medieval-looking town of Ypres, one of the most ancient and the deadest in Belgium... I felt that there, in that little town that had weathered the storms and hurts of many ages, peace and contentment dwelt in perfect harmony.'[6] With the unfolding of the first two battles, Ypres, it seems, translated its pre-war status as a city of the dead into an even higher state of being. Laurence Binyon appeared consciously to revisit his pre-war musings on the city in his 1916 poem 'Ypres':

> On the road to Ypres on the long road,
> Marching strong,
> We'll sing a song of Ypres, of her glory
> And her wrong.
> Proud rose her towers in the old time
> Long ago,
> Trees stood on her ramparts and the water
> Lay below.
> Shattered are the towers into potsherds—
> Jumbled stones.
> Underneath the ashes that were rafters—
> Whiter bones.
> Blood is in the cellar where the wine was
> On the floor.[7]

The *Sydney Morning Herald* recounted the dramatic history of Ypres for its readers before concluding, 'So the old city has witnessed its fair share of tragedy and heroism.'[8] 'You ought to see the cities and towns of this part, Ypres especially,' ran a soldier's letter published in the Dundee *Evening Telegraph*; 'it is a city of the dead, ruin and destruction everywhere.'[9] Quoting a French official communiqué, an article in *The Times* reinforced the image of a peculiarly violent and vindictive German culture, which also brought Ypres to its preordained condition as a city of the dead: 'This magnificent city was condemned to death on the day when the Emperor was forced to renounce the hope of making an entry into it.'[10] Such attention to the buildings and environment did not mean that the human cost, whether civilian or military, was being ignored. In fact, it was part of a process in which the landscape became a metaphor for the body.[11] Indeed, the association between Ypres and mortal sickness was already well established, at least in German and Dutch culture, in the phrase 'the death of Ypres', as noted in Chapter 2. The war then gave this phenomenon even greater circulation. A German infantry officer wrote to the *Berliner Tageblatt* in December 1914, pointing out the origins of the phrase in the Black Death of 1350, but adding that in 500 years' time it would refer to the current war.[12] Probably picking up on German reports, the British press also noted the phrase and its long use in Germany and the Netherlands.[13] Continuing the theme of sickness and physical distress, the *Daily Mail* reproduced diary extracts from a Corporal A. Sproston who referred to 'the stricken city of Ypres with its cathedral-like cloth hall in medieval magnificence, fallen masonry at its base like solid tears'.[14] As will be argued, this phenomenon accelerated and matured in pictorial representation during 1917 with the utter devastation caused by the Third Battle of Ypres.

In fact, by the standards of 1917, the 1914 battle caused relatively minor damage. Far more serious were the bombardments of April and May 1915 during the Second Battle. The advance of German troops brought the artillery closer to the city and ensured much more accurate and concentrated fire. Up to that point, a substantial number of citizens remained in the city, finding the servicing of soldiers' needs a highly lucrative activity. 'Sapper', the pseudonym of H. C. McNeile, wrote a piece for the *Daily Mail* in May 1915, describing Ypres as a place bustling with cafés, bars, and restaurants which provided British soldiers with a welcome touch of comfort, brought to an appalling end by the recent bombardments and gas attacks.[15] 'Sapper' was among the earliest writers to use the term 'Wipers' in print. Entitled 'The End of Wipers', the article reveals how quickly this British colloquialism had entered the common language, eventually becoming part of Ypres's mythology which endures to this day in the anglophone world. The first reference to the term seems to have been in the *Daily Express* on 27 October 1914 under the short note 'Tommy's French', where it was announced that British soldiers were operating near Ypres, but they pronounced it 'Wipers'.[16] Others pointed out the correct pronunciation. In Australia the *Midlands Advertiser* told its readers that 'EE'p'r' was the actual way to say it, but the *Daily Mail* insisted on the Tommy argot, stating it was not 'EEpre' but 'Wipers'.[17] In Canada the *Toronto Star* brought Belgian linguistics into play, announcing (incorrectly) that the French call it 'Eepres', whereas the British use the Flemish 'Eye-per'.[18] 'Wipers' certainly caught on among home-front audiences across the Empire, probably because it helped reinforce the image of a simple, unaffected, downright British Tommy with little time for sophisticated niceties of correct pronunciation. So deep into the consciousness did it seep that it could even be deployed in completely different spheres. In 1916 'Zog' cleaning products ran a press campaign under the title 'The New Battle of "Wipers"'.[19] Another label emerged early on in the war: the 'Ypres salient', but it was far from the sangfroid flippancy of 'Wipers', having instead the resonance of military high command. Its first use in the public arena appears to have been in the British graphic journal *War Illustrated* on 5 December 1914, when it was stated that 'The British salient at Ypres fascinated the Kaiser'.[20] Usage increased during 1915, most notably in *The Times* article of 5 May 1915, which was headed 'German Pressure on the Ypres Salient', and became much more common during 1916.[21]

As the destruction intensified during the Second Battle, Ypres gained another element of notoriety as the location for the first use of gas on the Western Front. Generally, the French press reacted to this event more quickly than the British, revealing much about the censorship processes of both nations. As early as 24 April, just two days after its first use, *Le Matin* was reporting the appearance of gas at Ypres.[22] Two days later the *Journal des débats politiques et littéraires* labelled it a 'barbaric' act by the Germans.[23] The first major comment in a British newspaper occurred on 29 April when an editorial in *The Times* attacked it as the 'latest discovery of German civilization. The wilful and systematic attempt to choke and poison our soldiers can have but one effect upon the British peoples and upon all the non-German peoples of the earth. It will deepen our indignation and our resolution, and it will fill all races with a new horror of the German name.'[24] It took a further three months before the first full British account of the Second Battle appeared when John Buchan's narrative was published by *The Times*.[25]

In Germany the press coverage was full of ambiguities. On 23 April German newspapers carried an official communiqué about the deployment of poison gas. However, it said nothing about the grand military and scientific experiment with chlorine gas of the previous day. Instead the communiqué suggested that this weapon had been used by the Allies for several months and that Germany would be able to strike back with much more effective gases.[26] A few months later the *Kölnische Zeitung* published an eyewitness account which contained a rare admission of gas being a German initiative. 'We owe the great success to ... asphyxiant gases', the proud soldier stated.[27] But this was a lone voice. By and large, the German public sought refuge in images of traditional warfare, as had been established by the descriptions of the Langemarck fighting in November 1914 which will be discussed later. Further public image problems were created for Germany by the introduction of another new weapon on the Ypres front: the flame-thrower, or 'liquid fire' as it was known in the British press. *The Times*

Figure 3. Victims of gas attack of 22 April 1915. German photograph, April 1915.

published details of the weapon and its use in early July, as did many other papers, and the *Illustrated London News* carried an engraving depicting its deployment the following month.[28] The reputation of Ypres as a place of death, violence, and almost ceaseless activity was underlined by these stories.

* * * * *

The focus on Ypres also helped shape an intimate knowledge of the landscape's human and natural features. A host of names began to enter the public arenas of Britain, France, and Germany. For France the Yser front and the zone immediately to the north of Ypres became the focal points. In an excellent example of the Great War's ability to throw up uncanny resonances and strange coincidences, the French deployed a brigade of marines to the Yser front which promptly found itself in the peculiarly apt circumstances of a flooded landscape caused by the Belgian's deliberate opening of the coastal sea sluices so as to slow the German advance. In defending the high ground of the railway embankment outside Dixmude, the French brigade of marines turned this nondescript geographical feature into a site of glory. 'Never was such heroism displayed as by the marines . . . in keeping the Yser unbroken,' was the judgement of *Le Matin*; they were the 'heroes, who, under Admiral Ronarc'h, outnumbered, managed to halt the Germans'.[29] A similar sense of glory and excitement was seen in the winter of 1915 when a play was staged in Paris celebrating the role of the marines, and before the war was over a number of books and pamphlets about the French defence of the Yser were published. Chief among them were Charles Le Goffic's *Dixmude: Un chapitre de l'histoire des fusiliers marins (7 Octobre–10 Novembre 1914)* in 1915 and Jean Pinguet's *Trois étapes de la brigade des marins* in 1918. Both works stressed the qualities of the marines, and the weird and wonderful landscape of the flooded zone, making a combination of unique soldiers in a unique environment. Le Goffic encapsulated French conceptions of the Yser on the very first page of his book: 'The name of Dixmude will henceforth shine with a legendary aura.'[30]

In 1918 Henry Frichet's *La Bataille de l'Yser: Dixmude, la maison du passeur* was added to the literature. His work appears to have been aimed at a younger readingship and told the story as a breathless adventure. The front cover had a coloured illustration of French troops advancing across a flat landscape past a ruined barn and onto a house from which rifles are firing in the upper storey windows. The other significant location was the countryside around Steenstraat, Langemarck, and Saint-Julien where the colonial Moroccan troops were caught by the initial gas attack on 22 April. *Le Matin* carried a front-page article by 'Commandant de Civrieux', remarking on the 'barbarian methods' of the Germans.[31] The *Journal des débats politiques et littéraires* stated the same, adding that it was the act of an enemy entirely without scruple.[32]

For the Germans Langemarck had already emerged as an iconic microsite within the wider Flanders front. The small village to the north-east of Ypres was established in the German consciousness by an army press communiqué on 11 November 1914, which was distributed via the national wire service and printed verbatim in the evening editions of national and local papers throughout the country. However, typesetters seem to have been confused by the spelling of the village: 'Langemarck' sounded too Germanic to be correct, and so some decided to Gallicize it as 'Langemarque'. But at this stage it was not a focal point and editorial comment was minimal. Instead, the initial focus was on Dixmude. 'Good News from the West! Dixmuide Taken by Storm', announced one regional newspaper.[33] Likewise, 'Dixmuide Taken by Storm' was splashed across the Berlin *Vossische Zeitung*, the foremost organ of liberal opinion in Germany, on page 1. This doubtless reflected the fact that forcing a way through in the northernmost coastal region and taking the higher ground at Dixmude was of much more immediate military importance.

Langemarck featured, but only as an additional detail to the stories about fighting in the west. Even so, the press statement contained the key elements that would—with astonishing speed—gather into the contours of a myth. It is doubtful that the Langemarck story evolved as part of an intentional plan to create a national myth, as official propaganda was ineffective and ill-coordinated in the early stages of war.[34] Rather, the commercial press can be identified as the main motor behind the construction of the Langemarck myth. Starved of exciting news from the Western Front for two months, journalists were desperate to break out of the 'orchestrated silence' that had followed the debacle on the Marne in early September.[35] It took them just twenty-four hours to realize the symbolic potential of that one sentence buried in the army communiqué. On 12 November the liberal *Frankfurter Zeitung* carried a short patriotic poem by Heinrich Zerkaulen (probably written before 11 November) and prefixed it with a quotation from the communiqué of the previous day: 'West of Langemarck, young regiments broke forward singing "Deutschland, Deutschland über alles" against the first line of the enemy's positions and took them.'[36]

'West of Langemarck' suggested that German troops surged westwards. The location given was remarkably imprecise, but Bixschoote, where the fighting had taken place, does not roll off the tongue in the same way. Imaginative names for battles were the order of the day: the other famous battle of 1914, the German army's famous victory over the Russians in August, had not exactly taken place at Tannenberg either. '[Y]oung regiments' was phrased ambiguously, too; it could refer either to those four newly created army corps deployed in Flanders or to soldiers of a young age. The communiqué was, however, unusually specific about one detail, namely the adopted battle song 'Deutschland, Deutschland über alles'. Fuelled by these stories, Langemarck began to serve as a symbol not only of youth but also of unity. The singing of 'Deutschland, Deutschland über alles' demonstrated youthful enthusiasm for the nation's cause and triggered memories of the wave of 'war enthusiasm' that had apparently swept through the land in summer 1914. The collective singing of patriotic songs had been a key feature of the 'spirit of 1914', palpable in the streets of German cities. Consisting largely of urban-based educated youth and well-to-do *Bürger*, these patriotic crowds acquired a new centrality to the iconography of the nation at war. The nationalist press gave such demonstrations a great deal of space, and newspapers suggested that the newly found sense of purpose and belonging had transformed a divided society into a homogenous community.[37] The reporting about Langemarck in November 1914 rekindled the imagined 'spirit of 1914' that was already in danger of evaporating into history. While the official communiqué referred merely to 'young regiments', in the press they were identified as 'students' and 'volunteers'. The fact that students had volunteered to serve in the ranks—giving up the privilege that the army granted men of academic and social distinction to serve as *Einjährig-Freiwillige*—was something unheard of before 1914 and seemed to show true commitment. Their baptism of fire in November 1914 would become the nucleus of a new national community that transcended the divisions of class.[38]

The story of troops singing the 'Lied der Deutschen' in the midst of battle became a reality in the process of newspapers citing each other. The wartime media formed a self-referential system in constant conversation with itself; every shred of 'news' was recycled several times. Thus, a local newspaper from Westphalia cited *Deutsche Tageszeitung* which in turn referred to an article in *The Times* which quoted an eyewitness of the fighting in West Flanders: 'He praised the heroic bravery of the attacker, which was unparalleled in world history.'[39] Called on to corroborate the German account of Langemarck, the enemy press proved instrumental in transforming a press statement into a national myth. And yet, the myth-making was not as linear and inevitable as it might appear in hindsight. Not all organs of the press joined in. Influential weeklies such as *Die Gartenlaube* or *Die Woche* did not single out Langemarck. In fact, the latter published on 21 November a map of the West Flanders theatre of operations but omitted to sketch in the now famous village.[40]

Of course, military insiders had no illusions that Langemarck meant anything other than the 'pointless death' of young men, as one staff officer bluntly put it.[41] The fighting in Flanders was immensely costly in lives of soldiers; 80,000 Germans were killed in 1914. Among

German commanders, Erich von Falkenhayn's decision to prioritize the assault on Ypres and, moreover, to deploy poorly trained units was controversial. But also people back home were able to read between the lines of the army communiqué. Some relatives of young soldiers were filled with indignation at receiving the news. In an effort to silence the critical voices, newspapers started publishing extracts from *Feldpostbriefe* (soldiers' letters from the front); the moral authority of the eyewitnesses was called on to reinforce the official version of events. The campaign was led by the quasi-official *Norddeutsche Allgemeine Zeitung* which printed the letter of a wounded soldier on 14 November. He did not mince his words in denouncing the 'base liars' who doubted the soldiers' enthusiasm, and he had little understanding for timid parents who wished their offspring could avoid front-line service. Significantly, the letter continued the circle of citations by invoking a paean to the German soldiers' bravery published in *The Times*.[42]

Less conventional stories about Ypres speaking of loss and bereavement found it harder to reach the public domain than tales of heroism. But exist they did—alongside the emerging Langemarck myth. The book *To My Dead Son Ernst Alexander Leipart Who Fell as a 17-Year Old War Volunteer near Ypres on 9 December 1914*, published privately in 1915 by the father, a trade union leader, provides a perfect example. A widower, Leipart senior seemed to have formed an especially close relationship with his only child. He had, of course, tried to talk his son out of volunteering, but once the young man had made up his mind the father stood by him and proudly carried his son's rifle to the train station. 'My dear son! As much as my inner self rears up against the thought, it remains the horrible truth: You are dead now!' Contrary to all clichés about public mourning as essentially female, we see in this commemorative brochure an outpouring of emotion and fatherly grief: 'I will hear never again your lovely voice—nobody will call me "father" again!' There is a hint of pacifism when Leipart senior complains that the 'awful murder' continues at Ypres. Yet, this booklet is a personal, not a political, statement. It is an attempt to enter into a dialogue with the dead son, to bear witness to the young man's bravery, to reconstruct the circumstances in which he was killed and, above all, to find closure: 'You have done your duty! But I have not accomplished mine yet. My duty calls me to work. Sleep in peace, my dear, brave son. Your father.'[43]

In 1915 different—less ephemeral—media of memory began to perpetuate the Langemarck story. Books were an important vehicle for consolidating the myth. Olaf Heinemann's *Der Tag von Langemarck* (The Day of Langemarck) set the trend. It was the first of many books that were to carry Langemarck in the title—somewhat misleadingly because in this anthology of ten short stories only one was actually about the legendary assault. The story which gave the book its title is a tale of generational conflict and of youth coming into its own. In a fictitious town called Banausia (Philistinia), two grammar-school pupils are caught smoking and drinking. The old headmaster's diatribe on the moral degradation of young men is disrupted by the news of the outbreak of war. The town is swept by a wave of war enthusiasm, and the two sinners volunteer for the army. At the front they are reunited with their favourite teacher, a fatherly friend who had saved them from being expelled. Under his command they storm forward singing 'Deutschland, Deutschland über alles'. When the headmaster receives word of their heroic deaths, he starts sobbing and regrets bitterly his harsh words about 'the youth of today'.[44]

By the time Heinemann's book hit the shelves, the Ypres salient had seen another major battle. The Second Battle of Ypres was fought in a landscape thick with memory. Naturally, the village of Langemarck featured prominently in the coverage of the action of spring 1915. The army communiqué of 23 April announced plainly that Langemarck 'was taken' the previous night—somewhat to the surprise of readers who believed that it had been in German hands all along. The heroics of 22 April were embellished in various *Feldpostbriefe* and in artists' impressions. Notably, the painter Fritz Grotemeyer, who had already produced an oil painting of the fighting in November 1914, returned to the theme of the *Sturmangriff deutscher Infanterie bei Langemarck am 22.*

April 1915 (Storm Attack of German Infantry near Langemarck on 22 April 1915).[45] His two pictures are strikingly similar, thus showing continuity between the fighting of autumn 1914 and spring 1915. Similarly, journalists rhapsodized over the return of the war of movement. Yet the layout of newspaper pages suggested the very opposite: between 24 April and 10 May 1915 the *Vossische Zeitung* featured four maps of the Ypres salient, including one contour map covering half a page. By contrast, in October and November 1914 the newspaper had not produced a single map of the area. Six months later there was no pretending that the German troops would soon overrun the enemy's positions; the area map became the symbol of stalemate.

A similar, but more extensive, microgeography of Ypres was emerging in the British Empire as the battles of Ypres, and associated minor actions, dragged in units from across the Britannic world. This brought into wartime discourse the myriad of villages and features making up the salient. With battlefield maps regularly printed by the newspapers and available to purchase, people had the opportunity to become familiar with places such as Poperinghe, Vlamertinghe, Hooge, Langemarck, Wytschaete, Ploegsteert, Saint-Julien, Zandvoorde, Zillebeke, Zonnebeke, and the Menin Road. Most of these names were reduced to pronunciations easy for the British palate and sat alongside the army names imposed on the landscape like Glencorse Wood, Inverness Copse, Mouse Trap Farm, Battle Wood, and Sanctuary Wood.[46] This filtering of original names and renaming made the salient seem like some kind of British imperial backyard and infused British plans for Ypres in the immediate aftermath of the war. At a regional level, communities could imagine a particular locale as belonging to them through the actions fought by local men or units. In the case of Worcester it was the village of Gheluvelt, recaptured by the 2nd Battalion, Worcester Regiment at a pivotal moment in the First Battle of Ypres. Under the headline 'The Charge of the Gallant 500: How the Worcesters Saved Calais. Heroes of Gheluvelt', the *Daily Mail* recounted 'how 800 British soldiers barred the Kaiser's road to Calais; how fewer than 500 English linesmen charged right into the mouth of a veritable inferno, drove back a twenty times stronger force of Germans, and for ever freed England from the menace of the Hun on Calais sands'.[47] The association between Worcester, its regiment, and a small Belgian village on the Menin Road was sealed in December 1917 when Lieutenant Colonel E. B. Hankey was presented with the freedom of the city during a ceremony in which he told the story of the charge to his large audience.[48]

The war also emphasized the oldest link between the home nations and Ypres in the form of the Irish Nuns of Ypres. Expelled from Dublin by William III, the nuns had settled in Ypres and had been solely Irish until the 1840s. During the nineteenth century Irish antiquarians and historians had kept alive the history of the convent and were particularly interested in determining the status of the abbey's most famous possessions: the flags of English units captured by the Irish brigades during the War of the Spanish Succession. Irish newspapers provided a regular diet of stories about the nuns and the flags from the 1890s, doubtless inspired by the latest evolution in Irish nationalist thinking.[49] The two were fused in 1905 when John Redmond, leader of the nationalist Irish Parliamentary Party, travelled with his niece to Ypres and witnessed the ceremony of her formal acceptance and entry into the convent. In 1908 this renewed interest was most strongly expressed in Revd Patrick Nolan's monograph *The Irish Dames of Ypres*, which provided a full history of the convent and is members.[50] Far from becoming a rallying cry for more extreme Irish nationalists, the British defence of Ypres allowed the convent and its flags to be co-opted into an overarching imperial narrative during the conflict. Forced to flee by the advancing Germans, the nuns became a symbol of Prussia's wanton aggression, allowing their defence to become the task of a united British Empire. Building on Nolan's work, Barry O'Brien provided a graphic account of the nuns' harrowing flight from Ypres in his 1915 book *The Irish Nuns of Ypres*, complete with a special introduction by John Redmond.[51] Drawing attention to their utter destitution, O'Brien's work was a fundraising venture for the re-establishment of the convent, whilst also pointedly noting that the nuns had found refuge in (Protestant) England, underlining the sense of affinity between English and Irish sentiment over the war. The point did not go unnoticed by the *Freeman's Journal,* which stated that the nuns were 'dependent on the benevolence of kindly English strangers', and then linked the nuns to Ireland's self-identity: 'The story of the Irish nuns of Ypres is bound up with the story of Ireland. They represent not only a religious order but the national ideal as well. They stand for Faith and Fatherland.'[52] In effect, Ypres became the agreed common ground between Catholic Ireland and the United Kingdom during the conflict.

With the British government and moderate Irish nationalist opinion keen to stress Irish loyalty in the wake of the 1916 Easter Rising, the press made much of the 7 June 1917 attack at Messines where the 16th (Irish) Division fought alongside the 36th (Ulster) Division. Quoting the *Daily Express,* the *Irish Independent* deemed it 'a triumph equally for the (Irish) troops—Catholics, Protestants, Home Rulers, and Orangemen went up the ridge together'.[53] The *Irish Examiner* used Philip Gibbs's observation that 'Irish troops, Nationalists and Ulstermen, not divided in politics on the battlefield, but vying each other in courage and self-sacrifice stormed their way up to Wyschaete'.[54] For the *Skibbereen Eagle,* the battle was proof of the 'gallantry of Irish troops' and of the 'most cordial' relations between Catholic and Protestant soldiers.[55] Somewhat ironically, the damage caused by the fighting in Dublin a year earlier saw the city compared with Ypres, and the comparison was made again in 1923 as a result of the destruction caused by the civil war in the new Irish Free State.[56]

Among the overseas components of the British Empire, Canada was the nation with the longest history in the salient and arguably it shaped the dominion's entire conception of the war, notwithstanding its stunning victory at Vimy Ridge in April 1917.[57] As with much British imperial coverage of Ypres, the dreadful hardships of life in the salient were translated into further reasons to wonder at the courage and determination of 'our boys'. For Canada three sites became particularly important: Saint-Julien and its immediate environs, being the area in which its troops were caught in the 1915 gas attacks; the crater zone near Saint-Éloi where the Canadian Corps fought in 1916; and finally Passchendaele itself, captured by the corps in November 1917. Deploying an implicitly Christian understanding of triumph achieved through suffering, Canadian press coverage, largely fuelled by the expatriate owner of the London *Daily Express,* Max Aitken (Lord Beaverbrook from 1916), told Canadians to take pride in this national baptism of fire and maintain their focus on victory. This concentration on Ypres as a place of suffering and purification was underlined by being the location where the Germans were alleged to have crucified a Canadian soldier, and as the site where Canada's greatest contribution to war remembrance was conceived: John McCrae's poem 'In Flanders Fields', which merged the region with the very meaning of the war, urging his readers not to 'break faith with us who die'.[58] Saint-Julien also allowed Canadians to assume the same mantle as the original BEF, and in so doing transformed volunteer amateur soldiers into equal status with revered professionals: Aitken reported that the actions of the Canadians at Saint-Julien had given them 'the right to stand side by side with the superb troops who, in the First Battle of Ypres, broke and drove before them the flower of the Prussian Guards'. As a result, it provided Canada with a legacy for future generations: 'The Canadian soldiers at the front have shown that they are second to none... The fight of Canadians at Langemarck and St Julien makes such a battle story as has sufficed, in other nations, to inspire song and tradition for centuries.'[59]

Fuelled by Aitken's London-based Canadian War Records Office, the British press also found it easy to obtain a diet of excellent material about Canada's war effort, which was especially in evidence during the Third Ypres campaign. According to the *Manchester Guardian*'s correspondent, the capture of the Bellevue Ridge 'should ring throughout the Empire, with special resonance along the roads between Nova Scotia and British Columbia'. Although a day of hard fighting, at its end 'the Canadians were still insatiable' as they methodically organized their defence of the position.[60] The wresting of Passchendaele a few days later saw fresh praise heaped on the Canadians. The *Manchester Guardian*'s correspondent stated: 'After an heroic attack by the Canadians this morning, they fought their way over the ruins of Passchendaele and into ground beyond it.'[61]

Although the Canadians had the longest association with the salient after Britain, the immensity of the efforts made at Messines and then Passchendaele in quick succession during 1917 also served to ingrain Ypres in the national war experiences of Australia and New Zealand. Previous to this, both nations had been exposed to the city mainly through British coverage, which gave it a profile and in the process ensured that Australians and New Zealanders shared the same vision as the imperial metropolis, but a deeper emotional pull was added once their own men became involved. Further, it also meant a distinctive microgeography consisting of the districts around Messines, Polygon Wood, and the Gravenstafel and Broodseinde ridges. Precise chronology here becomes important, for exposure to the salient by Australian and New Zealand soldiers in 1917 meant that they were experiencing it at the most intensive phase of fighting during the entire war. In turn, this had the ability to inform post-war remembrance and conceptions of Ypres. A further element influencing Australian and New Zealand perceptions was the military success won by their men, which counterbalanced the sheer horror of the fighting in terms of public discourse. Every achievement of the Australian and New Zealand units could then be celebrated on two levels. The first was the simple fact of military victory, and the second was the deeper spiritual connotation of having won through despite the appalling conditions of the battlefield. In combining these elements, home-front audiences could be presented with the truth about the dreadful nature of the battlefield because the rhetoric around it was so carefully shaped. Thus, the New Zealand official correspondent admitted the fact that the 'weather has been simply appalling', turning the battlefield into a 'sea of mud and water-logged shell holes', whilst stating that 'in the attack on Gravenstafel...many heroic deeds have also to be recorded such as will make the victory live in our history'.[62] Pride could then flow from these achievements. 'The 26 September will long be one of the red-letter days in Australia's calendar in memory of the superb achievement of our boys at Polygon Wood,' the *Farmer and Settler* told its readers. A few weeks later the *Barrier Miner* reported the advance on Broodseinde, crowing, 'No army in the world contains five more magnificent units than those in this Australian force, which was concentrated with the New Zealanders for the first time in the battle before Ypres.'[63]

* * * * *

Running alongside the ever more detailed understanding of the geography of the salient was the emphasis on its extreme strategic significance. Only through constant repetition of this point could both sides justify the commitment to the area. In the German public arena this element emerged only slowly with the initial focus being on Dixmude due to its commanding position over the coastal plain and key to the Yser riverfront.[64] By contrast, the British and Dominion press quickly focused on the importance of Ypres as the gateway to the Channel. John Buchan noted in *The Times* that 'the first battle of Ypres... [was] the greatest and most critical struggle of the Western war'; whilst the *Toronto Star* told its readers that during the Second Battle 'the Canadians had kept shut the gate to Ypres. They had barred the road to Calais.'[65] As the casualties rapidly piled up around Ypres, the strategic was combined with the sacred which gradually ensured that a self-fulfilling circular mantra was forged about Ypres: Ypres was significant because it blocked the way to the Channel; Ypres was significant because it was soaked in so much imperial blood; Ypres could not be abandoned because of this significance; Ypres blocked the way to the Channel. *The Times,* regardless of any reputation for sober reporting and reflection, was actually at the heart of this myth-making, starting in November 1914: 'The centre of the struggle has been Ypres, the defence of which will certainly be reckoned in history as one of the most striking episodes in the annals of the British Army.' A few weeks later another editorial averred that 'the Battle of Flanders has been the greatest in history', and a few weeks later still, 'What that stand has meant to England will one day be recognized. What it cost these troops and how they fought will be recorded in the proudest annals of their regiments.'[66]

Embedded in this rhetoric was a veneration for the original BEF. Initially eulogized for their stand at Mons, the pre-war professionals of the British army were given even greater status by the adoption of the nickname 'the Old Contemptibles', a deliberate mistranslation of a remark the Kaiser is alleged to have made about the British army. Despite the natural public interest in the newly raised units of Kitchener's volunteer army, the cachet of the old BEF remained strong, and with Mons, the birthplace of its reputation left way behind German lines, Ypres became the spiritual home of the original army. The minor poet, and future co-founder of the Ypres League, Beatrix Brice, was fixated on the connection between Ypres and the pre-war British army. Her poem 'To the Vanguard' eulogized those who had 'Stood fast while England girt her armour on', and was published by *The Times* in November 1916.[67] By 1917 a potent distillation was maturing as *The Times* led a campaign to officially recognize 31 October, the anniversary of the first crisis moment in the First Battle, as a day of solemn remembrance and observation.[68] A parallel was also drawn with a site sacred to the soul of France: 'The country around Ypres is to the British Army what Verdun has become to the French. It is the scene of the hardest and most desperate fighting our troops have known in the war, and nowhere have they gained greater glory.'[69] Post-war, the Ypres League took up these sentiments and ensured they maintained a high public profile. With the introduction of the whole Empire to the salient by 1917, *The Times* could also begin to present it as a palimpsest on which a host of imperial narratives were written:

> Nor should it be forgotten that these low ridges on which our troops are fighting are already hallowed ground to the old British Army, as they will also be consecrated henceforth in the eyes of Australia and New Zealand, of Canada and Newfoundland. On these very slopes fifty thousand men of the original Expeditionary Force laid down their lives or were wounded in the epic conflict of October 1914... To France belongs the glory of the

> Marne, to Great Britain the deathless pride of Ypres; but to both nations the two victories are a common heritage.[70]

As the grim casualty statistics of the Third Battle began to emerge on the home fronts of Britain and the Dominions, there was even more reliance on a compound language of clinical military evaluation and spiritual values. On the capture of the Passchendaele Ridge, both the *Manchester Guardian* and *Daily Mail* deemed that the savagery of the fighting, which demanded the heights of heroic self-sacrifice by men of the Empire, revealed the value placed on it by the enemy.[71] Ypres became the supreme testing ground of British imperial military mettle. *The Times* stated: 'Not even the records of high fighting in the great battle of the Somme excel the story of the endurance and valour shown by the British Army under incredibly difficult and baffling conditions during the last three months... It is not without reason that the name of Passchendaele has already become historic in the last few weeks.'[72] In April 1918, when the region was threatened by the German spring offensives, the *Daily Mail* once again summoned up the spiritual and the prosaic in explaining the recent fighting in the area. After a brief statement on Ypres's strategic significance, an editorial went on to state:

> It also has a moral importance. It was the scene of repeated and furious battles in which our troops always in the end drove back the enemy. No ground on the whole front has been more lavishly watered with our blood, and there was no destination which the German soldier so dreaded to be sent. The loss of Ypres at this moment would therefore possibly revive the drooping hopes of the enemy and might encourage him to continue his northern thrust for the Channel ports.[73]

* * * * *

The only real dissenter from the extreme importance of Ypres as the first line of defence for the Channel, and therefore by implication the sanctity of Britain, was Captain Hugh B. C. Pollard in his 1917 work *The Story of Ypres*. Although admitting that it was 'the key to Calais', he added: 'For political reasons it was essential that not a scrap

Figure 4. Book cover of the German-language edition of *The Story of Ypres* by Hugh B. C. Pollard, 1917.

more of the soil of Flanders should be surrendered, although the position was an unfavourable one for the Allies and a much better line of defence could have been sited on the slightly higher ground further back.'[74] Published in the immediate aftermath of the Battle of Messines, but before Third Ypres reached its conclusion, Pollard's book used an emotive and evocative tone and diction, reinforcing the images rapidly coming into sharp focus in anglophone discourse of Ypres as the most appalling battlefield on the Western Front. He opened by stating: 'Some of us laid down our lives at Ypres; there, too, many of us said farewell for all time to our careless youth. No one of us will ever regret his sacrifice or forget the terror and splendour of those days.' To have fought at Ypres was then deemed the true mark of the British soldier: 'Of those who have fallen, write only upon their monuments, "THEY FELL AT YPRES"—It is immortal honour.'[75] These statements contain hints of the poetry of W. N. Hodgson and Binyon's 'Fourth of August' combined with the acceptance of death, but firmly counterbalanced by the value of sacrifice and the nobility of army life in the service of a great cause. Finally, the supreme significance of Ypres as the prime battlefield of the war is made clear. However, the reason for the profile of Ypres is left ambiguous. Whether its strategic significance was so important that defending it became tantamount to saving Britain itself, or whether it had become sanctified simply by having so much British blood spilt over it, is not defined. In effect, it is the encapsulation of the post-Somme discourse in which the casualties become the reason for fighting the war to a victorious end; they become intermingled with the British justification for being at war. Here can be seen Geoff Dyer's identification of the paradox at the heart of the Great War's enduring grip on the British imagination: 'the Great War urges us to write the opposite of history: the story of effects generating their cause'.[76]

Maintaining this rhetoric of sacrifice as a reason for continuing the struggle, Pollard called Ypres 'holy ground', and dabbled with apocalyptic visions in describing the city as 'blood-drenched' and 'flaming in red ruin...the blood-red sky reflected the surging rage of war', but also hinted at the spiritual redemption that would inexorably follow: 'The great beauty of Ypres has passed to destruction, the great glory of Ypres has attained immortality.' The construction of this image closely parallels the language of the Church in the deliberate juxtaposition of death and regeneration: 'Christ has died. Christ is risen.' Similar use of Christian imagery can be seen in the poetry and prose of two well-known writers of the time. John Oxenham made Ypres one of his high altars of sacrifice whilst exploring the Western Front.[77] Wilson McNair went further still, outstripping Pollard in his insistent parallels with Scripture and Christianity:

> Ypres is more than a place name of our history; Ypres is more than the most splendid and the most bloody of our battle-fields. Ypres is the new altar of our nation, red with sacrifice; the covenant-shrine of a new Britain builded [*sic*] by the hands of those about to die, sanctified by their agony, embellished by their devotion. Ypres is holy ground, the supreme sacramental place of our nation.[78]

This prefiguring of the post-war language of pilgrimage was also used by the war correspondent G. Valentine Williams. On visiting Ypres he remarked that it 'was for me a pious pilgrimage to the place of sacrifice of the best of England's sons'.[79] Prior to 1914 Ypres was the city of the dead; Ypres was now the city of the martyred dead and their spirits were added to its mystical aura.

Other variants on pre-war guides and studies of Ypres were taken up in these works. Pollard consciously made the link by referring the reader back to '1914 [when Ypres] stood but little touched by time, as quiet and serene as, let us say, the Cathedral Close of Wells. It was rather out of the way for tourists' visits.'[80] The gaze, the intellectual and emotional outlook of the tourist, was therefore maintained in the public sphere. Some authors grasped the opportunity to make a few revisions to their pre-war works and capitalize on the public interest in Belgium generally and Flanders in particular. This also meant the repetition of familiar messages about Ypres. According to Joseph E. Morris's 1915 work *Belgium*, for the 'Beautiful Europe' book series, travelling between Nieuport and Dixmude provided a 'prospect of innumerable towers and spires, just as you have if you travel by railway between Spalding and Sleaford, or between Spalding and King's Lynn'. Having deployed this standard pre-1914 British image of Flanders, he maintained it in an extended comparison with East Anglia.[81] One guidebook placed the war at the heart of its narrative and was aimed at 'tourists' created by the war, *Ypres—Yper: A Few Notes on Its History before the War*. The guidebook of the Young Men's Christian Association (YMCA) was written by its leading agent in the salient, C. J. Magrath, with a foreword by the town major (local military administrative head), Captain James Lee. The work was largely aimed at the military and civilian services that operated in and around the city 'who make an enforced sojourn here, and can neither procure a guide book nor read long histories in Flemish'.[82] Somewhat ironically, the book was published in April 1918 just as the latest German attacks on the city were pressing the Allied defences back still further. Magrath's book encouraged his readers to imagine the former glories of Ypres, but also looked forward to the post-war world when it would inevitably be restored through the deliverance of Allied military victory. In his foreword, Lee wrote:

> I am often asked whether Yper is to be rebuilt. I greatly misunderstand the Flemish spirit if it should not be . . . I hope in the near future to revisit it in its new glory, and when the carillon of the restored belfry again rings out as old, to raise my voice with its people in their beautiful *Tuindaglied*—Juicht, Yper, Juicht, en viert den blijden dag [Welcome, Ypres, Welcome and celebrate the happy day].[83]

Lee here inverted the pre-war discourse of Ypres as a city of the dead by implying that it would only come back to life when it was fully restored to its old self. For him, at least, this would wipe out the horrific effects of war. This is a British vision very different to that of Winston Churchill's 1919 plan where the sepulchre of ruins was the only fitting outcome (see Chapter 4). Lee also showed a sympathy for Flemish culture and character in his desire to take part in the *Tuindag* (Palisades Day) festival and song. *Tuindag* commemorated the raising of the 1383 siege by the forces of England and Ghent, and in a further example of an unwitting foretelling of similar events, it was—and still is—celebrated on the first Sunday in August: ironically enough, in 1914 this overlapped with the first stages of the German invasion on the eve of another and far more terrible siege.

The tourist viewpoint was also consciously conjured up in German imaginings. Contained in its initial fixation on Dixmude, the German press carried numerous reports in the winter of 1914–15 detailing how significant buildings in the town had been destroyed (allegedly by the Allies) and how the debris of daily life littered the streets of the town. 'Dixmuiden is dead; it is a grave of ancient culture', wrote one war correspondent.[84] He went on to describe the destruction of the town's institutionalized memory—its archives—with medieval manuscripts lying around the ruins of the former guildhall. This report still relied on graphic description rather than visual images, but the 'before/after' perspective was already there. The newspaper even quoted an officer who allegedly had his Baedeker on him; the tourist guide told him that Dixmude was 'a quiet town on the Yser'.[85] Correspondents and soldiers alike approached Dixmude with the mindset of a traveller. One *Feldpostbrief* that gives a vivid account of the house-to-house fighting concluded by saying, 'Now there was also a bit of time left to visit the town'. But, disappointingly, the war had spoilt the sightseeing.[86]

For German soldiers, Dixmude was seemingly inviting visitors, whereas Ypres was out of reach. With its spires visible yet so distant, the city captured the imagination of both German war correspondents and soldiers. The painter Max Beckmann, who described himself half-jokingly as a war tourist, wrote in a letter home dated 7 June 1915 (and published in the same year) that 'I saw Ypres like a mirage in the hot mist in the distance'. In expressionist language he describes the 'fire-yellow craters', the 'sallow violet, hot sky', and the 'cold rose-coloured skeletonised church' of a village that barred his way to the city.[87] A rising star of the avant-garde, Beckmann served in Flanders as a medical orderly in 1915 and 1916. For a 1915 commemorative booklet of XV Army Corps, he contributed inter alia a drawing entitled *Towards Ypres* which depicts a rural scene with an alley leading nowhere. The city, it suggested, was a distant prize.[88] A dark obsession with urban Ypres grew between 1915 and 1917 as photographs of the burning Cloth Hall and aerial views of the ruined city became widely available in Germany. Ypres—the city—became a byword for destruction just as Langemarck—the rural village—symbolized regeneration.

Possession of Ypres—physically and spiritually—became an obsession for both sides, but was perhaps more pronounced on the part of the British Empire. In this struggle for possession, the need to define precisely what was being contested and the nature of the contest itself put a great strain on written language. Trying to conjure up word pictures of such scenes of devastation placed Ypres at the centre of one of the war's enduring cultural legacies: the problem of describing the indescribable. In his memoirs, the German writer Carl Zuckmayer reflected on why he had never written an expansive war novel. It seemed to him not only impossible but even futile to attempt to capture the experience of the war in words: 'I have also almost never spoken about the war, and especially not with people who were not in it. With the others, a phrase sufficed: "Somme, 1916." "Flanders, July '17." After that we preferred to fall silent.'[89] What Zuckmayer did not realize was that the assertion that the war was 'untellable' was in fact *the* code in which soldiers' expressed themselves. The very idea that an experience was beyond words is the leitmotif of numerous accounts of the Third Battle, simply known as 'Flanders' in Germany. The battle between the desire to find the right words on the one hand, and the recognition that the limits of language might have been reached on the other, became a quintessential feature of the age of 'total war', born in the sodden morass of Passchendaele.

* * * * *

Ypres was the place where the groping for words came together with an image to make the essential vision of the Great War. Passchendaele was peculiarly suited for this merger, being the ultimate onomatopoeic term for Western Front fighting and an iceberg of a name—its tip sticking above the sea of mud is only a tiny bit of the whole sunk deep in the Flanders clay. As Percy Wyndham Lewis, the war artist, later remarked: 'the very name, with its suggestion of *splashiness* and of *passion* at once ... was very appropriate. The moment I saw the name on the trench map intuitively I knew what was going to happen.'[90] Painting, sketching, and photography provided insights into the awful reality of fighting in and around Ypres which have endured to this day, although the message attached to them has often changed radically. To paraphrase the historian John Terraine, the visual road to Passchendaele commenced early in the war. It was during 1915 that visual images transformed Langemarck for German audiences from a geographical place name to a symbolic site. In the absence of photographic images, publishers commissioned artworks that showed the German troops storming forward—very much in the manner of nineteenth-century battle paintings.[91] Conscious reference to this inheritance was made by the Canadian artist Richard Jack, in his *The Second Battle of Ypres, 22 April to 25 May 1915* (1917). His huge canvas depicts a wounded officer calmly giving orders whilst his men steadfastly stick to their duties. Lord Beaverbrook was very impressed with his first commission for the official Canadian War Memorials scheme: it fitted his dual desire to create works that were both of immediate propaganda value and a heritage for Canada, memorials to inspire generations to come.[92] W. B. Wollen produced another iconic moment of Canada's involvement in the salient in *The Battle of Frezenberg* (1915), depicting the action of Princess Patricia's Canadian Light Infantry in the Second Battle of Ypres. Like Jack, Wollen's work was technically and aesthetically utterly different from the avant-garde artists commissioned by the state, but his vision was easily understood and digested by the public at large.

A significant number of images were brought together in the official British publication *The Western Front*, published in the spring of 1917 in the immediate aftermath of the battle of the Somme. Consisting of officially commissioned sketches and drawings by the Establishment artist Muirhead Bone, the booklet opened with a two-page introduction entitled 'The Western Front', which was probably written by Charles Montague, a distinguished journalist who achieved even greater fame through his post-war memoir *Disenchantment* (1924). The immediate effect was to domesticate the landscape in a sustained parallel with Britain. Working his way up from the Somme, each landscape is described in turn before reaching Ypres—*the* destination, the arrival, and terminus point of the British Western Front:

> The next change is not abrupt, like the first; but it is as great. Near Ypres you are on the sands, though yet twenty miles from the sea. Here you have a sense of being in a place still alive but pensioned off by nature after its work was done. You feel it at Rye and Winchelsea, at Ravenna, and at any place which the sea has once made great and then abandoned... But this countryside has the brooding quietude of a sort of honourable old age, dignity and pensiveness and comfort behind its natural rampart of sand dunes, but not the stir of life at full pressure.

The introduction to the Ypres section then concluded:

> There are dead cities, but with their bones still above ground: Ypres is one—many walls stand where they did, but grass is growing among the broken stones and bits of stained glass on the floor of the Cloth Hall, and at noon a visitor's footsteps ring and echo in the empty streets like those of a belated wayfarer in midnight Oxford. 'How doth the city sit desolate that once was full of people!' [Lamentations 1:1][93]

This vision contains much of the pre-war rhetoric in that Ypres had long been conceived as a city whose great medieval glories had gone, to be remembered in a warm halo of autumnal light. It also contained the link with England, particularly the south-east and Rye, which was already famous for its Ypres Tower. It was a city and region in the autumn of its years and had been abandoned, but such an interpretation of Ypres could have been written in any English text from about 1880 onwards. It was dead before the war; it is dead now. In this narrative the war was simply the next step in the preordained progression of Ypres. But this book is about snapshots taken in the middle of a war, and so the unspoken implication is that all will change with its end. Britain was fighting for the literal and spiritual restoration of Belgium, and Ypres had become its crystallization. The irony was that the vision existed long before 1914, and in the obsession of feeling the ghosts of Flanders' glorious past it made a link with later writers on Flanders such as R. H. Mottram.

Bone's first vision of Ypres in *The Western Front* is of the 'Grand' Place and Ruins of the Cloth Hall'.[94] It is unclear whether the accompanying description is his, but it encompasses 'the gaunt emptiness of Ypres' and stresses the grass creeping through the ruins. 'The only continuous sound in Ypres is that of birds, which sing in it as if it were the country.' The pastoral persists here and ruins remain romantic and serve their pre-1914 function of reminding the beholder of their own mortality and urging them to consider their own contribution to the world and its likely legacy. It begins to seem that Geoff Dyer's idea that 'the Great War ruined the idea of ruins' is just a little too emphatic.[95] 'A Village Church in Flanders' shows a scene in which 'there is the quiet of a desert' dominated by the picturesque ruins of the church.[96] 'A Street in Ypres' depicts a solitary figure walking along a road.[97] Towering above him to his left is what appears to be the remaining section of the main facade of St Peter's church. Used to thinking of Ypres as an inferno of noise in which shells fall incessantly, here 'the visitor starts at the noise of a distant footfall in the grass-grown streets'. Again, the pre-war conception lingers. Fitzgerald and Binyon had been awed by the shattering silence of Ypres which was especially felt at night. Here, both the description and the image have the overtones of the Gothic imagination. This world of ruins and fragments could be a city that had been abandoned and decayed over centuries, as Bone gives absolutely no hint as to how it reached this condition. The war is the given in the background, the all-dominating fact that needs no comment, which therefore meant nothing had to be said about justifications for its continuance.

The next image, 'Distant View of Ypres', shows a landscape without features apart from the almost insignificant silhouette of its ruins in the middle distance.[98] Here the shock of war's reality is achieved by the avoidance of what a viewer expects from a landscape image—something to which the eye is drawn as a focus point. When it comes to views of Flanders, the empty horizon was expected, but it was usually punctuated by some kind of standard feature such as a windmill or church spire. Here Bone shows very little, despite the fact that it is obvious that 'the fields are covered with crops, varied by good woodland' in the ground behind the lines. Such details merely serve to emphasize the devastation of the battle zone. But then comes the punch: 'To a visitor from the Somme battlefield the landscape looks rich and almost peaceful.' Such an interpretation was very much confined to the war, and the particular circumstances of 1916, and would not survive it. Post-war, the roles were reversed. The Somme was the landscape thought to be recovering more quickly, whereas Ypres held about it the reek of death. Here, a precise chronology of the war is extremely important. Although the battles around Ypres in 1914 and 1915 had been intensely violent, and there was further military activity in 1916, they were fought before both sides had truly refined and augmented their killing technologies. For all Western Front combatants, 1916 marked a sudden, wrenching lurch through the gears at Verdun and on the Somme and as such made Ypres seem a quaint backwater by Christmas 1916. It was Passchendaele that saw Ypres take centre stage, the dominant panel in an awful triptych of battles, allowing it to dominate the British vision of the war over the next twenty years.

The pause in the destruction of Ypres after the Second Battle of 1915 was captured by the British official newsreel in February 1916. Released in March under the title *Ypres: The Shell-Shattered City of Flanders*, and subsequently added to and rereleased in at least two further editions with new material, the film concentrates on the Cloth Hall and cathedral.[99] Both buildings are shown in a very badly damaged condition, gutted and roofless, but they are not yet the haunting ghosts of 1917 and 1918. Capturing this progressive destruction of the landscape and buildings became a particular obsession of the artists commissioned by the Canadian War Memorials scheme, who poured out paintings and drawings of the salient during the war, as revealed in the first full exhibition of their work in 1919.

The caesura and watershed represented by the Third Battle of Ypres, at least in terms of visual representations of the salient, is most clearly seen in the contrast between Bone's work and that of Paul Nash. Nash's vision of the Great War, which is also one that has a good deal of influence over contemporary understandings of the emotional and physical reality of that conflict, was one almost entirely shaped by the Ypres salient in 1917. In fact, Nash's only real experience of the Western Front, both as a serving officer and then as official war artist, was in the salient. He saw no other section of the front in great detail, and when he returned as a war artist, it was to the Third Battle. In his determination to confront the experience of modern battle, he then became even more intimately aware of the topography of the salient. Allocated a 'mad Irish chauffeur', the pair successfully navigated their way up the Menin Road, allowing Nash to engage with the intensity of the struggle in the fields beyond, whilst also taking him very close to the Hill 60 sector where he had seen out his brief period of active service with the 15th Battalion, Hampshire Regiment.[100]

His focus provides yet another example of Ypres's status as the concentrated essence of the Great War, the eye of the storm, the heart of all British imperial activity. He was also very much aware of the microgeographies, and, like others, was an obsessive identifier of precise locations in this new holy ground—'the topography of Golgotha', to steal from Wilfred Owen. In the combination of his precise titling and arresting visual images, Nash helped ensure the interchangeability between the terms 'Ypres salient' and 'Great War' whilst underlining the essential geography of the salient: *Sunrise Inverness Copse* (the basis for *We are Making a New World*); *Crater Pools Below Hill 60*; *Hill 60, From the Cutting*; *The Caterpillar Crater*; *Rain: Lake Zillebeke*; *Nightfall: Zillebeke District*; *The Landscape—Hill 60*; *The Field of Passchendaele*. Other images, although not ostensibly identified as the salient in the title, were clearly interpretations of its landscapes, including

Void; *Mule Track*; *Wire*; *After the Battle*; *Marching at Night*; and *Landscape, Year of Our Lord, 1917*.

For Nash the landscape artist and nature lover, the desecration of the physical environment during the 1917 fighting provided a metaphor for all the suffering and misery caused by the war. Seemingly appalled by the calamitous effects of modern weapons, he appears to have shed the status of artist in favour of direct spokesman for the front-line soldier, bringing home the appalling realities of war to those ignorant of its nature. Describing the front as 'unspeakable, godless, hopeless' in a letter to his wife, he went on to outline his new self-proclaimed role: 'I am no longer an artist interested and curious, I am a messenger who will bring back word from the feeble men who are fighting to those who want the war to go on for ever. Feeble, inarticulate, will be my message, but it will have a bitter truth, and may it burn their lousy souls.'[101] Such statements make it easy to equate Nash with poets like Owen; both men felt the need to suppress their role as artists in favour of something far more immediately relevant, and both men experienced a sense of crisis in their own medium of communication to encapsulate the titanic dreadfulness of the war.

It might, however, be going too far to deduce from this that Nash had identified himself unambiguously as a dissenter and protester.[102] The artist and art critic Sir John Rothenstein believed Nash never achieved a clear, solid position on the war, and in allowing room for this instability it is easier to understand the propaganda potential in Nash's work for the British and Canadian governments which commissioned it. Most of Nash's output, feverishly produced during the summer and autumn of 1917, was exhibited in London in May 1918 and included in *British Artists at the Front*, published at the same time. Displayed on its front cover was the painting *We are Making a New World*, which some take to be the ultimate expression of Nash's protest mission. However, in this context it was, instead, a powerful statement about the sanctity of British sacrifice because the spilling of blood, as reflected in the red sky, is ensuring regeneration.[103] As McNair wrote, 'they did not die in vain. For here in the fields of Ypres the world has been reborn of their blood.'[104] In this way the landscape of the Third Battle was made sacred through sacrifice and became the next chapter in an unfolding British imperial narrative about Ypres.

Nash added his sketches and paintings to the rapidly expanding photographic record of the fighting in the salient, which also acted as a precursor to his exhibition and the publication of *British Artists at the Front*. Although Nash admitted the shortcomings of war reportage, it was a process he appeared comfortable with, and he even believed that the newspaper coverage and images did at least attempt to give the home-front public a sense of life at the front and the nature of battle. 'We all have vague notion of the terrors of a battle', he wrote to his wife, 'and can conjure up with the aid of some of the more inspired war correspondents and the pictures in the *Daily Mirror* some vision of the battlefield; but no pen or drawing can convey this country—the normal setting of the battles taking place day and night, month after month.'[105] Two notable points arise from this comment. First, in accepting the role of war correspondent, Nash placed himself in a distinctly different category to men like Siegfried Sassoon with his angry contempt for the press. This should perhaps caution us against too simplistic a categorization of Nash, his attitudes, and his perception of his role. Second, the term 'this country', rather than a more generic label such as 'the front', reveals the highly particular vision of Nash in which Flanders and Ypres became *the* Western Front.

* * * * *

The Ypres salient allowed for visual records and interpretations that foregrounded both the destruction of the natural landscape and the ruin of the ancient fabric of the city. This was, to some extent, a reflection of pre-war anxieties about the impact of a future war on urban communities. However, the availability of visual images of pre-war splendour and wartime plight was crucial, notably photographs that could be juxtaposed to highlight the deadly power of modern artillery. The genre of the 'before/after' image—which later would become an integral part of the iconography of the bombing campaigns in the Second World War—originated, inter alia, in the wartime representation of Ypres. This technique was used in Macgrath's guide to Ypres and was picked out as a special point of interest by the reviewer for *The Spectator*.[106] Likewise, German soldier newspapers as well as commercial magazines featured illustrated articles on 'Ypres: Once and Now'.[107]

Other publications patiently monitored the progressive destruction through photographs. In France, the Roman Catholic booklet *La Guerre allemande et la catholicisme* (1915) carried photographs of the nave of St Martin's with damage to its roof and rubble strewn around the altar caused by German artillery.[108] In November 1917 *Le Monde illustré* devoted a double-page spread to photos of Ypres showing the Cloth Hall in ruins, under the title 'The joys of great art destroyed by the Boche'.[109] German guilt for the destruction of Ypres was never doubted, as shown by the *Illustrated London News* which provided regular visual updates on the accumulating damage. On 5 December 1914 it carried images under the emotive titles 'The Town in Which the Kaiser Proposed to Proclaim a German "Belgium": Ruined Ypres' and 'Among the Monuments to German "Culture": The Ruins of Ypres'.[110] Just over a month later it published a photograph of the roofless Salle Pauwels in the Cloth Hall on its front page and in August 1915 produced its most arresting image so far in an aerial shot showing the extensively damaged Cloth Hall, cathedral, and main square under the stark headline 'Ypres, 1915'.[111] The same image was reproduced in the *Daily Mirror* a day earlier, under the caption: 'Ruined Ypres as it is today. What would happen to St Paul's if the Huns came to London.'[112] The ruins of St Martin's and the aura of medieval piety that also infused the secular Cloth Hall then allowed the architecture to become a metaphor for the stoic suffering of the troops emulating Christ in their steadfast dedication. These sentiments were expressed by the *Illustrated London News* in December 1916 when it carried another front-page image, this time of St Martin's, under the headline 'In

Ypres the Wound: The Shattered Cathedral. A Fragment of the Cloisters'.[113] The term 'wound' evoked not only the injuries to the soldiers, but also those inflicted on Christ, and the use of 'fragment' perhaps resonated with the medieval world of holy relics.

As with much else in the Ypres salient, Passchendaele saw a spike in photographic activity. For the British Empire this was partly the result of the creation of the Department of Information, and a greater attention to propaganda by the Dominions with the Canadian War Records Office maturing and Australia paying much more attention to its visual record and media profile. Between 1 August and 30 November 1917 the *Daily Mirror*, the British daily built around visual images, carried photographs of Ypres battle scenes in thirteen separate editions. William Rider-Rider, the former *Daily Mirror* photographer, became the lead official Canadian photographer in 1917 and produced a series of memorable photographs. One of his personal favourites was the now iconic image of Third Ypres showing men of the Canadian 16th Machine Gun Company occupying a series of shell holes in a lunar landscape, first published in the *Daily Mirror* in early 1918. The photograph was labelled 'A Dog's Life at Passchendaele'. Underneath, the longer caption commenced with a quip from Bruce Bairnsfather's famous wartime comic creation, Old Bill: 'They wish they knew a better 'ole. The Canadians who are holding the line at Passchendaele have no trenches, but just mud holes. Some are dry, but on the other hand some are not.'[114] The first official Australian photographs of the battle appeared in the *Daily Mirror* on 5 October 1917.[115]

Just over a week later came a powerful front-page image showing the smashed landscape with water-filled shell holes and in the middle distance a cluster of concrete pillboxes. Headlined 'Complete Rout of General Mud', the caption read: 'The public will be better able to realise the wonderful achievements of our Army when they see this Australian official photograph. It shows the quagmire over which troops advanced in Flanders, while in the background is a German strong point which fell into our hands. Despite the bad weather we made another advance yesterday.'[116] No attempt was made to deny the dreadful state of the ground, nor the difficulties it created, which should cause us to question the extent to which the home front was deliberately misled about conditions at the front. Instead, this very fact is used as a way of encouraging admiration and respect for the troops whilst drawing a veil over the precise nature of the advance and its human cost. Three days later three more Australian official photographs appeared on the front page, including Frank Hurley's powerful profile silhouette of men marching across a slight crest with their reflections glinting in a shell hole full of rainwater.[117] But perhaps Hurley's finest achievement during Third Ypres was published by the *Daily Mirror* on 13 December 1917 under the headline 'The Sceptics: A Battlefield Story' and captioned: '"How I did it." An Anzac infantryman tells his comrades of an exploit, but the story was received with a good deal of persiflage.'[118] The now famous image showed men gathered around a blazing brazier, concentrating intently on one man who is addressing them. Some of the men have grins on their faces, which, thanks to the captioning, helps imply that they are not taking the story seriously.

Here was the flip side of the high diction—the essential good-humour of British imperial troops which set them apart from the automaton German enemy. The language and visual imagery associated with this set of characteristics did nothing to undermine the hallowed aura of Ypres. In fact, the two were intimately entwined, for it was precisely because the British soldiers were perceived as good-natured, simple, earthy chaps that their heroism, stoicism, and patient endurance were even greater qualities. In addition, this image was born and flourished in the Ypres region under the cartoonist Bruce Bairnsfather who created the famous Old Bill character, the soldier who embodied all the qualities of the BEF 'Old Contemptibles'. Originally published in the *Bystander* illustrated magazine, Bairnsfather provided his fans with a full insight into his experiences in *Bullets & Billets*. First published in December 1916, it was a bestseller running through numerous editions. However, far from focusing on the Battle of the Somme, which had just come to an end, Bairnsfather's entire text took place in the stretch of line between Ploegsteert and Ypres. Shot through with a very British sense of humour, Bairnsfather emphasized a particular microgeography of the Western Front in which Ploegsteert was very definitely not the salient proper. Instead, the immediate area around Ypres is the real heart of the war. He wrote:

> I was mighty keen to see this famous spot. Stories of famous fights in that great salient were common talk amongst us, and had been for a long time. The wonderful defence of Ypres against the hordes of Germans in the previous October had filled our lines of trenches with pride and superiority, but no wonderment. Everyone regarded Ypres as a strenuous spot, but everyone secretly wanted to go there and see it for themselves.

For Bairnsfather, Ypres was the ultimate test of the soldier: 'If one has ever participated in an affair of arms at Ypres, it gives one a sort of honourable trade-mark for the rest of the war as a member of the accepted successful Matadors of the Flanders Bull-ring.'[119]

* * * * *

Many other books about Ypres were published during the war, among them Frederic Coleman's *From Mons to Ypres with French* and Lord Ernest Hamilton's *The First Seven Divisions: Being a Detailed Account of the Fighting from Mons to Ypres.* Both were very popular with the public, going through multiple editions by 1918, and both kept the focus on the earliest engagements in the salient. A Canadian account was provided by Henry Beckles Willson's *In the Ypres Salient: The Story of a Fortnight's Canadian Fighting, June 2–16, 1916,* which put a highly positive spin on the rather mishandled struggles for the craters around Saint-Éloi.[120]

In early November 1917, while the Third Battle of Ypres was still being fought, the Württemberg daily *Schwäbischer Merkur* began publishing a new series of articles about the history of the battles of Messines and Passchendaele, and especially the contribution made by Württemberg's troops. It suggested that these battles were 'more gruesome and more enormous' than those waged at Verdun and the Somme. It stressed the 'iron' endurance of Württemberg's soldiers and how their 'bitter humour' helped them cope with the 'tough-flowing yellow mud'.[121] Needless to say, there was no room for even alluding to the indiscipline and panicky reactions that bore testimony to the cumulative strain of fighting a third major battle over the same terrain.[122] However, the content itself is less interesting than the fact that these articles were commissioned in the first place: an attempt to write history while the events were unfolding. This first draft of history was indirectly endorsed by the War Archive of Württemberg, which incorporated the newspaper articles into its collection, alongside primary sources such as war diaries.

The War Archive had been given the task of overseeing the publication of the official history, *Schwäbische Kunde aus dem großen Krieg* (Swabian Tale from the Great War). The title is borrowed from a humorous poem by Ludwig Uhland, a leading protagonist of German romanticism in the early nineteenth century. His 'Swabian Tale' is about the Gallant Swabian, a paladin of the crusader Frederick I Barbarossa, who always remains cool, calm, and collected in battle. He endures the assaults launched on him with disdain and plays a passive role up to a point when he unexpectedly, but vigorously, strikes back with his sword: the *Schwabenstreich* (Swabian blow or trick). During the First World War the Gallant Swabian dealing out *Schwabenstreiche* was turned into the symbol of Württemberg's contribution to the war effort, memorialized in a statue unveiled in Stuttgart in autumn 1915. Thus, the title of the official history represented a fusion of myth, medievalism, and memory of the war.[123]

The first two volumes appeared in 1918, covering inter alia First Ypres. That battle is described as one between enthusiastic German war volunteers and hard-nosed British professional soldiers: 'The enemy's superior number and firepower could not cause a notch in the German sword. It hit sharply . . . in the enemy's armour, powerfully it knocked the offensive weapon out of his hand. The haughty commanders French, Haig and Foch ducked behind their shield.' However, the narrative is also peppered with metaphors of modernity; 'iron hail' (*Eisenhagel*) and 'storm of iron' invoke the industrial nature of modern warfare.[124] The same metaphors were utilized by the official Prussian account of the history of First Ypres. Published in 1918, it appeared in English translation in the following year. Interestingly, the translator struggled to render the metaphorical language into English; 'iron hail' is translated rather clumsily as 'the continuous shelling of the enemy's artillery'.[125] It is worth noting that in 1914 no one had used this kind of language. The official histories, published in the aftermath of Third Ypres, drew on a repertoire of images furnished in 1917 to describe the events of 1914.

Historical accuracy was not the main concern of these two official accounts. Both were essentially propaganda publications. The series in which *Ypres, 1914* appeared had been the brainchild of propagandists within the general staff. The author himself made no bones that his was merely a sketch rather than a proper history—something that must have been lost on the Historical Section of the Committee of Imperial Defence which treated it as *the* official German history. What the Historical Section apparently did not know was that the institutional structures of military history in Prussia had been liquidated by the end of 1916; it was a reflection of the dire military situation in which all personal and material resources had to be thrown into the actual campaigns.[126] A German legend would therefore play into the post-war British imperial myth of Ypres, for that is what it was becoming as each chapter in the unfolding history was underpinned by the qualities of epic literature.

* * * * *

By 1918 Ypres had evolved into an extremely complex narrative consisting of a mainly British imperial text coloured by significant additions from the other combatant nations present in the region. It was also a series of polarities: it was the city of the dead, but infused with an unconquerable, immortal spirit; it was the city of medieval glories now turned to rubble; it was the heart of the horror and filth of war and the site of sublime nobility. Underpinning this wartime discourse about Ypres was a Janus-like quality, insofar as it consciously and unconsciously drew upon ideas and themes current in pre-war popular culture about the city and region, whilst also framing the post-war cult of remembrance. By the end of the war Ypres was also a site in which a British imperial construction of meaning and value was gathering immense power, establishing a moral and spiritual—not to mention physical—grip on interpretations of events and the landscape. Within this overarching narrative there was space for detailed and competing visions based upon a very fine-grained geography: Canadians at Saint-Julien and Passchendaele; New Zealanders and Australians at Messines and Passchendaele; Germans at Langemarck and Dixmude; French and Belgian at Dixmude and the Yser front. Although Dixmude and the Yser front were strictly speaking outside the Ypres salient, they were incontestably part of the wider definition of Flanders over which Ypres predominated as the patron saint of the West Flemish martyrs.

4

The New Battle for Ypres, 1919–1927

The ending of hostilities did not bring the struggle for Ypres to an end. Rather, a new battle commenced which combined the material with the metaphysical since the remaining fragments of the city and the landscape around it were inscribed with new messages. Already invested with meaning during the war, in its aftermath Ypres became the site of a new contest centred on reconstruction and the extent to which this should be allowed to obliterate what remained of the old. The landscape was reified as a highly significant silent witness in its own right with each of the combatants, but most particularly with the British, who were determined to impose their own imperial narrative on that witness. Indeed, by virtue of being quickest to respond, the British Empire utterly outstripped any French and German activity in the salient, ensuring it an advantageous position which did not really alter until the end of the 1920s. A host of media were used to express the narratives, with their implicit and explicit moral values, including a range of literary and visual forms, and—most potently—imposing and permanent interventions in the landscape itself in the form of memorials and cemeteries. This resulted in occasionally strained relations with local people who mainly wished for a return to the pre-1914 world.

* * * * *

Revealing the immense significance of Ypres as *the* British imperial battlefield of the war, its ruins became the focus of British and

Canadian attention very soon after the Armistice.[1] As early as January 1919 Winston Churchill, the secretary of state for war, proposed acquiring the ruins of Ypres as a permanent memorial to the sacrifices of the British Empire.[2] On the ground itself an imperial occupation was effectively in place as the region was still under British military control and the town major, Henry Beckles Willson, a Canadian writer, formerly a member of Lord Beaverbrook's Canadian War Records Office, was determined to safeguard the ruins and rapidly exceeded his authority. Starting with the staking out of a section of the ramparts as a Canadian zone, on which he built a small bungalow, Beckles Willson tried to enlist Field Marshal Sir John French in a campaign to block any Belgian attempts at rebuilding. Most potently, he also rushed out the first post-war guidebook dedicated to Ypres which encapsulated imperial sentiments about the city and in the process struck the crucial leitmotif for the next twenty years. Poignantly and powerfully entitled *Ypres: The Holy Ground of British Arms*, the opening declared:

> There is not a single half-acre in Ypres that is not sacred. There is not a single stone which has not sheltered scores of loyal young hearts, whose one impulse and desire was to fight and, if need be, to die for England. Their blood has drenched its cloisters and its cellars, but if never a drop had been spilt, if never a life had been lost in defence of Ypres still would Ypres have been hallowed, if only for the hopes and the courage it has inspired and the scenes of valour and sacrifice it has witnessed.[3]

Operating largely on his own initiative, Beckles Willson added to the number of agencies attempting to control the future of Ypres. In Britain alone three separate but interlinked authorities were at work: the War Office, the IWGC, and the Battle Exploits Memorial Committee. The Australian, Canadian, and New Zealand equivalents of this last body were also busy with their own plans. Eventually, the IWGC emerged as the most important British imperial authority in Ypres and this at least concentrated all discussion through one channel.

In Belgium the pre-war civic authorities of Ypres were re-emerging, most notably in the form of the mayor, René Colaert, and the city architect, Jules Coomans. At the same time, the Belgian government in

Brussels was trying to make sense of the devastated zone and maintain a dialogue with all interested parties. The atmosphere was particularly tense among the Belgians as opinions divided on the precise form of the rebuilding style. Ideas had been batted around during the war, with the exiled Ypres city authorities addressing a conference in Paris in 1916 in which they argued for rebuilding along existing lines. Such statements disturbed the Bruges modernist architect Huib Hoste. Based in the Netherlands, where he had fled after the German invasion, he had visions of a bold new city neatly delineated into separate zones for commerce, industry, recreation, and housing. In 1918 Hoste polled fellow architects and artists as to the future treatment of the Cloth Hall and the ruins. He received a range of responses, but very few believed it would be fitting or tasteful to reconstruct the ruins of the major buildings exactly as they were. This put him on a collision course with the city authorities led by Colaert and Coomans who were concentrating on restoring Ypres to its pre-war condition. They, along with many others, were fearful of a rebuilding programme in the 'new Dutch' modern style, believing it to be too Netherlandish and not truly Flemish, which also hinted at Catholic fears of a Protestant influence making itself felt in a key West Flanders city. The question of reconstruction was therefore far from simple or focused on a few key authorities.[4]

The 1919 visit of President Woodrow Wilson to the Belgian coast and Ypres was a further indication of the region's significance in the (post-) war period, and also illuminated the way discourse about correct behaviour in the devastated zone rapidly established a standard of codes. As described in the *New York Times,* the terms used still included those of the tourist trip, encapsulated by the picnic lunch at Houthulst Forest and the visit to see the 'tank graveyard'. Ypres itself was at the heart of the conundrum with its 'dozen or more frame buildings... erected to serve as hotels, restaurants, drinking places and small shops'. The contrast between regeneration and desolation was summed up in the headlines 'Wilson Deeply Moved by Belgium's Ruins' and 'Witnesses the Abomination of Desolation along the Battle-front in Flanders'.[5]

Figure 5. Temporary housing in Ypres. Postcard series 'The Ruins of Ypres', c.1920.

In Ypres the American president was pulled into a British imperial orbit, which on the ground was represented by Beckles Willson and his self-declared mission, as was perceptible in the British press. The *Daily Mail* noted that the Belgian royal couple and President Wilson were taken to the Menin Gate 'which has been presented to Canada . . . for a memorial building'. Wilson is then said to have exclaimed: 'What a splendid idea to gather together here the records and memorials of the Canadian fighting! Surely we, too, ought to do something of the same sort for American pilgrims at the front.'[6] The Church Army also used the visit to reinforce a sense of British ownership. Clearly thrilled at the opportunity to serve tea to the party, the Church Army representatives saw a validation of their work and the need for its permanent presence in the city, for it 'will always be a centre of pilgrimage, and a place to which English people will come to visit the graves of those fallen in the war'. They shared with the locals 'memories as sacred to England and the dominions'.[7]

The British imperial presence in the region was given an even greater profile when George V and Queen Mary visited the salient as part of their battlefields tour in May 1922. The royal party stopped at Tyne Cot cemetery where they met the gardeners and exhumation teams, and also visited the grave of their cousin, Prince Maurice of Battenberg, in the city's communal cemetery.[8] Their Majesties made a deliberate point of visiting the burgeoning Tyne Cot cemetery that was home to thousands of unknown soldiers before that of their own relative. Ypres thus served another unique function for the Empire in linking the highest and the lowest of the imperial dead and in doing so highlighted the key principles of the IWGC. Quite possibly the lowliest of the imperial dead was the soldier exhumed and chosen as the Unknown Warrior for repatriation to the United Kingdom and reburial in Westminster Abbey. There his tomb was filled with 100 sandbags of battlefield soil; it was draped in a Union Jack that had flown at Ypres, and the coffin had a posy of flowers cut on the Ypres battlefields. Ypres therefore dominated the associations and accoutrements that accompanied the body of the Unknown Warrior.

Figure 6. Tomb of the Unknown Warrior in Westminster Abbey in London. Postcard, *c.* October 1921.

At the other end of the scale was Prince Maurice of Battenberg. Killed in the First Battle in November 1914 and buried in Ypres town cemetery, Prince Maurice's grave became a contested site. His mother, Princess Beatrice, campaigned for the right to erect her own memorial on his grave. All such approaches were politely but firmly rejected by the IWGC's vice chairman, Fabian Ware, who noted in a letter for Winston Churchill's attention that if the request was granted it might lead to 'bad feeling among the working classes and many others who are in favour of equality of treatment'.[9] The Ypres League remembrance movement co-founded by Beckles Willson, despite having the Princess as an influential member, reported her case sympathetically, but ultimately without giving it sanction. Instead, its journal, the *Ypres Times,* recounted the story under the headline 'All Treated Alike'.[10]

Figure 7. HH Prince Maurice of Battenberg's grave at Ypres Town cemetery. Photograph, May 2014.

With the British insistent on their right to a major say in the reconstruction of Ypres, it is perhaps fortunate that they appeared to remain oblivious of the German wish to engage in the restoration as part of a 'great cultural memorial of... reconstruction', as the German Armistice Commission put it in 1919. Walther Rathenau, minister of reconstruction from 1921, argued that restoring the war-ravaged fabric of Europe would not only stimulate the German economy but also potentially 'count as the greatest positive creation of Germany in centuries to come'.[11] Future generations would remember the rebuilding rather than the destruction. This is a remarkable statement, considering that it came from the mouth of a man who had lent his support to the deportation of Belgian labourers during the war. Unsurprisingly, the Belgians would have none of this, and would not allow the Germans to take credit for the rebuilding effort. In the end, German visitors to Ypres witnessed a 'completely new... clean, beautiful city'—on which they congratulated the local planners.[12]

Figure 8. St Martin's Cathedral and the law courts. Postcard series 'The Ruins at Ypres' with handwritten note ('This is a ghastly city'), 1919.

Of great concern in Britain and the Empire was the speed with which local people were returning who were seemingly oblivious to the sensitivities of the Empire to this most sacred of spots. The elevation of the diction about the transfiguring of the city through the spilling of imperial blood ensured that the sense of shock at any attempt to return the city to normal was profound. Once again, Beckles Willson set the rhetorical standard in emphasizing the holy status of the city:

> No fire or steel or poison-fumes can rob it of its new glory in the annals of the British Empire. It is the words of the soldier-poet, Rupert Brooke, 'a corner of a foreign field forever England'.
>
> What Jerusalem is to the Jewish race, what Mecca is to the Mohamedan [*sic*], Ypres must always be to the millions who have in that long conflict lost a husband, son or brother, slain in its defence and who sleep their eternal sleep within sight of its silent belfry. Ypres and the expanse of earth spread out eastwards is in truth the 'Holy Ground of British Arms'.[13]

* * * * *

In an editorial, *The Times* set out Ypres's position as the pre-eminent 'memory site' of the Empire:

> Ypres is more than the name of a city or a battlefield. It is a symbol—and the fittest symbol—of the pride of the Empire in the achievements of its sons in the war; for there is no part of the Empire that does not claim some of the 250,000 dead who fell in defence of the famous Salient.[14]

In this rarefied emotional atmosphere the re-establishment of the city's annual summer fair caused deep dismay, as did the mushrooming of a souvenir industry. Both were regarded as the sacrilegious desecration of a shrine. A reader of *The Times* complained about the hawkers who have turned it into a 'sort of second rate country fair'; another correspondent, a bereaved Canadian mother, urged licensing of the souvenir sellers to deter disrespectful practices, and an article referred to the hustle and bustle of the city which already contained some 135 cafés and bars (rapidly put together from scraps of timber), postcard sellers, tourist buses, and souvenir hunters.[15]

Figure 9. 'No Man's Land Canteen' at Hill 60. Photograph, 1928.

Figure 10. Hotel 'Ypriana' and 'War Souvenirs' shop in Ypres. Postcard, *c.*1928.

Much of this rhetoric centred on the Belgians and rather ignored the reason for their industry: the fact that so many British and Dominion visitors were already arriving, thus stimulating a vibrant hospitality trade, and were to remain continual visitors despite fluctuations in the

Figure 11. Hotel 'Excelsior' in Ypres. Postcard, *c.*1920.

exchange rate with the Belgian franc. Prurient engagement with the battlefields as a spectacle was very much frowned upon, but regardless of whether a visitor regarded her/himself as a reverent pilgrim or an interested tourist, both required a supporting infrastructure. As such, a new industry was spawned in and around Ypres and the Westhoek generally in which established players competed with newer, smaller enterprises. On the grand scale Michelin famously responded with great speed in producing guides to the battlefields, including Ypres, by 1919. Commencing with a summary of the major actions around Ypres and accompanied by well-designed maps, the text moved on to provide an itinerary for a battlefield tour which made lavish use of photographs, many of them continuing the established trope of juxtaposing pre- and post-1914 images. Little overt comment on the nature of the destruction was made until the section on Ypres itself which is described as 'now but a memory'.[16] It then moved on to describe in great detail the Ypres that remained, with the tourist directed to what survived of that grandeur in much the same way as the wartime YMCA guide. In maintaining a focus on the medieval fabric of Ypres, the guide also implied that there was likely to be some kind of continuation of pre-war tourist interests rather than a focus on the effects of the war. This was reinforced by the inclusion of itineraries for the surrounding hinterland going as far into France as Estaires and Bethune.

When Ward, Lock and Company produced its revised guide to Belgium in 1921, it added a new element to the title and main text: *Belgium and the Battlefields*. Although it gave primacy to the bereaved wishing to visit graves of loved ones, it also encompassed a more general interest and covered a wide battlefield area going up to the Yser front. Realizing the desperate desire of many visitors, but particularly the bereaved, for the familiar and reassuring, the Château des Trois Tours at Brielen was highlighted as the base of the Battlefields Bureau, a specialist travel agency with its headquarters on London's Piccadilly, as well as the Ypres League and the Anglo-Belgian Union. At the same time, the guide also walked the tightrope between reverential advice on how to visit the cemeteries on the one hand and the tourists' interest in spectacle on the other by noting the so-called 'tank cemetery' which abutted the Menin Road beyond Birr Crossroads. This site had already been made famous through photographs showing the wrecks of many tanks caught by German fire whilst trying to advance. Thus, a novel 'attraction' was inserted into a wider framework of respectful remembrance.[17]

In the same year the Belgian Ministry of Railways and Telegraphs produced a guide to the Yser front emotively entitled *Aux champs de gloire: Le Front belge de L'Yser*. After noting that Belgian forces on the Yser undertook a 'sacred guard', it turned to a relatively straightforward account of the battles. The illustrations, however, are detailed in depicting the ruins and trenches and have a similarity with Bone's wartime work. The main bulk of the text was in gazetteer format with brief entries on each location listed in rough geographical order from north to south. Although the entries are generally rather sober, they are not stripped of all emotion. Ypres is said to be the place where the 'rage of the enemy was vented on the ancient city and its inhabitants as

Figure 12. 'Red Cars' battlefield tours itinerary. Advertisement, c.1925.

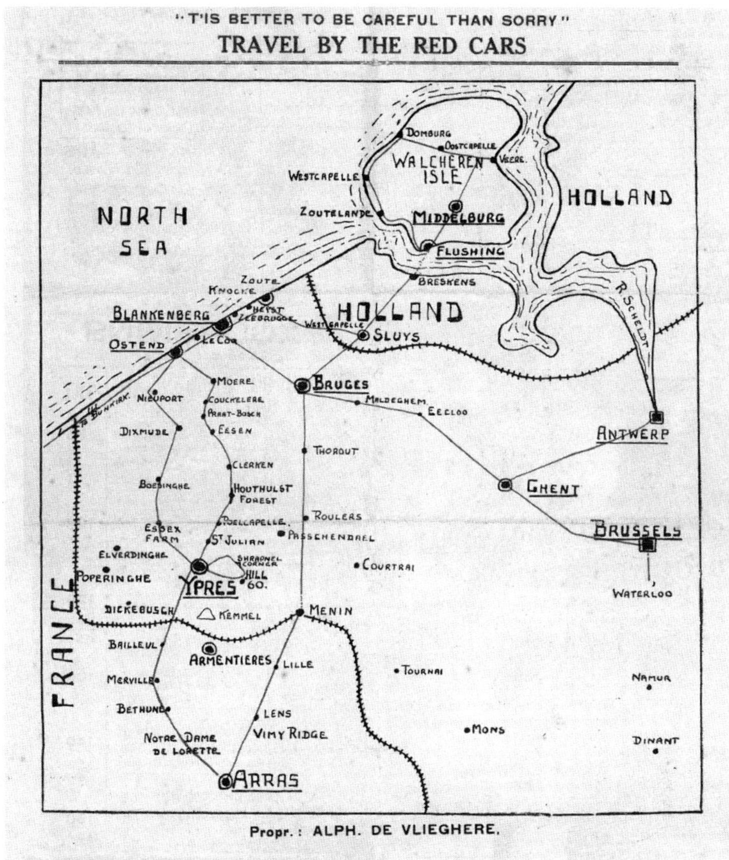

Figure 13. 'Red Cars' battlefield tours map. Advertisement, *c.*1925.

a result of which it was totally destroyed'. Similarly, Dixmude is the site of the 'heroic resistance' by the French marines at the spot where the Germans came closest to crossing the Yser in force; whilst Steenstraat was made famous by the 'bloody fighting' that took place in 1914 and 1915.[18]

Until the late 1920s very few Germans visited the former battlefields on the Western Front. Nevertheless, a visit to the former theatres of war, and particularly to the grave of a loved one, was an almost

Figure 14. 'London' garage and tea rooms near the Menin Gate memorial. Postcard, *c.*1927.

universal aspiration of the bereaved—even before the war had come to an end. During the war the press had reported how meticulously the location of every burial was recorded so that 'everyone will one day be able to visit the grave of their relatives'.[19] An unstable currency combined with strict visa regulations were practical obstacles to a journey to Flanders after 1918. And yet newspaper readers were made aware that 'a wholly new kind of battlefield tourism' existed. One article of 1920—which compared war-ravaged Dixmude with the sublime beauty of Pompeii—highlighted that many new bars and cafés catered for the thirsty tourist in Ypres.[20] In practice, however, only the well-to-do could afford such a trip, while the overwhelming majority were armchair tourists who travelled virtually in the company of press correspondents.

Consequently, in the early 1920s it was mainly a small number of individual travellers who ventured on their own initiative to the former Western Front. For the German tourist a typical tour of Flanders with a local chauffeur included stops at Ypres, Kemmel, Wytschaete, Comines, Werwicq, Hill 60, Saint-Jean, Saint-Julien, Langemarck, Bixschoote, and Steenstraat. Publishers of guidebooks must have considered this market insignificant, for the main publishing houses did not bring out new editions of their Belgium guidebooks until the late 1920s or early 1930s. To be sure, a brief guide to German cemeteries in the west appeared in 1927, but this booklet contained neither maps nor photographs. The author recommended that the bereaved should first pay a visit to the war graves office located in half-destroyed barracks in Ypres in order to track down the precise location of a grave.[21] Those who did so were often dismayed to find graves desecrated by horse manure and cow dung. Significantly, from 1926 onwards battlefield tourists pointed the finger not at Belgian farmers but at the German state. 'Where are our authorities, who finally, now that the war is almost eight years over, take care of the dignified burial of our fallen???', one angry veteran wrote to a military journal.[22] He had visited German cemeteries shortly after the Belgian–German war graves agreement of 1926. It was of course unrealistic to expect the

German authorities to transform the cemeteries within a matter of weeks but even so the war graves issue had important domestic ramifications. Previously a diplomatic tool in the campaign against the Versailles Treaty, the shocking condition of German war graves came to undermine the legitimacy of the Weimar Republic. Foreign tourist guides, too, did their best to hammer another nail in Weimar's coffin by telling their audiences—primarily British and American tourists—that the condition German war cemeteries were in showed that the Germans lacked respect for their own war dead.[23]

Regardless of the nationality of the visitor, a certain code of conduct was expected to be observed. Ensuring that all visitors maintained a respectful tone was essential across the battlefields, but was felt to be especially important at Ypres and this helped the rapid transformation from tourist to pilgrim.[24] Leading the process in the region was the emerging Christian movement Toc H, based at Talbot House, Poperinghe. In 1920 it established the tone by producing *The Pilgrim's Guide to the Ypres Salient*. With accommodation in and around Ypres so scarce, agencies like the Salvation Army and the Church Army then contributed to the guarding of sacred memory by prioritizing space for relatives of the dead, particularly mothers and widows, at their hostels. Colaert and the city authorities also did their best by agreeing to a British plan for the fencing off of the Cloth Hall and cathedral ruins and the erection of a sign instructing all to behave decorously and refrain from removing souvenir fragments of stone in what the British called 'the zone of silence'.

* * * * *

In their desire to maintain a sepulchral silence around the ruins, and in the stubborn refusal to accept rebuilding and rehabilitation of the devastated Ypres, the British perhaps revealed that they were a nation in shock unable to think of a future. However, this vision was undermined from two directions. The first was the inability to stop people returning and demanding reconstruction, and the second was the vision of the IWGC itself which, having inherited the Battle Exploits

Memorial Committee's initial planning for a great memorial in Ypres, was finalizing an alternative vision in which the British Empire would leave an entirely different indelible footprint on the city: the Menin Gate memorial to the missing. Somewhat ironically, at no point did the British ever stop to consider whether their lack of concern over local wishes undermined their role as liberators and defenders of a people made vassals of a dictatorial enemy. A rare concession to the fact that the British defended Ypres on behalf of Belgian liberties was provided by the BEF's first commander during his visit in 1922. Arrayed in his striking new title of Lord French of Ypres, he stated that 'we defended this bulwark and bastion, this almost final fragment of *uninvaded Belgian soil*, to the end'. For much of the 1920s, Ypres was viewed as something akin to the south-easternmost county of England, and not a corner of an independent sovereign state.[25]

Indeed, throughout the twenties, the British reminded everyone of their indisputable claim to Ypres by continuing the wartime insistence that Ypres was the final outpost of British imperial security. Reverting to this trope, Lord French followed exactly this pattern in another 1922 speech: 'The fate of the Empire was never in greater peril than at these two battles of Ypres.'[26] Every trail of imperial blood shed on every battlefield eventually led back to Ypres, the crucible and chalice of imperial sacrifice; as Beckles Willson wrote in an *Ypres Times* editorial:

> There were those amongst us who fought under the shadow of the Holy Places in far-off Syria; there were those who marched amid the ruins of dead empires to the city of the caliphs; there were those who fell in their thousands in the effort to reach Byzantium, Constantinople of to-day; there were yet others who fought and fell on the seven seas of the world; but to England on the whole, the War is summed up in the one word 'Ypres', the gate of Flanders.[27]

Such a reliance on high diction allowed for the continuation of the wartime rhetoric in which Ypres far exceeded its 'mere' strategic value and became instead a symbol sanctified in blood, defended entirely because it was a site of sacrifice. It was the elevated and spiritual version of the soldiers' prosaic, ironic, and resigned song, 'we're here because we're here because we're here': a self-fulfilling, circular prophecy.

Boyd Cable, ex-serviceman, journalist, and writer, understood this meaning and definition of Ypres, stating that it 'came to mean from the first days of the war more than a mere town to be held or lost, a square of the great chess game to be yielded or taken. For the Empire and the whole world, "Wipers" became a sign and a symbol.'[28] When both the spiritual and strategic significance of Ypres were combined, it allowed the British Empire to indulge in solipsism about the war, foregrounding its own experience and role above all others, particularly when compared to that of France. The *Daily Express* told its readers that 'it was there, more than at Verdun, that the war was won and Europe and the Empire saved'; whilst an article in *The Times* claimed that 'it detracts nothing from the splendour of the achievement of our Allies to say that not Verdun itself nor any other place saw anything comparable with the four years-long agony of Ypres'.[29] Some adopted a more reflective mode, understanding Ypres as the British equivalent of Verdun. C. J. Magrath, long-time YMCA representative in Ypres, wrote in *The Pilgrim's Guide to the Ypres Salient*: 'Ypres! It is not easy to convey what this word meant to the British Army. It was a symbol—as Verdun was to the French—of the tenacity of the race, of the certainty of victory. From the first to last Ypres figured in the war.'[30] The Bishop of Bury, who was also Anglican bishop for north and central Europe, similarly declared Ypres a 'great name to our race, as Verdun is to France'.[31] King Albert of the Belgians underlined the point during his speech at the Menin Gate unveiling ceremony in which he reassured everyone present that he both fully understood and agreed with British imperial sentiments about Ypres: 'If bloodshed in a noble cause sanctifies the ground where it is spilt, no ground in the world is more sacred than the Ypres salient. For fifty months Ypres was the threshold of the British Empire; its name stands forever as a symbol of British courage and endurance. Ypres was for the British Empire what Verdun was to France.'[32]

Reginald Blomfield's Menin Gate stamped a massive, and permanent, British imperial footprint on the city which not only served as an alternative focal point to the ruins of its medieval Cloth Hall and cathedral, but also acted as the funnel through which pilgrims would access the salient. Rich in classical allusion, the gate contained the names of some 56,000 missing up to August 1917 with the rest included in a memorial forming the rear wall of Herbert Baker's massive Tyne Cot cemetery near Passchendaele. The decision to build a major memorial on the site of the old Menin Gate was hardly surprising given its wartime significance as the portal to the battlefields. However, the initial conception had nothing to do with IWGC plans to commemorate the missing. The project was actually conceived by the Battle Exploits Memorial Committee. Formed under the auspices of the War Office with the intention of erecting memorials to the British and imperial forces on the most important battlefields of the war, the committee instantly identified Ypres as of paramount importance and despatched Reginald Blomfield to investigate. Blomfield quickly settled on the Menin Gate site, and deeply aware of the city's Vauban inheritance, found inspiration in the gate erected in the city walls of Nancy. Thus, Blomfield decided to make deliberate allusion to the history of Ypres and its role as a military bastion. Further, as a project of the Battle Exploits Memorial Committee, his design reflected its imperatives to mark the achievements of British imperial forces on the battlefield. Blomfield achieved this by marked reference to the triumphal arches erected by Roman emperors, and thus the foregrounding of classical motifs.

Unveiled in front of a huge crowd on 24 July 1927, the ceremony combined imperial pride with heartfelt mourning, especially as a large contingent of bereaved wives and mothers attended under the auspices of the St Barnabas Pilgrimages. Lord Plumer, who had commanded the Second Army in the salient for much of the war, told the crowd that no man remained missing: 'He is here!' The British and Dominion press picked up on the poignancy of this remark given the large number of bereaved women present, implying that grief and remembrance had a distinct female significance which formed one particular strand of the overall emotional and spiritual atmosphere. Pathé Gazette's newsreel gave a gendered account: 'Mothers from every part of Britain tread the path—where once their dear ones trod—to the Menin Gate...to place their tributes on the gate of a million memories.'[33] Lieutenant General Sir William Pulteney, a senior figure in the Ypres League, consciously made the link between service to the crown, encapsulated in his own masculine military service, and the character of imperial womanhood:

> While there is no need to describe here the Pilgrimage or the ceremony at the Menin Gate, it is not possible to pass over the fortitude displayed by the pilgrims, especially the mothers. With such parents, one ceases to wonder at the heroism and endurance of their sons who laid down their lives for King and Country.[34]

In faraway Queensland, the *Townsville Daily Bulletin,* using syndicated material, told its readers that the pomp and circumstance was underpinned by the emotions of ordinary 'British fathers and mothers, brothers and sisters' who 'throughout the night... [had] poured into Ypres', causing such a crush in the city 'that many were forced to spend the night in the open air'.[35]

Unique among British newspapers, the *Daily Express* made the 700 women whose sons were missing or in unknown graves the central point of its coverage. Referring to the ceremony as the most moving event since the burial of the Unknown Warrior in Westminster Abbey in 1920, it emphasized the humble backgrounds of the women, most of whom were taking 'their first adventure in travel', clutching their wreaths of English flowers. Their naivety and innocence infused the piece with sentimentality and in the process imposed an almost childlike status on the women who were 'a little dazed by the foreign turmoil' of arrival in Ypres. When sittting down in their special enclosure at the gate, 'they did not know that they were sitting on the road to Hell Fire Corner', and then they were called upon to lay their wreaths: 'They came to it bravely, so bravely and calmly, holding their little posies of English flowers. All one could do was to put one's arm in theirs, as if they had been one's own mother, and pointing high up on Menin Gate, spell out a name to them.' Looming over the whole event were the ghosts of the dead, thus exploring the same spirit that inspired Will Longstaff's famous painting *The Menin Gate at Midnight*. The correspondent asked these ghosts, 'what sight could amaze you more than "Dear Mother" so near to Hell Fire Corner holding a little bunch of flowers from the front garden at home?'[36]

The most remarkable testimonial to the power of the Menin Gate memorial came from the Austrian pacifist writer Stefan Zweig. Writing in awe-filled tones in the *Berliner Tageblatt* in September 1928, he praised the memorial for its remarkable fixation on the names of the dead, literally referring to them as 'entrenched on the gate', which stripped it of any other meaning. Clearly either unaware of, or deliberately downplaying, its multifaceted function, Zweig saw in this 'Roman simplicity' a monument 'more moving than any triumphal arch or monument to victory that I have ever seen'.[37] Therefore, not all who might be expected to be troubled by the gate fell into line with Siegfried Sassoon, who condemned it as a 'sepulchre of crime' and a container of endless 'nameless names' in his 1928 poem 'On Passing the New Menin Gate'. On insisting on the primacy of the disillusioned veteran as the only true judge and interpreter of the war, Sassoon totally ignored its myriad faces and meanings.

On the same day as the unveiling of the Menin Gate, Lord Plumer laid the foundation stone for another important focal point of the British presence in Ypres: St George's memorial church. Also designed by Blomfield, the intention behind the church was to provide a place of worship for pilgrims and the city's burgeoning permanent British community, mostly working for the IWGC and in the hospitality trades catering for British visitors. The project had a long gestation, having its origins in 1919 when the Church Army originally suggested the need for a permanent Anglican chapel, with one of the islands in the moat or the Lille Gate considered as sites. Perhaps unsurprisingly, there had been some disquiet from the Roman Catholic clergy who were concerned that it would impose Anglican rites on all British pilgrims to the city. Nonetheless, the idea maintained the support of the Church of England, and the Ypres League threw its weight and energy behind the scheme which resulted in the purchase of land close to the Cloth Hall and cathedral ruins. Although very understated in its design, with a typical Flemish gable ensuring that it was consistent with the facades of the rapidly restored buildings, St George's did, in fact, emphasize the dominance of the Anglican Established Church and maintained a distance from the Roman Catholicism of the local people.[38]

In the Irish Free State a reverence for Ypres was partially maintained because of its shared Roman Catholicism, with much of the press interested in the Irish nuns of Ypres as they became settled in their new homes, first at Macmine Castle, Wexford, and then Kylemore Castle, Galway. The erection of the Munster cross in the shadow of the cathedral ruins in July 1924 then provided a perfect balancing act of loyalties, motivations, and sentiments. Inscribed with the message that it commemorated the fight for the freedom of all nations, and unveiled with speeches proclaiming Ireland's long-standing connections with Flanders, it spoke to Irish nationalists and Catholics. At the same time, because it was unveiled by George V's son, Prince Henry, it was also a reminder of the ultimate unity of the Empire tried and tested in the Ypres crucible.[39] The unveiling of the 16th Division cross in Wytschaete also helped maintain the profile of Ypres, and in particular the Messines district, as also symbolized in the Messines Park homes for veterans in Londonderry.[40] Imperial metropolis visions and local identities could merge.

From Ypres itself, the imperially shaped landscape fanned out across the old salient in the huge number of memorials and cemeteries. Eventually, some 169 permanent cemeteries were built in 56 square miles, or three for every square mile. This represented a new departure in commemorating war dead through the systematic creation of sites designed for the immediate comfort of the bereaved and as a lasting legacy to the efforts of the British Empire. Reflecting the crucial significance of the region to Canada was the decision of its government

Figure 15. Irish Munster cross and the ruins of the cathedral. Postcard, 1925.

to erect three memorials, at Saint-Julien, Mount Sorrel (Hill 62), and Crest Farm, Passchendaele.[41] The judges of the Canadian war memorials competition deemed two designs to be of outstanding quality: the pylons and sculpture combination of Walter Allward and the so-called 'Brooding Soldier' obelisk of Frederick Chapman Clemesha. Both were deemed to be of such striking quality that they should be used once only, whereas the other designated memorial sites were each to be marked by a simple octagonal stone plinth. The centrality of Ypres was such that the Mount Sorrel site was very carefully considered as a possible location for Walter Allward's grand memorial scheme eventually constructed on Vimy Ridge. That Mount Sorrel was a serious proposition reveals that Vimy Ridge was by no means regarded as the entirety of the Canadian Western Front experience in the interwar period. Then, in choosing Saint-Julien as the site for the Clemesha design, its unique significance as the place where the Canadians had not just endured battle for the first time but had also been exposed to the appalling new weapon of gas in 1915, was fully underlined. Infused with a striking spirit of mournful, respectful repose and reflection, the memorial made a deep impression from the moment it was unveiled. A correspondent of the London *Evening Standard* described the mysterious effect of the memorial as the visitor approached:

> A mile or so further on stands a monument which affected me beyond the power of stone. From a grey and giant sheath grew the head and shoulders of a Canadian soldier... It is by far the finest memorial of the late war that I have seen, and the one that will tell future generations most about the Great War.

He then added that the simple inscription

> has almost the power of the Greek: 'Stranger, depart and tell the Lacedemonians that we lie here obeying their laws.' One bows the head in humble acceptance; the bravest ornaments were not out of place. There is a mysterious power in this brooding figure, drawing you from the things that are to the things that were. It does more than command the landscape, it orders the spirit.[42]

The Canadian memorial at Crest Farm produced an equally sobering effect through its inscription, which carried out the subtle trick of turning the dreadful reality of Passchendaele into spare, but noble, prose: 'The Canadian Corps in Oct.–Nov. 1917 advanced across this valley—then a treacherous morass—captured and held the Passchendaele ridge.' Here, on a memorial, there was a strong indication of the true topographical conditions of the battle transformed into an affirmation of Canadian endurance and courage which should be saluted by all. Australia and New Zealand also erected memorials at locations intimately connected with actions by their troops. For New Zealand this issue became extremely important as, alone among the Empire, it opted to commemorate its missing in cemeteries rather than at central memorials. In taking this decision it remained faithful to a solution to the problem thrown up by the missing discussed early on by the IWGC, but in the process excluded itself from the Menin Gate. The governments of Australia and Canada were likewise attracted by the idea of commemorating the missing in cemeteries, but once the plans for the Menin Gate with its immense scale and grandeur became clear, both realized that to stand aloof from this grand pan-imperial scheme ran the risk of dimming their roles in the salient.[43]

Indeed, New Zealand subsequently came to the same conclusion which resulted in an additional plaque being added to the Menin Gate listing the sites where its men were remembered.[44] Commemorated at Tyne Cot, Polygon Wood, and Messines Ridge, New Zealand's memorials to its missing were accompanied by two obelisks at Messines and Gravenstafel designed by London-born New Zealand architect Samuel Hurst Seager. Like Canada's plinths, they impressed by their simplicity, but perhaps made their greatest punch through the powerful inscription: 'From the utmost ends of the earth.' The memorials to Australia's contribution to the battles around Ypres also had their own inherent drama. The first was in the form of an obelisk given a looming presence by virtue of its position on the top of the old Belgian army firing range butts at Polygon Wood, and the second was at the heart of Tyne Cot cemetery. Here the remains of the battlefield were not entirely swept away, for three great German blockhouses were left in place. The central one then became the site of the Cross of Sacrifice, but Herbert Baker (or more correctly, his assistant on the project, J. R. Truelove) left a small portion of the original rough concrete exposed, and a bronze wreath was added, stating that the position was captured by the Australian 3rd Division. Thus, Australia gained a significant presence in the largest IWGC cemetery in the world, on arguably the most dramatic site, with its clear vistas all the way to Ypres reminding visitors of what the imperial armies had endured to reach this crest.

Almost completely marginalized in this British-dominated memorializing programme were the Germans. The first German war cemeteries were planned in the immediate aftermath of First Ypres. This was a subject covered in some detail by war correspondents who tried to reassure people back home that the dignity of the individual mattered in an age of mass death. In November 1915 the *Frankfurter Zeitung* featured an article about 'The Graves of the Regiment "Deutschland, Deutschland über alles"', near Becelaere. After recounting the story of the already legendary assault on Langemarck, the article went on to describe how the dead of this imagined regiment had been buried in a disused trench, their graves marked by white crosses blown awry. And yet it was not a pitiful sight, but a 'triumphal song of heroism' with the grave markers blending into the Flemish countryside. The emphasis on nature and landscape here is significant; it was to become a salient feature of post-1918 discourses.[45] While these were provisional war graves, the Germans also began to lay out semi-permanent war cemeteries, often extending communal cemeteries such as the one at Roeselare in 1915. With row upon row of wooden 'Iron Crosses' painted black, one war correspondent described the Roeselare cemetery as a 'field of seeds of the German future'. At the same time he conjured up images of a mythological past filled with Valkyries carrying the fallen soldiers to the hall of the slain in the afterlife, Valhalla.[46] But the war dead rarely did rest in peace in the Ypres salient. Many a war grave was battered during the Third Battle. A war correspondent revisiting the cemetery near Herenthage in autumn 1917 was shocked to find absolutely nothing left, not even fragments of skeletons and coffins. The whole place looked 'as if ground by a colossal mortar'.[47]

The dilapidated appearance of German war cemeteries would not change much in the early 1920s. The monthly journal of the Volksbund Deutsche Kriegsgräberfürsorge, the German war graves association, provided regular updates on the state of every single war cemetery abroad. Again and again it recorded that grave markers had been destroyed in combat and not replaced. North Langemarck cemetery, it noted in March 1922, 'is full of shell-holes and remains in the same condition in which it was left'. In addition, the journal highlighted the ongoing neglect; new fences had already disappeared and cows had been allowed to graze on several cemeteries.[48]

The Volksbund—in contrast to the intergovernmental IWGC which followed civil service practice—was a private association. Individuals could join, yet the membership was dominated by corporate members such as municipalities and associations. Although the Volksbund collaborated closely with the German authorities, especially the Foreign Office, it managed to convey the impression to the public that it was the sole organization looking after German war graves. In practice, though, there was little the Volksbund could do apart from reporting back home, for its resources were limited and, moreover, the upkeep of German war cemeteries on Belgian soil was—according to the Versailles Treaty—the responsibility of the Belgian state. To be sure, the much-lamented state of disrepair became a useful tool in the hands of both the Volksbund and the Foreign Office: it demonstrated that the Allies themselves were not serious about fulfilling their responsibilities under the peace treaty and provided ammunition to those who demanded a revision of the Versailles settlement. Thus, moral outrage went hand in hand with political cunning.[49]

The main problem with the German war graves in the Ypres salient was that, in contrast to other sections of the former Western Front, 'the population can less easily forget the war events', German diplomats suggested. Very few local people were apparently willing to maintain the graves of the former occupier.[50] By 1925 the situation had become critical. The cemeteries in the salient were in an extremely poor condition compared to those in northern France; German public opinion, the authorities claimed, was enraged; and Belgium, by invoking national law, threatened to remove the soldiers' graves after a statutory period of five years.[51] Eventually, the Belgian and German governments concluded a special treaty in 1926, and the German Foreign Office assumed responsibility for the German war graves in Flanders. In the following months the Brussels embassy tried to gain an overview, carry out essential repairs, and formulate basic principles for the construction of cemeteries. Lessons were to be learnt above all from the IWGC's designs. While German architects were impressed with the lavish and orderly appearance of the British cemeteries, they considered them too manicured, their entrance halls too bombastic, and the white headstones too alien-looking in the Flemish landscape. By contrast, it was argued that German cemeteries must look natural and avoid the appearance of a botanical garden.[52]

Different architecturally and horticulturally from the German examples, British distinctiveness was matched by sheer number, allowing the work of the IWGC to overshadow the activities of all others. The siting of the memorials underpinned an 'imperial gaze' over the landscape in other ways, for it also contributed to the process of maintaining the wartime microgeography. As early as July 1919 the British Battle Exploits Memorial Committee had drawn up an extensive list of locations likely to see memorial activity, including 'Boesinghe, Bixschoote, Pilkem, Langemarck, Poelcapel [*sic*], Passchendaele, St Julien, Grafenstafel [*sic*], Zornebeke [*sic*], Polygon Wood, Sanctuary Wood, Gheluveelt [*sic*], Hooge, Hill 63, Neuve Eglise, Messines, Wytschaete, St Eloi, Hill 60, Kemmel, Ypres, Klein Zillibek [*sic*]'.[53] At only one site can the British be said to have 'lost' the battle for meaning, largely because it was peripheral to the imperially defined landscape, and that was Langemarck.

* * * * *

For Germans, and particularly for German youth, Langemarck retained its wartime aura. Showing Germany's marginalization from the actual salient, the initial focus on this particular site was expressed in acts of reverence conducted in the Rhön Mountains. There the middle-class youth movement, the Bündische Jugend, held commemorative rallies which established it as the principal custodian of the memory of Langemarck during this period. The appropriation of Langemarck by the youth movement was a natural development, given that since autumn 1914 Langemarck had become a symbol of youth and the sacrificial death of young men to guarantee the nation's future. Note that the term 'youth' had a special resonance for Germans. It did not simply describe an age cohort but connoted qualities such as vigour, energy, and purity; it stood for a departure from convention and a return to nature or, literally, regeneration. In Imperial Germany tensions between the generations had been more pronounced than in any other European society at the time. An anti-urban (male) youth movement had emerged among the middle classes of the cities at the turn of the century. They had rejected the shallowness of Wilhelmine society and the ugliness of industrial modernity. In 1913 the young ramblers (the Wandervögel and other like-minded groups) had congregated on the Hoher Meissner mountain massif in protest against the establishment's double commemoration of the centenary of the Battle of Leipzig and the Kaiser's silver jubilee. Against this backdrop, the events at Langemarck promised to bring about the spiritual renewal of society as a whole that the bourgeois youth movement had longed for over many years.[54] While 'youth' had been a term to conjure with in Imperial Germany, it gained even greater symbolic presence in the Weimar Republic. The notion of the teenager did not exist at this time, and 'youth' described a cohort of adolescents and young men, roughly between the age of 13 and 30. A demographic revolution meant that the proportion of young people among the population had never been as high as during the Weimar years. These young males were in a precarious position; the centre of much public attention, they also faced socio-economic marginalization. For many—but by no means all—members of this so-called 'superfluous generation', the Langemarck myth proved immensely attractive.[55]

However, the evolution of the Langemarck myth within the bourgeois youth movement was not as linear as has often been suggested. The speaker at the 1923 Rhön rally warned of the danger of turning Langemarck into a 'cult': 'Langemarck, as it was, must never be again.' His wrath was directed at the officers who had failed to stop hot-headed youths from advancing into certain death in 1914. This indictment of the officer class and, by extension, the old system of Imperial Germany, is significant. Generally speaking, the years between 1919 and 1923 marked, according to historian Benjamin Ziemann, 'a short period of insight' during which critical recollections of the war—and especially of the role of the officer class in the war—struck a chord with many people. The youth movement was not immune to this critical atmosphere, as the 1923 speech shows. Nevertheless, the debunking of the myth actually ends up buttressing it. The assault is pronounced 'futile', but the memory of the dead is considered 'holy'. The reckoning with the guilty men went hand in hand with a reassertion of the integrity of the dead.[56] Within a year the critical impetus was completely gone. On the tenth anniversary of First Ypres, the author and war veteran Rudolf G. Binding visited an encampment of 2,000 youths in the Rhön mountains. In his address he recounted how a generation had come into its own in Flanders fields; how this band of brothers leapt forward with 'a thundering song on their lips' in those days in late October 1914. Binding's dating of the events and his reluctance to name the song must have raised a few eyebrows, but he put a stop to controversy by stressing that Langemarck 'belongs no longer to history': it had transcended history to become a mythos that would eternally rejuvenate the nation. Thus, there was no need, or indeed room, to quibble over historical details.[57]

With the exception of Langemarck, the British were dominant in every aspect of the microgeographies of Ypres and its environs. They also tended to perpetuate the British wartime nomenclature with guidebooks continuing to list such locations as Clapham Junction, Salvation Corner, Hell Fire Corner, Tower Hamlets, Tattenham Corner, and Glencorse Wood. The most fervent in their desire to preserve the old salient were the members of the Ypres League.[58] Although by no means a huge organization—the evidence suggests it peaked at around 10,000 members worldwide—it was nonetheless a potent propaganda machine and, by virtue of having a permanent presence in the salient and branches across the Empire, had the ability to maintain a link between the actual sites and those who might never get the opportunity to visit themselves. Assisting Beckles Willson in getting the organization into life was Beatrix Brice, who was his equal in passion for Ypres, energy, and drive. During the conflict Brice had served in the Voluntary Aid Detachment (VAD) nursing wounded soldiers whilst also composing poetry, the most famous of which was her 1916 paean to the original BEF soldiers who fought at Mons and First Ypres, 'To the Vanguard', published in *The Times*. Her association with the 'Old Contemptibles' was strengthened in 1917 through her organization of a grand pageant at the Royal Albert Hall in their honour.[59] Combined, Beckles Willson and Brice formed a formidable force, and the Ypres League duly came into being in October 1921.

Deeply aware of the need to ensure good relationships with all major players, the IWGC was initially somewhat wary of the Ypres League and its headlong pursuit of projects driven by the energy and determination of Brice and Beckles Willson.[60] Within a short space of time the league had committed itself to the construction of a hostel and a carillon tower in Ypres—although in the event neither project was realized—and erected signposts across the salient pointing out important sites. Most significantly, it joined forces with the automobile Touring Clubs of France and Belgium and their scheme for the erection of small memorials to mark the furthest limits of the German 1918 advance.[61] The league with its broad membership of veterans, relatives, and friends of ex-servicemen, including quite a few children, eventually funded and oversaw the completion of six Demarcation Stones (which marked the limits of the German advance in 1918) in the salient. As part of this scheme, the league ensured a physical reminder of a key location on the Menin Road, Hell Fire Corner.

Probably its greatest contribution of all was the production of three guidebooks, each with a highly resonant title: *The Immortal Salient* (1925), *The Battle Book of Ypres* (1927), and *Ypres: Outpost of the Channel Ports* (1929). The guides took the form of gazetteers stuffed full of information about each and every site and included detailed maps. The tone was a curious mixture of the flatly factual and synoptic with the reverent and commemorative, which made them not only invaluable to the visitor, but also a memorial which a relative or veteran could keep in the home and thus imagine, or revisit, the salient from afar. In these works distinctions between gazes and psychological modes were collapsed. At one and the same time, the person was the spiritually engaged pilgrim *and* the historian looking for, and examining, the traces of the past. The cool detachment of the objective onlooker was merged with immersion of the emotionally-engaged. It was a position reinforced by the resonant titles which very firmly steered the reader as to their moral and spirit, and in the case of *The Immortal Salient* was given even greater weight by its subtitle, *An Historical Record and Complete Guide for Pilgrims to Ypres*. Reviewers often noted this dual stance; one stated that 'No such record has been made before, and it will probably be treasured by those who read it like a family Bible or an old copy of Homer.'[62]

* * * * *

The first comprehensive, and reflective, histories of the war in English were completed by John Buchan, the popular author and one-time director of British propaganda during the conflict, in his four-volume account published in 1921–2, which built upon his earlier part-time work for Nelson's press that had run throughout the war. Buchan lauded the achievements of British and imperial forces in all the major actions at

Ypres and venerated the ground. At First Ypres the BEF had 'opposed the blood and iron of the German onslaught with a stronger blood and finer steel'.[63] At Second Ypres the Canadians made the crossroads between Poelcappelle and Zonnebeke their 'Thermopylae'.[64] By the end of the Third Battle it could be said that 'Ypres was indeed to Britain what Verdun was to France and the hallowed soil which called forth the highest virtue of her people, a battleground where there could be no failure without loss of honour'.[65] However, Buchan did not allow rhetoric to undermine his critical faculties and he passed harsh judgement on Third Ypres. Whilst lavishing praise on the endurance of the soldiers, he questioned the wisdom of maintaining the offensive in a quiet, but nonetheless clear, manner.[66]

Buchan's stance was a very early, and very rare, example of dissent over British generalship in the war, and at Third Ypres in particular, made especially notable coming, as it did, from an Establishment figure. It was an equally Establishment figure, rather than a radical voice, who picked up on his comments. Ralph V. Woods, who gave his address as the Cavendish Club, wrote to the *Saturday Review* in fulsome support of Buchan, stating that he had revealed that 'our Generals may be brave and "pukka" Sahibs, but are pitiably deficient in military genius' and were particularly amiss in ignoring the state of German defences at Ypres in 1917, the condition of the ground, and the apparently well-known fact that the region was notorious for wet summers.[67]

The most detailed historical overview was provided by the British official history programme under the direction of Brigadier Sir James Edmonds. In March 1925 the first two volumes were published, covering the first five months of the war including First Ypres, and in 1927 the third volume appeared, containing an account of the Second Battle. Perhaps revealing that traditional attitudes to battle were still very much part of the popular culture, the first two volumes sold in much higher numbers than any other part of the series, possibly because they covered a period of the war marked by successive actions as part of a fluid campaign. J. M. Bulloch reviewing them for the *Sunday*

Times certainly implied that this was part of their appeal, noting that they recounted 'the glorious work of our little Expeditionary Force in bringing to a standstill, and then rolling back, the great German onrush'.[68] When the future field marshal Archibald Wavell examined the third volume for the *Times Literary Supplement,* he deemed it a great success and noted how the Ypres sections revealed that accurate artillery fire rather than gas was the true reason behind German effectiveness in the assault.[69] He passed over the other great controversy—the removal of Lieutenant General Horace Smith-Dorrien from command of Second Army—without comment. Edmonds had, in fact, freely admitted the breakdown of relations between Smith-Dorrien and Sir John French largely because avoiding such frankness was practically impossible due to French's notorious memoirs, *1914,* which contained an open assault on Smith-Dorrien's judgement at Le Cateau.[70] A public controversy followed and Andrew Bonar Law, the acting prime minister, called French to account, reminding him of his responsibilities as an employed state servant. Smith-Dorrien may have taken the moral of this controversy, for his own memoirs, *Memories of Forty-Eight Years,* published in 1925, were largely tactful and only hinted at the depth of his dispute with his commanding officer.[71]

The French official historians, preoccupied with unpicking Verdun, had comparatively little time for Ypres, although in France perhaps the single greatest contribution was Admiral Ronarc'h's memoirs.[72] *Mercure de France,* like many other journals, praised Ronarc'h for telling his story with great modesty and instead stressing the qualities of the marines under his command who had maintained the prestigious history of the corps.[73] For the writer in *La Nouvelle Revue,* Ronarc'h revealed that the battles of the Yser had decisively halted the German advance and stood alongside the Marne as the moment when the enemy ran into an impenetrable barrier.[74] Here was a distinct French variant on the metanarrative about the battles of the Yser–Ypres region.

For the Germans, the historiographical battle over the legacy of Ypres commenced shortly after the guns had fallen silent. Erich Ludendorff opened the debate with *My War Memories,* published in both German and English within months of the Armistice. Controversially, the master of German strategy declared the fighting at Kemmel and around Armentières in 1918 a victory: 'We had beaten the English army'—a statement that was later cited, and thus indirectly endorsed, by one of the official historians.[75] Yet, there was something for everybody in the two massive tomes. 'Ypres mud was worse shell hole than Verdun', splashed the Louisville *Courier Journal,* one of the anglophone newspapers that had secured the rights to serialize the book.[76] Ludendorff's nominal superior, Hindenburg, echoed this point in his 1920 autobiography. The fighting in Flanders in 1917, he stressed, 'put all our battles on the Somme in 1916 completely in the shade'.[77] Despite the rift in their relationship in autumn 1918, both Ludendorff and Hindenburg had a vested interest in foregrounding Third Ypres and downgrading the battles of 1916, thus showing that their task had been infinitely greater than that of the man they had driven out of office in 1916. Erich von Falkenhayn himself published his war memoirs in 1920, too, although his are confined to his time as chief of the general staff from 1914 to 1916. Written in the style of a military history (in which he refers to himself in the third person), Falkenhayn was anxious to clear his name in relation to First Ypres. During the war he had come under criticism for having thrown newly trained troops into battle. In his book he asserts that logistically he was left with no choice but to deploy the inexperienced troops in this crucial assault before the stalemate set in. What is more, experienced contingents were not only unavailable but also *abgekämpft* (weary), in contrast to the 'fresh' new regiments.[78]

The first full-scale history of Ypres had appeared in 1917, albeit in a censored version, as the author subsequently claimed. Wilhelm Schreiner's *Der Tod von Ypern* (The Death of Ypres), though not a towering bestseller, proved popular enough to go through several editions between 1917 and 1937. In the post-1917 editions, Schreiner aimed to cut down on historical details (such as the names of regiments and tactics used) and instead to expand on the phenomenology of battle. 'Now only the colourful experience talks' through the book, he claimed.[79] This was decidedly not a sober *kriegswissenschaftlich* (war studies) account. The occasional use of the first person lends the narrative an immediacy and intimacy. The text even conveys the feelings and thoughts of soldiers, both German and British. The use of dialogue and quotations from soldiers' letters and diaries are stylistic devices employed to further reduce the gap between the reader and the text. But how did Schreiner come by this information? According to the author himself, the book is largely based on 'non-printed sources'. In fact, the original 1917 publication contained an appeal to readers to supply the author with material for later editions.

As a popular writer Schreiner had no access to official documents. These were kept under lock and key at the Reichsarchiv in Potsdam, a newly created institution charged with the task of cataloguing the files of the wartime army and editing the official history of the war. Published in eighteen massive volumes comprising a total of 9,343 pages, the dry-as-dust official history was never going to be a popular success. Moreover, it was slow to appear; the volume covering First Ypres did not hit the shelves until 1929. In the meantime something short and snappy was needed; therefore the Reichsarchiv launched 'Battles of the World War' as the semi-official series of popular histories, mostly penned by middlebrow writers (whose names appeared neither on the book cover nor on the spine, but in small print on the title page). One inspiration for this series was Buchan's *Nelson's History of the War*. The author commissioned to produce *Ypern, 1914* was Werner Beumelburg, a veteran who had embarked on a career in fiction writing and journalism after the war, eventually becoming managing editor of the *Deutsche Soldatenzeitung*. His client encouraged him to dispense with operational details and to concentrate on a 'naturalistic' representation of the *Erlebniswucht*, the impact of the war experience. The author himself saw it as his objective 'to paint a truthful picture'. The metaphor is important here: Beumelburg's history is an artistic account, in which he switches frequently from past to present tense. It defies all categories of genre, combining travelogue, fairy tale, action novel, and history in one.[80]

Official history could be stranger than fiction. It fell to the most prominent writer of his generation, Thomas Mann, to highlight the implausibility of the idea of soldiers singing the 'Deutschlandlied' in the midst of battle. In the final scene of his 1924 novel, *The Magic Mountain,* the central character, Hans Castorp, descends from his Alpine sanatorium to the plains of the battlefield. Having joined a 'volunteer regiment, fresh young blood and mostly students', Castorp stumbles rather than storms forward, tripping over the hand of a dead comrade, all the while singing Schubert's lied 'Der Lindenbaum'. He sings, first in a low voice and later 'unconsciously'. 'And thus, in the tumult, in the rain, in the dusk, he vanishes out of our sight. Farewell, honest Hans Castorp, farewell, Life's delicate child! Your story is over.'[81] Mann refers to his character as 'our hero', though he is anything but. Castorp's war experience is tragicomic rather than glorious, and the battlefield is described as hell's antechamber rather than a field of honour. Despite Mann being deliberately vague about the theatre of war where Castrop sees action ('East, west? It is the flatland, it is the war'), *Hochland*'s critic was in no doubt about the precise location: Langemarck.[82]

* * * * *

It was not solely in literature that those unable to visit the salient were reminded of its importance. Specific annual commemorations, such as the German youth rallies, were also held, and as with the German Langemarck observations reinforced understanding of the microgeography of the region. Throughout the 1920s the Ypres League emphasized the importance of 31 October. Labelling it 'Ypres Day', and arguing for its significance as the crisis moment in the First Battle, it was the herald for Armistice Day and the special Sunday church services that accompanied it. As it had done during the war, *The Times* enthusiastically supported the observation of Ypres Day and with it a veneration for the men of the original BEF.[83] A similar sense of respect for the original cohort can be seen in Canada's observation of 22 April, marking the moment when its first contingents went into action. On 22 April 1919 the *Toronto Star* argued that it should be kept as a national holiday whilst urging the immediate response of public displays of the flag.[84] 'Saint-Julien balls' were held annually by many regiments, usually preceded by a parade and church service in which pride at being the bulwark of the Empire was often expressed.[85] Clearly competing strongly with Vimy Ridge as the linchpin of Canadian commemoration and public memory, Saint-Julien was regarded as a name that would resonate down the generations. A *Toronto Star* editorial declared: 'When the last veteran of the war has made his exit, where the years have thrown a cloak of forgetfulness around the heroic struggle in which he played his part, some names will linger, as far off stars of miraculous brightness enrich the heavens long after they have died, and not the least of those fair names, St Julien will evoke the homage of the ages.'[86] In Australia, 22 September was noted for its soldiers' advance in the battle of the Menin Road and their role in the capture of Polygon Wood during the Third Battle. The *Sydney Morning Herald* called it a 'day of sad but proud memories for many families throughout Australia' and added the rapidly solidifying fact that 'Ypres . . . was to Britain what Verdun was to France—"the hallowed soil which called forth the highest virtues of her people"'.[87]

The salient also came home to the Empire in another potent manner: the continual reference to the poppy as the 'Flanders Poppy'. Although this flower flourished across the broken ground of the Western Front, it was anchored to Ypres by this very particular attribution. First sold to support the British Legion in 1921, commemorative poppies were an instant success, gripping the public imagination, and the appeal has never lessened. Within a short space of time, the term 'Flanders Poppy Day' was also in use as an alternative label for 11 November, and was particularly deployed by the British Legion in its appeals for purchasers and volunteer sellers.[88]

* * * * *

Along with the poppy, probably the most important medium for maintaining the profile of Ypres across the Empire was the circulation of powerful visual images. These had the ability to counterbalance the testimonies which claimed that reconstruction was rapidly stripping the region of its former associations, freezing its ruins forever as poignant memorials and silent witnesses. In the process this maintained the status of Ypres as the battlefield above all others. Nowhere was this more so than in Canada where a striking number of its officially commissioned pieces related to the salient. Indeed, a large-scale painting of the ruins of the Cloth Hall by James Kerr-Lawson was even chosen for permanent display in the Senate Chamber of the Canadian parliament alongside its companion piece, *Arras, the Dead City*. Before final installation, both paintings were exhibited in 1919 and 1920 at the Royal Academy in London, and in New York, Ottawa, and Toronto. Although some younger and more experimental artists were highly unimpressed by the conservative style, and both canvases ignore the gruesome carnage of the trenches, the paintings nonetheless left a haunting impression of the devastation caused by war.[89] Paul Konody, the noted art critic whom Beaverbrook employed as consultant to his war artists' scheme, assessed the Canadian collection, including the large number of Ypres images, in a special edition of the art journal *Colour Magazine*, in September 1919. Of Kerr-Lawson's two grand canvases, he noted:

> His special task is to depict the ruins of Ypres and Arras. Fortunately he collected his material for the first of two large paintings in the autumn of last year, before the stately Cloth Hall at Ypres was turned into a shapeless heap of debris. The ruins, as depicted by him, still retain a good deal of the erstwhile magnificence and much of the exquisite Gothic details for which the building was cherished by generation after generation.[90]

Three important points emerge from Konody's analysis: that ruins remained romantic; that there was a continuation with the pre-1914 fantasy of Ypres; and that the real devastation of the region came in 1917 with the Third Battle, underlining the sense that Passchendaele marked the true caesura.

Konody also produced an overview of the war artists' scheme in the official guide, *Art and War: Canadian War Memorials*, published in 1919.

Of the fifty-six reproductions included, ten were of battle scenes and zones, and two of artillery in action. Among these, no fewer than seven were specifically located in the Ypres salient. The ruins of Ypres were strongly represented in *The Gate of St Martin, Ypres* and *The Cloth Hall, Ypres November, 1914*, both by Alfred Bastien, a Belgian artist commissioned by the scheme, and Cyril Barraud's *Evening (on the Ypres–Poperinghe Road, near the Asylum) November 1st, 1917*. The most disturbing image of the entire publication was the reproduction of William Roberts's *The First German Gas Attack at Ypres*. The accompanying text described the scene: 'The French infantry, Zouaves and Turcos, thrown into disorder by the German gas attack, are seen retreating wildly past the guns of a Canadian Field Battery, while Canadian gunners endeavour to stay the advance of the German Infantry, who are within 200 yards of the Canadian Batteries.'[91] The painting has a nightmarish quality made all the more disturbing by the violent contrast of the brightly coloured uniforms of the French colonial troops with the dull khaki of the Canadian gunners. Here was no shrinking from the horror of war which had been experienced at its worst in the Ypres salient.

The British official scheme also saw Ypres at the heart of its images. In the spring of 1919 Nash began work on the largest of his war compositions. Originally entitled *A Flanders Battlefield*, Nash soon made the topographical reference definitive: *The Menin Road*. He depicted a brutalized landscape in which the eye is led between a discordant geometric mess of stubby, shorn trees, diagonals of light cutting through brooding clouds polluted by explosives and gas. A dead German suppurates in a shell hole whilst two British soldiers, rendered inconsequential by the troglodyte landscape, pick their way between the craters. Although insistent that the piece was a protest—'it is on these I brood for it seems the only justification of what I do now—if I can rob the war of the last shred of glory, the last shine of glamour'—it was nonetheless an official commission and as such was a war memorial as well as a historical representation.[92] With so many other sources candid about the horrors of the Ypres salient and using the landscape as a metaphor for the trials and agonies endured by brave men, it was possible to ignore the protest and co-opt it into a language of sacrifice for the noblest of causes. It was precisely this balance that Will Longstaff achieved in his *Menin Gate at Midnight*.

Longstaff, a noted Australian landscape painter, was one of the few Australian guests present for the unveiling of the Menin Gate. During the war he had served as a camouflage officer and had direct knowledge of conditions on the Western Front. Deeply moved by the ceremony, he was unable to sleep that night and around midnight got up and went for a walk. At the Menin Gate he had a vision in which he saw the dead soldiers of the salient rise and march out towards the battlefields. Unable to escape the power of the scene, he decided to commit it to canvas and rapidly completed his most famous painting, *Menin Gate at Midnight*. It quickly achieved a legendary status through being publicized in the *Graphic Weekly* on Christmas Eve 1927, encapsulating the mystical, spiritual value invested in Ypres by people from across the Empire. Riding high on a wave of publicity, the painting was bought by Lord Woolavington for 2,000 guineas, the highest sum paid for an Australian painting at the time, and was donated to the Australian government. It was initially displayed at Australia House where a group of VIPs, including Blomfield, took the chance to study it. George V requested the chance to view it at Buckingham Palace and it was duly lent for his private scrutiny. In April 1928 the painting began a tour, commencing with Manchester before moving on to Glasgow where 2,000 people saw it daily over its two-week exhibition, and on 10 November the *Illustrated London News* published a centre-page-spread reproduction. When the painting reached Australia, public curiosity was even greater. Over 35,000 people viewed it during a three-week period in February 1929 at Melbourne's town hall. It then commenced a tour of major Australian cities and in Sydney was displayed alongside a scale model of the memorial. A poster reproduction was hugely popular and helped fund the Australian War Memorial in Canberra.[93]

An equally dramatic effect was achieved by Alfred Bastien with his *Panorama de l'Yser*. Following in the nineteenth-century tradition of grand panoramas, Bastien produced a scene 115 metres long by 14 metres high based on a plethora of preliminary sketches, drawings, and photographs. It was originally exhibited in Brussels where over 800,000 people saw it, including George V and Queen Mary, before being moved to Ostend for permanent display in a specially constructed building. Here it proved an equal success, drawing huge audiences, including British visitors making for the battlefields. The scenes were of great topographical accuracy, showing the inundations, breastworks, and piers over which the soldiers traversed the swamps. The entire front was linked by Bastien's inclusion of a scene of the Cloth Hall under bombardment, as well as the ruins of St Martin's Cathedral in Ypres. Revealing the extent to which the war had become a tourist trade, Bastien's fees, the cost of production, and the erection of the building were all met by a consortium of businessmen and banks.[94]

In Germany the written word did more to shape the mental image of Ypres in the 1920s than visual media. This was a post-war development. The original 1917 edition of Schreiner's book had featured a number of photographs and drawings, principally of the city of Ypres. But all illustrations were expunged from subsequent editions. While Beumelburg's (semi-)official history contained seven plates, the most striking visual elements are the decorative vignettes that frame each chapter. These little line drawings show battlefield scenes, war-torn landscapes, and soldier's graves—images that appear uncanny and picturesque at the same time. They lend the book a contemplative, almost religious quality.[95] To be sure, Beumelburg accepted that photographs had uniquely captured the reality of war that had been hidden from the ordinary soldier's view. In the preface to a German volume of photographs taken by Allied photographers, he suggested that these images lifted finally 'the iron curtain' on no man's land.[96] But one can detect a reluctance to let the photographs speak for themselves. Publishers of illustrated volumes engaged

A PART OF THE PANORAMA.

It is most realistic and is well worth a visit.
(The Morning Post.)

A work of truth and life magisterially executed.
(The Times.)

That moving painting commemorates facts and events of which the artist has been a witness, as an officer in the Canadian army.
(The Daily Chronicle.)

Magnificent work that gives faitfully incidents in battle between Nieuport and Ypres.
(The Times.)

741.372 *visitors to the* 1st *of April* 1924. *The King and the Queen of England, when in Brussels in* 1922, *visited the Panorama with Sir Douglas Haig and Admiral Sir Beaty.*

Figure 16. Part of the war panorama by Alfred Bastien. Postcard, *c.*1924.

wordsmiths such as Beumelburg to introduce the images and frame them with words.

Even in slide shows the verbal could overwrite the visual. Consider the slide series 'Ypern 1914' that was shown in schools in Westphalia. It came together with an extensive commentary that borrowed heavily from Beumelburg's eponymous book and indeed cited him directly. Like Beumelburg, the author of the slide show goes out of his way to demonstrate that Belgian civilians violated international law by firing from behind closed shutters at the invaders, and that reports about German atrocities were a product of 'mendacious propaganda'. The massacre at Esen (the execution of forty-seven inhabitants and deportation of 275 others) is discussed at length, and yet the slide shown to the children was a photograph of the locks at Nieuport. Thus a striking gap opens up between the images and the commentary. There is, however, a slide entitled 'The Shelling of Ypres', showing the still-intact Cloth Hall shrouded in smoke. The accompanying text suggests that this was another punishment dealt out to the Belgians, and also a necessity: 'The lives of German men have higher value than the beauty of Gothic monuments!'[97]

* * * * *

The moving image also maintained the high profile of Ypres. It was film that helped make Bastien's panorama an even greater attraction. When the Belgian minister for war visited the site, it was captured by the official Belgian newsreel which included extended close-ups of individual scenes. The official newsreel also produced the *Yser Journal/IJzer Journaal* series, which were compendia of material shot during the conflict. Newsreels also allowed people to witness the unveiling of memorials and other commemorative ceremonies and established a visual shorthand for Ypres and its environs: Ypres was a city of ruins and the surrounding countryside was flat and featureless, dotted by the odd hastily built house. By the time the Menin Gate was unveiled, there was much evidence of rebuilding in Ypres with only the Cloth Hall and cathedral still undergoing extensive renovation. The gate seemed to be part of a healing process and revealed an acceptance by the British that the wartime landscape could not remain indefinitely.

Most potent of the moving images was the full-length film *Ypres* (1925). Made by British Instructional Films, which had already completed a series of battle reconstructions, *Ypres* was its biggest box office success. Narrating the story through a series of vignettes, mostly built around the actions of Victoria Cross winners, Walter Summers, the director, ensured that *Ypres* told a story of human endeavour and will shaping the course of the battles. These men were no powerless playthings of fate, but made their own destinies through sheer courage and endurance. Britain's role as the defender of Ypres as the key narrative theme was reinforced through the film's balance, which was heavily weighted in favour of the earlier battles, and not the offensive action of Third Ypres. A stunning success throughout the Empire, it linked veterans and relatives eager to understand what their loved ones had gone through at the front. The Perth (Western Australia) *Daily News* review translated the film into a celluloid war memorial:

> The film will live as Ypres will live. It will be handed down for generations and shown with pride to our children's children. It will tell them that the enormous sacrifices at Ypres were not in vain, and it will show them what war really was in our time.[98]

For the *Cape Times* film reviewer, moral and emotion were in perfect balance, for Ypres was the essence of war, the definition of combat, and the film had found a way of interpreting it:

> The sadness, the glory, the pathos and the valour of the Great War are epitomized in one word, Ypres; memories whose splendour of devotion and sacrifice will never be excelled are enshrined in the salient of immortal remembrance; and it is to the infinite credit of the film industry that it has been able to give the world a moving and impressive record of the epic adventure.[99]

The fact that the IRA led a campaign against the film in the Irish Free State serves to underline its status as a truly powerful war memorial.[100]

Powerful and enigmatic photographic images also helped maintain Ypres's status as the imperial crucible of the war partly through the excellence of the images captured and created by the official photographic teams, especially those of the Canadian War Records Office and the Australian War Records Section. However, these were significantly supplemented by the fact that Ypres contained two highly active and effective private photographers who survived the war and re-established their businesses. Daniel and Antony of Ypres produced a huge range of postcard images showing ruins, cemeteries, and memorials; abandoned military materials; and the gradual re-establishment of civilian life and activity in the region. Their output, an overtly commercial enterprise, also ensured a merging of the respectful with the tourist gaze of spectacle.[101]

* * * * *

During the 1920s Ypres was largely rebuilt, but at the same time it was further encased in its wartime rhetoric. Although the British reluctantly accepted the fact and increasing pace of reconstruction, the Empire actually became a part of the process through its extensive programme of cemetery and memorial construction, which far outstripped the activities of all others who had fought in the region. These massive, permanent physical reminders of the imperial commitment to Ypres became the essential navigation points of the area, further stamping the wartime microgeography into imperial popular culture and life. Heavily buttressed in a rich language of sacrifice, duty, and nobility, the region was also associated with the hardest and most horrific fighting of the war which was especially expressed in widely circulated visual images. Exposed to such images, and informed by a range of guidebooks and histories, British visitors to Ypres came to the sites with a well-developed intellectual and emotional framework in which to absorb the surroundings. The experience of visiting sometimes caused friction, as British visitors believed occasionally that local people did not display an appropriate degree of respect towards the war dead of the Empire, but by the mid-1920s the ever-burgeoning permanent British community in the city helped keep visitors in a partial Britannic bubble. At the same time, a distinctly German vision of the salient, also built around a microgeography, was reinforced through books and images but, lacking permanent memorials on anything like the scale of the British, there was not the same degree of focus for visitors during the early to mid-1920s. However, by the end of the decade impressive Belgian, French, and German memorial schemes were underway which were to provide alternative national narratives of the region, even if the essential messages were to remain remarkably similar.

5

New Battles for Langemarck, 1928–1944

The year 1928 marked the beginning of a new phase in the history of Ypres. The major British imperial memorials and cemeteries had been completed in the previous year; over the next decade the emphasis would shift from the dead to the living by establishing Ypres as a 'colony' of British settlers and visitors. The German presence in the former salient had hitherto been negligible. The 'Langemarck' of post-war discourses had been an imagined site, not a geographical place. That was about to change as the intention to build an imposing war cemetery at Langemarck was announced with great fanfare in 1928. The same year saw the publication of the first new tourist guidebook for German visitors to Belgium and also the first naming of a street in Germany after Langemarck. It was a year of many firsts. Belgians aimed to regain the initiative in two contradictory ways. Within the space of a few days in July, the first Last Post was sounded at the Menin Gate in honour of the British defenders of the city, and the foundation stone of the massive Yser Tower at Dixmude was laid in an effort to rewrite the history of the conflict from a Flemish nationalist viewpoint. In the following year French veterans staked their claim to the blood-drenched landscape with the unveiling of a memorial to the victims of gas warfare at Steenstraat. In 1927 the new battle for Ypres had ended in a resounding imposition of British markers of memory on the landscape; in 1928, as commemorative activity shifted to the north(-east) of the city, and with new groups trying to carve out a niche for themselves in this part of the salient, the new battles for Langemarck and Dixmude were about to begin.

* * * * *

The Menin Gate continued to be a focal point for British and imperial remembrance. Tens of thousands signed the visitors' book every year between 1928 and 1939, and many used the amenities of the new Haig House of Rest next to the gate.[1] In August 1928 the British Legion organized a pilgrimage, led by the Prince of Wales, for over 11,000 participants, the highlight of which was a ceremony of remembrance at the gate, attended by an additional 26,000 local day-trippers.[2] Foreign observers were struck by the outpouring of (gendered) emotions, dispelling the image of a nation of repressed stoics that had emerged in Victorian times: 'some men broke down and silently wept, while many women sobbed aloud'.[3] Like the unveiling ceremony, the event was broadcast live by the BBC, linking the pilgrims in Ypres to people at home. Reflecting the subtly changing atmosphere, the Archbishop of Canterbury in his address stated that they should learn the lesson of Nurse Edith Cavell and realize that patriotism in itself was not enough, as they needed to dedicate themselves to Christ and his message of love and peace in order to build a better Britain. But this did not mean disillusionment with the war or a questioning of the sacrifices made, as the archbishop made the battle for a new Britain a continuation of the same noble struggle, concluding: 'Let the Last Post sound our message of remembrance to the dead! Let the Reveille sound Christ's summons to the service of the living.' *The Times* coverage pointedly referred back to the war by quoting Rupert Brooke's 'The Soldier' and saw the gate as a fitting memorial creating that corner of a foreign field forever England.[4]

German visitors lacked such a focal point prior to the completion of the war cemetery at Langemarck in 1932. Perhaps they did not need a physical monument in order to remember; the German soldier's memorial was 'The Invisible Memorial', as the title of a 1930 book suggested. The landscape itself was supposedly their memorial.

Figure 17. The Menin Gate memorial during the British Legion pilgrimage in August 1928. Press photograph, 1928.

One had only to visit the village with the suggestive name Verlorenhoek (Lost Corner) to conjure up the German 'unknown soldier'.[5] Even so, the itineraries of German visitors suggest that they toured the former battlefields somewhat aimlessly, without a ritualistic climax. Moreover, they eschewed the language of 'pilgrimage' so prevalent in British commemorative culture.[6] The first organized trip of German veterans to the Ypres salient took place in October 1929. The consulate in Antwerp urged them to keep a low profile and refrain from wearing military insignia.[7] One cannot know in what frame of mind Germans returned to Flanders. Veterans' associations were often right-wing, although this does not mean that German veterans per se were reactionaries. The majority simply picked up the pieces of their civilian lives and remained aloof from the veterans' movement. Moreover, the largest single organization to emerge after the war was the social democratic Reichsbanner. Its members were moderate pacifists who condemned the war as futile. Keen to reach out to like-minded French veterans, Reichsbanner members were, however, more likely to visit Verdun than Ypres.[8]

Hard on the heel of veterans, groups of university students ventured to Flanders. Scathing about the 'pompous' British memorials, one delegation made a point of stopping at the war memorials erected by local people in Flemish villages as a gesture towards the brotherhood of Germans and Flemings.[9] Student associations were hotbeds of nationalism and revanchism in the late Weimar Republic and yet—as with veterans' associations—one should beware of lumping them all together. A member of a Catholic fraternity visiting Langemarck made a forceful peace appeal to which others, the fraternity's magazine noted, reacted with 'a sour expression'.[10] The influx of a younger generation of visitors, both German and British, was noticeable after 1928. A 'battlefield tour' came to be considered an important part of the training of officer cadets in the British army, and a group of 700 Scottish schoolboys were taken to Ypres in 1933.[11]

Not only did group travel increase, but the number of solitary travellers also went up. With motoring becoming more widespread among the British middle classes during the 1930s, Ypres proved a particular magnet. Journeys by car to the former theatres of war were facilitated by the publication of specialist gazetteers and touring atlases. German visitors almost always arrived by train and preferred to travel in organized groups, even though the individual traveller could now rely on up-to-date guidebooks. The first post-war edition of Grieben's popular guide to Belgium appeared in 1928 and Baedeker followed suit in 1930.[12] Universally trusted before 1914, Baedeker tried to gain a new foothold in the lucrative anglophone market with its 1931 English-language edition. Interestingly, this was not a direct translation of the German original but a much revised version. While the German Baedeker dwells on the action at Dixmude and Langemarck in autumn 1914, that episode is covered in a half-sentence in the English edition. By contrast, the city of Ypres, which had 'acquired a certain English air', is treated in much greater detail than in the German edition. It is also significantly more upbeat about the reconstruction programme which the German guide rejects as 'an artificial rebirth' of a medieval city.[13]

By and large, Baedeker adhered to its traditional sober style. For those who liked their guidebooks more verbose, Toc H (the Christian movement that had emerged from a soldier's club at Poperinghe) brought out *A Little Guide for Pilgrims* with a preface by 'B.B.' who may well have been Beatrix Brice of the Ypres League. The unique status of the salient in the war is stressed throughout: no location saw more concentrated fighting, more blood spilt, drew in more British soldiers. For these reasons it was deemed to be 'A Name to resound for ages' and 'will never be missing out of the English history books'. As with so many other works published in the 1930s, it reveals the emergence of Passchendaele as the ultimate defining indicator of the salient's meaning—'that pregnant name which stands enshrined in the minds of the men who endured the Third Battle of Ypres'.[14] The emphasis on Passchendaele contrasts markedly with the 1920s focus on the First and Second battles.

Local publishers brought out more prosaic guides with a wealth of practical information. Typical among these publications was the output of the Ypres printer Dumortier. In the mid-thirties it produced guides in French and English; the English translation from the original was assisted by Major Paul Slessor, a British veteran of the salient and resident of the British community in Ypres who now ran tours. Ex-servicemen were clearly happy to play up the drama and engage the imagination of the visitor, as the testimonials for Leo Murphy's Ypres Salient War Museum illustrate. Married to a Frenchwoman, Murphy settled in the city pursuing a range of business interests including an electronics and radio shop, an information bureau for British visitors complete with café and essential supplies, as well as his museum, housed rather incongruously in the old Meat Hall. Advertising in the guide, this jack of all trades proudly showed off the comments of his highly satisfied, 'spellbound' visitors: 'Lt Col.

Graham Seton Hutchison "Author of the *W Plan*, etc." "A conducted tour by Mr L. N. Murphy, the curator, round 'The Ypres Salient War Museum' at Ypres is a cross between a Prime Minister's Speech and a First-Class Music-Hall turn."'[15]

Seeing alone was not enough. Many a tourist wanted to take something 'real' back home, and souvenir shops and street hawkers were doing a roaring trade. '[M]ore souvenirs have been produced from Hill 60 and such places than ever fighting put there', the writer R. H. Mottram remarked bitingly.[16] Then and now, it is easy to criticize or ridicule the souvenir trade and its trivialization and sanitization of war. However, the purchase and ownership of a relic from the war may have played a role in the working out of personal memories and emotions, and, generally, in domesticating war.[17] Yet criticism of the souvenir business and fairground atmosphere in Ypres was a staple of both British and German discourses. They disagreed on whether the (Belgian) vendor or the (British/American) buyer was to bear the blame. The German press came close to reviving a wartime propaganda slogan—'heroes versus merchants'—in their coverage of how the 'English tourism industry' was profiteering in the aftermath of war and desecrating the landscape.[18] But there was a darker side to the hunt for authentic remains. Shocked by what he had witnessed at Hill 60, one German visitor alerted the Foreign Office in Berlin to the tomb raiders' disrespectful treatment of human remains.[19]

* * * * *

A fierce critic of 'tourist armies' invading the former battlefields was the writer Stefan Zweig. A particular thorn in his side was the professional tour guides, one of whom had misled Zweig into reporting falsely in the *Berliner Tageblatt* in September 1928 that German officers and privates were buried in separate cemeteries, that even in death the class divisions of the imperial army prevailed. The article caused a minor scandal and eventually Zweig had to retract his statement and admit his naivety and gullibility.[20] Zweig's was not a singular case. The files of the German Foreign Office are full of complaints about tour guides' anti-German 'agitation'. But letter writers also vented their anger at the Weimar Republic for the apparent neglect of German war graves. The Amtlicher Deutscher Gräberdienst (Official German War Graves Service) in Belgium was overwhelmed by the massive task of looking after 134,000 war graves, a responsibility it had only inherited from the Belgian state in 1926. Although the Gräberdienst's record was respectable—within two years it had laid out or repaired 100 out of 400 (often small) cemeteries—public opinion was fixated on the work not done.[21] Implicitly or explicitly, complaints about German war cemeteries contrasted them with the splendour of British cemeteries. What these unfavourable comparisons passed over was the fact that until 1931 French necropolises looked rather unappealing, too.[22]

The war graves issue had proven politically corrosive since 1918, but reached crisis proportions in 1928 as the result of a carefully choreographed public outrage. A delegation of German students was on its way to attend an international congress in Paris in August 1928. On learning that the opening ceremony was to be held at the very chateau where the 'Versailles diktat' had been signed, the German deputies allegedly turned on their heels and travelled to Langemarck instead—only to find the graves of those who had supposedly died singing 'Deutschland, Deutschland über alles' in a dismal state of neglect. The German Embassy in Brussels was astonished to learn through the press about the delegation's detour to Flanders. Pointing out that there were in fact eight different war cemeteries scattered around Langemarck and, moreover, that major work was being undertaken, the diplomats suggested that the students had visited the 'wrong' cemetery and jumped to conclusions.[23] These qualifications fell on deaf ears. The students wanted a political coup to step in publicly where the state had failed. Thus was born the idea of a new charity, the Langemarck Donation (as a subsidiary of the German Students' Association), tasked with collecting funds for the construction of a war cemetery in Flanders. For the official launch on 11 November 1928 rallies took place in university towns throughout Germany. Local branches of the German Students' Association were instructed to leave no room for sadness but to restage the 'war enthusiasm' of 1914. The key message was that November 1914 rather than November 1918 represented the date of 'the true German revolution'.[24] What had started as an anti-Versailles demonstration became an indictment of Weimar's political system. The fact that the Prussian minister of education tried to prohibit the Langemarck Donation from collecting money in Germany's largest *Land* only added fuel to the flames.[25]

Two years after the establishment of the Langemarck Donation construction work began. Several smaller cemeteries in the vicinity were dissolved in order to concentrate graves in what was called the 'students' cemetery' or 'war volunteers' cemetery'—even though the dead had come from all walks of life and included volunteers as well as conscripts. The German Students' Association sidelined the official

Figure 18. 'Field of Honour' and moat with red poppies at Langemarck war cemetery. Commemorative volume, 1938.

Gräberdienst and enlisted the services of the private Volksbund to produce a design in the style of a 'heroes' grove' where nature itself provided something of a Germanic touch. The two outstanding features of the cemetery's architecture were the integration of surviving blockhouses and the creation of a moat (as a symbol of the flooded landscape caused by the opening of the coastal sea sluices). The use of the material remnants of war as a stylistic device was not entirely novel; the IWGC had experimented with it at Tyne Cot. The difference was that at Langemarck the concrete bunkers were part of an architectural arrangement that aimed to tell a story, a story about the final assault of German youth and the end of the war of movement in autumn 1914: after the heroic encounter with the enemy, the volunteers had ultimately succumbed to the elements. Tyne Cot was designed as a space; Langemarck as a narrative.[26]

Another sharp contrast between Tyne Cot and Langemarck concerns the treatment of graves. The principle of an individual grave was sacrosanct to the IWGC. Keenly aware of the stigma surrounding paupers' funerals since Victorian times, the IWGC erected a headstone for (almost) every single recovered body—even the nameless. What is more, the inscriptions are scrupulously precise. There are headstones for the dead saying 'Believed to be' a certain person, 'Known to be buried in this cemetery', or 'Buried near this spot'. For graves lost or destroyed through bombardment, Rudyard Kipling devised the motto 'Their glory shall not be blotted out'. The right to an individual grave was even extended to former enemies. Hence the two headstones (of a slightly different shape) to four German soldiers buried at Tyne Cot. It is an irony that the IWGC showed greater respect to the individual German soldier than the Volksbund. Concentrating over 10,000 graves in a cemetery only a fraction of the size of Tyne Cot meant that individual headstones or crosses were out of the question anyhow. But in the process of redesigning Langemarck the identity of graves was not preserved; grave markers were lost and randomly reassigned. The integrity of the architectural ensemble carried greater weight than the identity of the dead. If the press were to get wind of this practice, the Central Register of War Losses and War Graves warned the Foreign Office, it could lead to a public outcry.[27] Yet, to the Volksbund and its chief architect, Robert Tischler, it was not the memory of the individual that mattered but the creation of a community of the dead, thereby extending the camaraderie of the trenches into the postwar.[28] Characteristically, the Volksbund's rejection of individualism was mirrored in its working practices. While the IWGC worked with famous architects and artists, the Volksbund's employees were absorbed by the designers' collective, the *Bauhütte*. The way in which the Volksbund's workshops at Munich were set up drew inspiration from the organization of stonemasons who had built the cathedrals of the Middle Ages. The design of German war graves aspired, after all, to eternal fame matching that of medieval cathedrals.[29]

The Volksbund cultivated an aesthetic minimalism and an austere 'natural' style in opposition to the IWGC's 'silent cities' which refused to blend into the Flemish landscape. While thousands had witnessed the opening of the Menin Gate, the consecration of Langemarck cemetery on 10 July 1932 was a deliberately low-key affair attended by a small delegation. In 1928 'Langemarck' had been merely a word, now it was a 'sacred site', said the president of the German Students' Association. He also fantasized that in 1940(!) the cemetery would be 'the place of pilgrimage of the German youth'.[30] Simultaneously, commemorations orchestrated by the Langemarck Donation were held in all German universities. Simple in style, their message was massive. Two key themes emerged: the idea of the Reich (empire) and the notion of the *Volksgemeinschaft* (national community). First, in his oration, read out at the local events, the poet Josef Magnus Wehner conjured up a vision of the immortal dead—'they are more alive than we'—and of the medieval Reich restored. Second, the Langemarck Donation represented the dead of 1914 as the nucleus of the new *Volksgemeinschaft*. Anchored in a misty medieval past, the events of 1914 were presented not as history, but as a harbinger of future greatness and national unity.[31]

The construction of the Langemarck cemetery between 1928 and 1932 was accompanied by a concerted propaganda campaign. However, Langemarck was only one of seventy-seven German war cemeteries (as of 1935) in Belgium and the only one designed by the Volksbund. The other seventy-six cemeteries had been laid out by the official Belgian and German war graves services. They tended to be functional in design, dominated by rows upon rows of crosses. None received much media attention, except for the cemetery at Esen near Dixmude. Buried there along with 1,400 other German soldiers was 18-year-old Peter Kollwitz, son of the sculptor Käthe Kollwitz. Like so many patriotic middle-class youths, Peter had volunteered (against his father's wishes but with his mother's tacit encouragement) in August 1914. On 22 October he was dead. His mother kept a diary, but she wrote nothing about the devastating news for nearly six weeks: 'Conceived a plan for a memorial for Peter tonight...The monument would have Peter's form, lying stretched out, the father at the head, the mother at the feet. It would be to commemorate the sacrifice of all the young volunteers.'[32] Käthe sought consolation in the ambiguous language of 'sacrifice': her sacrificing Peter, her son's sacrificial death, and the self-sacrificing idealism of German youth. The process of creating the monument, 'the offering', was a painful one, often revised and put aside. The executed design, a compelling sculpture of two mourning parents side by side on their knees, was placed adjacent to Peter's grave in July 1932. Historians disagree whether Kollwitz's design shows parents united in grief or whether the gap between the two figures and their body language implied a trauma that could not be shared.[33] The design has always invited multiple interpretations. In a personal letter to the artist, the right-wing minister of the interior recognized it as a powerful representation of parental grief, but he also gave it a political spin by interpreting it as a 'pledge of loyalty of the entire people'.[34]

Not far from Kollwitz's memorial, the monumental tower erected by Flemish nationalists rose from the banks of the River Yser. The site marked the Belgian army's final defensive stand during the Battle of

Figure 19. Käthe and Karl Kollwitz with workers and *Grieving Parents* (father) sculpture at Esen war cemetery. Photograph, July 1932.

the Yser in autumn 1914. Fifty metres tall, it was built in the shape of a giant *Heldenhuldezerk* ('heroes' homage headstone'), the type of headstone erected on the graves of Flemish nationalist soldiers during the war. Bearing the motto 'Everything for Flanders—Flanders for Christ', the memorial posthumously divorced the Flemish from the Belgian dead and redefined their deaths as sacrifices for Flanders rather than Belgium. The Belgian government stood accused of showing scant regard for Flemish sensibilities when it began to replace *Heldenhuldezerkjes* with uniform Belgian headstones in 1925. This was grist to the mill of Flemish nationalist propaganda. What the nationalist press omitted, though, was the fact that all wartime grave markers and not just the Flemish ones were to be removed. Seemingly adding insult to injury, the disused headstones were reportedly ground up and recycled as tarmac for roads. The foundation stone of the Yser Tower was laid in July 1928 against this backdrop, ostensibly to provide a sanctuary for the surviving *Heldenhuldezerkjes*. The tower also counterbalanced the Belgian military cemetery at Houthulst, completed in 1924, and thus 'rectified' its pan-Belgian nature with its government-designed official headstones. The tower's true purpose, however, was to serve as a focal point for the annual Yser Pilgrimages which, by the time the tower was inaugurated in August 1930, had grown into the foremost gathering of Flemish nationalists and radical Catholics. Underlying these demonstrations of political firebrands was a vague commitment to 'peace'. At its peak, a reported 150,000 Flemings made the pilgrimage to the Yser Tower.[35] This 'Mecca of the Flemings', as one German newspaper put it, also became a site of joint commemoration for German and Flemish nationalist students. It was in many ways an unlikely alliance of two groups that had little in common apart from their opposition to their respective states. True, the Germans had wooed Flemish nationalists during the occupation, but they had also left behind a trail of blood in the advance through Belgium in 1914.[36]

The northern sector of the former salient and the stretch along the river was becoming a heavily contested terrain after 1928. At Steenstraat, some 8 miles south of the Yser Tower and not far from Langemarck, a memorial quite different in tone from all the others was unveiled in April 1929. It was erected by French veterans with the support of the highest echelons of the Third Republic to commemorate the first ever mass gas attack of 1915 and, implicitly, Franco-Belgian union. Designed by the sculptor Maxime Real del Sarte, who had lost an arm in the war, the memorial was extremely striking in its use of statuary.[37] Three soldiers were included. One stood clasping his throat, gasping and choking against the background of a crucifix, while at his feet lay two men dead from asphyxia. Extremely rarely for a military memorial, the soldiers were reduced to a helpless status lacking agency, which was fully underlined by the inscription: 'To the first victims of asphyxiant gas'. The hideousness of gas warfare was further stressed in the inscription which referred to it as an 'abominable' weapon. Picking up on this term, General Gouraud told the crowd that gas was 'abominable because it killed defenceless men;

Figure 20. Yser Tower at Dixmude. Postcard, *c.*1930.

it was abominable because it killed slowly and was still causing men to die prematurely'. The unveiling speech appealed to the deep-seated pacifism of French *anciens combattants*. Revealing the thaw after the Locarno Treaty in Franco/Belgian–German relations, little attempt was made to demonize the Germans as instigators with the emphasis on the evil weapon itself. Indeed, it was stated, 'let no one tomorrow talk about hatred. This monument has no other aim than to educate; it was not constructed and unveiled amid excitement, nor vain parades. Veterans are not vigilantes; we are witnesses.'[38] Ypres became a synonym for chemical warfare in France. Significantly, the French coined the word *ypérite* for mustard gas, first used in the salient in 1917.

The Ypres–Yser front's presence in the French imagination was reinforced a few months later when a memorial commemorating the actions of the marines was unveiled in their garrison town

Figure 21. French gas memorial at Steenstraat. Postcard, *c.*1929.

of Dunkirk. The famed resilience of the marines was lionized in the dedication speeches: 'You were told to hold for four days. You were still holding the line three weeks later when you were relieved.' It was a story encapsulated in the memorial which would ensure that the 'immortal tale [will be told] to future generations'.[39] In 1932 another memorial was added, this time in the south, at Mount Kemmel, in the form of an imposing obelisk looking out over the landscape and commemorating the actions of French soldiers in April 1918. Although in a striking position, and sitting among a cluster of rebuilt hotels which had restored Kemmel's reputation as a holiday spot, it was largely off the beaten track created by a British-centric remembrance circuit.

With the major British imperial memorials completed by 1927, in the following years the focus shifted towards building up a non-commercial infrastructure for the 'pilgrims' on the one hand and the community of British settlers in Ypres on the other. The most important scheme was the building of St George's memorial church opposite

Figure 22. French memorial at Mount Kemmel. German soldier's snapshots, 1940.

the cathedral, dedicated in March 1929. In a rare concession to vernacular architecture, Blomfield had given his design a Flemish character from the outside. Inside the church was cluttered with memorials, notably to officers, above all Lord French, the first Earl of Ypres. The church's interior was one of the last vestiges of class distinction and eccentricity in a commemorative landscape dominated by equality and uniformity. The Anglican church, complete with a pilgrim's hall, was to serve both as a memorial to the dead and as a meeting place for visiting relatives, supposedly of all denominations.[40] On their way to Ypres many would have passed through Poperinghe and stopped at Talbot House, the original seat of the Toc H Christian movement. It was in 1931 that Lord Wakefield purchased Talbot House and presented it to Toc H, thus confirming its position as a living memorial in the salient itself.[41] The famous chapel at the top of the house became not merely a place where people could see a genuine relic of the war, but also one where they could participate in an ongoing tradition of worship and reverent remembrance. The salient also came home in the activities of Toc H, for the movement was dominated by Ypres symbols: the Ypres cross appeared on the organization's banners and, more dramatically and emotionally, on the 'lamp of maintenance' which was lit at the start of every meeting. Christ, often invoked as the companion of the Tommy, was, through Toc H, even more closely associated with the particular battle zone of Ypres.

With the opening of St George's church followed by the completion of the adjacent school building, a local British Legion branch, and sporting and recreational facilities for IWGC staff and others, the British community in Ypres reinforced its presence and ensured that whoever visited the district was made fully aware of the fact that the British Empire held the primacy in terms of what might be called the right to remember. Those Britons not in full IWGC employment were usually involved in the hospitality and guiding occupations which again served to impose a British-centric interpretation on the history of the conflict, the contemporary landscape, and memorials. What was conventionally referred to as 'the British colony' became officially the British Settlement in February 1931 when it was given legal civil status in a bill passed unanimously by the Belgian Chamber of Representatives. The president and deputies remained standing throughout the presentation in order to 'salute the memory of those thousands of soldiers who came from England to fight at the side of our own for a common cause'.[42]

The cornerstone of the Ypres 'colony' was the Eton Memorial School, which opened its doors in April 1929. It served both utilitarian and symbolic functions. With the help of affluent donors the school was built as a memorial to the 342 Etonians who had been killed in the conflict.[43] The commemorative idea was simple but powerful. Eton College had produced men capable of faithful service, regardless of personal cost, inspired by a beneficial education in a nurturing environment, so founding a new school would honour their memory and produce a new generation of fine Britons in a location sacred to the Empire. Land adjacent to the site of St George's church was purchased with funds collected by two Old Etonians, Field Marshal Lord Plumer and Lieutenant General Sir William Pulteney, thus making a particular corner of Ypres the heart of the British Settlement. The school's mission was to educate the offspring of British ex-servicemen, the vast majority of whom had joined the IWGC after demobilization. Some brought out their wives and families, whilst others married local women. At school the children were constantly reminded that they were not Anglo-Belgian or Anglo-French but British through an educational programme that insisted on events like Empire Day being observed with great ardour. At the end of the first term the head teacher was confident that 'these children will grow up quite British in outlook and well able to maintain the spirit of the British Empire'.[44] The first inspector to visit the school believed a strict vigilance had to be maintained against the 'insidious influence of the foreign mother-in-law'.[45] The fact that these children were only half British and therefore other cultural influences were a natural part of their identities seemed immaterial. Questions of national identify became mixed up with religious affiliation. Roman Catholicism was to be checked by a regular diet of Anglican services in St George's. National and religious frictions notwithstanding, the school proved highly popular and, by 1933, 112 children were on the roll.

* * * * *

On 30 March 1929, just days before lessons started at the British school, the new municipal museum opened its doors to the public. The exhibition highlight was the Chinese room featuring ancient pottery. Shortly after the war Ypres had received a generous donation from the Chinese government to facilitate the rebuilding of the war-torn city. Originally, the money had been earmarked for a school or library building, but since no strings were attached to the donation the money was, in the event, invested in porcelain for the new museum (in actual fact the porcelain on display also included Japanese pottery and Delftware). The Chinese gift, brokered by the Royal Palace in Brussels, reveals the extent to which Ypres and its rebuilding programme had become an international symbol of the global war; and it shows China's determination to highlight symbolically its own role in the First World War, to which it had supplied labourers, many of whom were killed in the war or during the clean-up operations after 1918. Thus Ypres became the symbolic site where China marked its arrival as an emerging player on the world scene after the age of empire.[46]

The rebuilding of Ypres was advancing at rapid speed in the early 1930s. In July 1930 the restored St Martin's Cathedral was consecrated, less than eight years after the first stone of the new building had been laid on Armistice Day 1922. A memorial tablet to the million dead of the British Empire was duly unveiled there a few months later. Around the same time, the international media reported that the city had at last decided to reconstruct the Cloth Hall, too. Citizens were apparently tired of preserving the hall's ruins as an attraction for tourists, and rebuilding seemed to be the only way to halt the clandestine destruction through souvenir hunters.[47] British press reactions to the rebuilding of the city were highly ambiguous. On the one hand, urban planners were criticized for not being bold enough, for failing to lay out a city on modern lines. On the other hand, efforts to turn the city into a habitable place again met with resistance whenever they involved the clearance of former British dugouts.[48] Veterans in particular found it challenging to come to grips with the new cityscape. The poet Edmund Blunden, an acute chronicler of the effect of the war on the environment, admitted that reconstruction left him with ambivalent feelings, seen in the poem 'On Reading that the Rebuilding of Ypres Approached Completion'. On visiting Ypres the feelings were intensified and explored in the poems 'Flanders Now' and 'Return of the Native', in which he found the ramparts to be almost disturbingly serene given his memory of the place in wartime.[49]

'Ypres' became a byword for urban destruction. 'Like Ypres' was a catchphrase to describe phenomena as different as slum clearance in Manchester, the ruins of civil war in Dublin, and bombed-out houses from the Japanese occupation of Manchukuo.[50] But with rebuilding progressing, 'Ypres' seemed to have taken on more positive connotations. Thus a property company called Passchendaele Buildings was active in Toronto in the 1930s, and an Ypres Garage was operational in west London until it went bust around 1932 (shortly after a greyhound called Ypres Mist was crowned champion). Moreover, the microgeography of the salient was invoked, too; for instance, a boarding house named Zillebeke invited paying guests to chill out in Cleethorpes.[51] Two things are worth noting here. Firstly, there was not any hint of complaint that such profane usage of a sacred term was inappropriate. Secondly, and more importantly, 'Ypres' began to leave its mark on urban spaces far away from Flanders. In previous chapters we have seen how British soldiers imposed place names such as Clapham Junction on the salient and how British markers of memory overlaid the city. After 1928 more and more place names outside Belgium bore the name 'Ypres', notably in Germany and to a lesser extent in Britain and France. As early as November 1918, changing the name of Manhattan's Greeley Square to Ypres Square was mooted in New York City. Yet it came to naught, in part due to 'the difficulty that the great majority of the people would have in pronouncing the same properly'.[52] A small number of streets named after the campaigns in Flanders sprung up in interwar Britain. For instance, Ypres and Menin roads ran through a housing estate for disabled ex-servicemen in a suburb of Derby; and, in addition, the British Legion opened an Ypres House in the same town.[53] A Rue d'Ypres could be found in the French concession in the Chinese city of Tientsin; and a Jardin d'Ypres was planted in Le Touquet, the town to which Ypres citizens had fled during the war.[54] By contrast, squares and streets named after Ypres became ubiquitous in Germany. The very first Ypres, Langemarck, and Kemmel streets were named in Würzburg in November 1928.[55] Four years later Bonn created a Langemarck Way in close proximity to the Bismarck memorial and the sports grounds in the university quarter. While Würzburg's choice was a matter of convenience (the roads were located in a development area), Bonn's was politically motivated. The councillor who had come up with the idea stressed that Bonn students had participated in the assault on Langemarck and thus thwarted 'the plan of the English to invade the Rhineland'.[56]

* * * * *

The memory of Langemarck became embedded in the streetscapes of German cities after 1928. A parallel development, also beginning in 1928, was the establishment of Langemarck Day as a fixture in the calendar, above all in university towns. The date was deliberately fixed at 11 November as an antipode to both Armistice Day and 9 November, the anniversary of the proclamation of the republic in 1918. In his speech to students at Greifswald University, the publicist Hans Schwarz asserted that on 11 November the former Allies were commemorating the past whereas Germans were looking towards the future. The dead of Langemarck, the embodiment of the unbending will of 'a new aristocracy', were merely the vanguard of a 'third Reich' to come: 'A war lost? Yes! But a life gained', was the gist of Schwarz's speech that was later published under the title 'The Rebirth of the Heroic Man'.[57] This new man is cast as the very opposite of the Unknown Soldier: he represents true leadership rather than a false egalitarianism, and resurrection rather than death. Speeches given elsewhere on the same day might have been less emphatic but in essence followed the same script: 'It depends on you whether you want to be the end . . . or whether you want to be the beginning and the starting point of a new time', the rector of Munich University implored his audience.[58]

The exhortation 'Langemarck lives' reverberated through the Langemarck Day ritual. It did not pass unchallenged, though. In a letter to the editor of the liberal *Vossische Zeitung* published in November 1928, a veteran stated that only a word borrowed from the French language allowed him to sum up Langemarck: *merde*. Poking fun at students singing the traditional lament of the armed forces, 'I Had a Comrade', he asked 'What did you have 14 years ago? A dummy in your mouth!'[59] The letter writer alluded to the falseness of what he called the 'Langemarck legend', but it was *Vorwärts* that first labelled the story an outright lie. On 11 November 1929, the day of a mass rally in Berlin's Sportpalast attended by 15,000 people, the organ of the Social Democratic Party splashed 'The Lie of Langemarck: A Crime of the Army Command—Not an Act of Heroism'. The following day, under the headline 'The Idiotic Army Command', *Vorwärts* maintained that generals had used inexperienced troops as 'cannon fodder' and that the decision to deploy these units in 1914 amounted to a crime.[60]

The legacy of Langemarck, invoked by both the Left and the Right, helped polarize the political climate in the later Weimar years. This might explain the decision not to broadcast Langemarck celebrations on national radio in November 1930—a 'ban', as the opposition had it, that ultimately backfired on the government as it created its own controversy.[61] Earlier in the same year 'Langemarck' had left the realm of myth and become entangled in political debate, used as a propagandistic weapon against the Young Plan. 'In the name of the dead of Langemarck', the Kyffhäuserverband, a confederation of student fraternities, appealed to Reich President Hindenburg to reject the plan to restructure German reparations. Even though the Young Plan was advantageous to Germany (reducing the financial burden and ending the occupation of the Rhineland), it triggered a new wave of nationalist agitation. Hindenburg was caught in the crossfire of propaganda. Not even his nimbus as war hero was enough to sway right-wing agitators, and thus Hindenburg, once the figurehead of the political Right, became a target himself. The student fraternities' intervention in particular hit a raw nerve, for it pitted two myths about 1914 against each other: the Langemarck myth versus the mythical figure of the victor of Tannenberg. In an open letter to the students, published on the front page of many newspapers, Hindenburg himself tapped into the Langemarck myth to justify the plan: it was the memory of the spirit of sacrifice of 1914 that imposed a duty on the new generation to do its bit (and accept the Young Plan).[62]

The initiators of Langemarck Day were probably not aware of the Ypres Day observance in Britain. Both events commemorated the war in Flanders, especially the First Battle, but that is where the similarities ended. While Ypres Day was a conservative (with a small 'c') affair supported by the Establishment and the Church, the organizers from the Ypres League steered well clear of current politics. Observed every 31 October since 1922, the central event involved wreaths being laid at the Cenotaph and the tomb of the Unknown Warrior. The herald for Armistice Day, Ypres Day placed a somewhat greater emphasis on pride than on mourning, although this contrast should not be overemphasized. The notion of universal mourning permeated commemorations. Nonetheless, as historian Adrian Gregory notes, 'The main dynamic of post-war commemoration was not... a straightforward product of family grief, but rooted in a concern for the proper acknowledgement of the losses of *others*.'[63]

The pain of others was acknowledged in a new commemorative ritual first performed under the arch of the Menin Gate on 2 July 1928. The Last Post was not an officially instigated event but emerged, apparently spontaneously, from within civil society. The frictions over the rebuilding of Ypres in the early years after the war seemed long forgotten, as the introduction of the Last Post represented a moving tribute by local people to the British. The buglers were members of the local fire brigade but participated in the ceremony in a private capacity. The fact that they dispensed with pomp and circumstance, turning up in their ordinary work clothes, gave the ceremony a special poignancy. The unusual format was, in a sense, in keeping with the quotidian quality of the British ritual of remembrance, for the Armistice Day silence, too, was always held at the same time, regardless of what day it fell on. Some seventy people were present at the original Last Post ceremony in 1928, but within the space of a year attendance had risen to between six and seven hundred. In the first two years the ritual was performed between July and September, clearly to coincide with the tourist season. From 1930 the Last Post was played throughout the year, although turnout dropped noticeably during the winter cold. A committee was set up in May 1930 under the patronage of King Albert I to oversee formally the daily ceremony. On Armistice Day 1930 the bugle call sounded not only at the Menin Gate, but also in sitting rooms throughout Britain and Belgium, transmitted in a live broadcast by the BBC and Radio Belgique, creating temporarily something like a transnational community of remembrance. Music was better suited than words or stones to forge a commemorative alliance between the two nations.[64]

The Menin Gate featured in internationalist public ritual staged in Britain, too. S. N. Sedgwick's 1929 play *At the Menin Gate* sought to teach Britons a lesson in world citizenship. A melodrama written for use at League of Nations Union meetings and Armistice Day, the play focuses on working-class characters and is set in a café a few days after the 1928 British Legion pilgrimage. Centred on a middle-aged couple who have come to Ypres with their daughter Nelly to see their son's name on the memorial, they are accompanied by William, their son's best friend in the trenches. William makes unrequited advances to Nelly and then turns to emotional blackmail, stating that Bob actually deserted and is probably not memorialized on the gate. He threatens to let this secret out if Nelly refuses to marry him. At the same time, the family has become friendly with the waiter in one of the cafés. He tells them that he had acted as translator in the war. They discuss Germans only for the father to declare his abiding disgust for them. Nelly is different, though, and promotes the message of the League of Nations Union. At this point a German couple enter the café and, detecting the hostile atmosphere, ask for directions to the gate before leaving quickly. William now sees his threat through and tells Bob's mother that had he not been killed running away from his post, Bob would undoubtedly have faced court martial and execution. The German couple now re-enter the café accompanied by their disabled son, Otto. They explain that Otto was seriously wounded in the salient, but his life had been saved by a British soldier who was killed carrying Otto to an aid post. Every year they return to Ypres to place a wreath on the grave of an unknown British soldier. Otto had found the photograph of a girl among the man's possessions which is, of course, a photograph of Nelly, and thus the man who had saved his life was Bob. This turns the final scene into a grand act of Anglo-Belgian–German reconciliation in which the Menin Gate proves to be the crucial focal point where the competing memories of the war are combined. Here the gate became the site of an imagined international community.[65]

* * * * *

The Ypres League, founded in 1921, quickly established itself as the main custodian of the memory of the battles of Ypres across Britain and the Empire. Membership was open to those who had served or suffered the loss of a loved one in the salient. Although it never became a mass movement, the league and its activities received a high media profile throughout the interwar period. An organization solely devoted to the management of the memory of Ypres, it had no direct equivalent in Germany, at least not until 1928 when the Langemarck Donation was formed. An offshoot from the German Students' Association, the Langemarck Donation had a full-time secretariat and its own propaganda machinery. Hitherto the middle-class youth movement had acted as the keeper of the myth, yet without any organizational infrastructure to speak of. Moreover, while Langemarck was an important legacy to the Bündische Jugend, it was by no means its raison d'être. New developments occurred in the aftermath of the tenth anniversary of the end of the war when several organizations sprung up, vying to inherit the legacy of Langemarck.

The Langemarck Donation aspired to represent the entire student body. In contrast, the Stahlhelm Students' Circle 'Langemarck', founded in 1929, was an exclusive organization that catered for the ideologically committed elite. Its parent organization was the powerful Stahlhelm League of Front-line Soldiers, a hybrid between a veterans' association and a paramilitary force. Since the hated Versailles Treaty placed severe restrictions on the armed forces' manpower and weaponry, Stahlhelm students sought to bolster the nation's defensive capabilities by other means. Their main goal was the psychological rearmament of Germany. To this end, they put on a programme of lectures and *Wehrsport* (military-style physical exercise). Moreover, local branches lobbied university managers to establish chairs in *Wehrwissenschaft* (military sciences), that is, the interdisciplinary study of history, politics, and economics of war and the armed forces, with excursions into military engineering, chemistry, and physics. The example of the University of Münster shows how successful Stahlhelm students were in setting the agenda. Although numerically weak (counting a mere fifty-six members), the local branch managed to persuade the university's senate to apply to the Prussian Ministry of Education for extra funding for *Wehrwissenschaft* at Münster.[66]

The very name of the association—Stahlhelm Students' Circle 'Langemarck'—conjured up two different facets of the war: the war of movement of 1914 and the war of attrition of 1916. The *Stahlhelm,* the distinctive flat-topped steel helmet, had been introduced in early 1916 to replace the decorative but inefficient spiked one. It became the emblem of a new kind of warfare and a new type of warrior, hammered into being at Verdun. Hardened by industrialized mass warfare, this ultimate front fighter typified a dehumanized race, a war machine with an iron soul. Historian Bernd Hüppauf draws a sharp distinction between the myths of Langemarck and Verdun: enthusiasm versus hardness, idealism versus nihilism, youth versus maturity, nostalgia versus futurism, heroism versus technology.[67] In the commemorative practice of Stahlhelm students, though, these two myths proved complementary rather than exclusive.[68] The organization even tapped into a further war myth in 1932 when it sent a group of 150 students on a 'patrol' of East Prussia in order to stake German claims in eastern Europe vis-à-vis Poland and Lithuania. A visit to the monumental Tannenberg memorial was an integral part of the 'patrol'. Built in a style reminiscent of a crusader castle, the Tannenberg memorial commemorated the defeat of the knights of the Teutonic Order in 1410 *and* the German victory over the Russian army in summer 1914 on the same battlefield. This historical coincidence gave rise to one of the most powerful myths of the war, of a German crusade in the east. At Tannenberg, Stahlhelm students imagined themselves following in the footsteps of both the Teutonic Knights and Hindenburg's soldiers.[69]

Stahlhelm students freely mixed elements from various war-related myths to create their own commemorative cocktail. Their Langemarck stood for a vision rather than history. An essentially ahistorical devotion to the First Battle of Ypres was typical of right-wing organizations that used 'Langemarck' in their name. 'A Langemarck occurred at *all* fronts', asserted the 'Langemarck Committee (Academy and Army)'. Formed in 1929 with the aim of uniting students and soldiers in the fight against liberal democracy, the committee differentiated between *Langemarckgedenken* (Langemarck commemorations) and *Langemarckgedanken* (Langemarck ideas). With their eyes fixed on the future, it was the latter that mattered most to them. What had actually happened in 1914—'whether or not the "Deutschlandlied" was sung'—was of secondary importance. In another respect, however, the committee saw the need to set the historical record straight by pointing out that those killed during First Ypres were not all students but, in fact, represented a cross-section of German society. At the same time, the committee acknowledged the prerogative of students to exercise 'the priesthood of Langemarck commemorations and ideas'.[70]

The reactionary Langemarck Committee (Academy and Army) was capable of making a great deal of noise; this has been picked up by the historiography, which has tended to equate the Langemarck myth with right-wing agitation. However, other more moderate organizations named 'Langemarck' inserted their voices into the cacophony of the public sphere in the later Weimar years, for instance, the Catholic Student Corporation 'Langemarck'. Established at the University of Bonn during the academic year 1928–9, its members not only accepted the political settlement of 1918, but even pronounced the war a 'madness', never to be re-enacted—all in the name of Langemarck.[71]

* * * * *

As the commemoration of Langemarck was gathering momentum in the late 1920s, the Reichsarchiv released its long-anticipated official account of the autumn 1914 campaign. While the British volumes covering First Ypres had hit the shelves in 1925, its German counterpart required another four years of gestation. Behind the dense descriptions of military operations, delivered in a factual and seemingly detached prose, lurked a historiographical bombshell. Langemarck—the village made famous in the war's most cited bulletin and over which so much ink had been spilled since 11 November 1914—is relegated to a sideshow. The communiqué itself, the text of which many, if not most, Germans knew by heart, is not even referred to. What is most striking about the official history is what is *not* mentioned: the students leading the assault and the singing of the anthem 'Deutschland, Deutschland über alles'. Nothing that elevated Langemarck to an iconic event is corroborated here. On the contrary, the official history concludes that no ground was taken in the 'overhasty attack' of underequipped and ill-fed troops in November 1914.[72]

How can one explain this implicit debunking of the Langemarck myth by no less an institution than the Reichsarchiv? Firstly, the veracity of the communiqué had come under scrutiny for some time. Eyewitnesses stepped forward claiming that the singing of the 'Deutschlandlied' was an act of desperation when German troops had come under friendly fire. Furthermore, it seemed increasingly implausible that advancing soldiers could have had the stamina to sing.[73] Secondly, within the Reichsarchiv a group of 'reactionary modernists' were gaining the upper hand. They had little time for the false romanticism of the 'childrens' crusade'. Committed to a 'scientific' examination of the lessons of war, one of the archivists argued that First Ypres was 'the most irrelevant' of battles. 'On the battlefield near Ypres the old concepts of valour, male bravery and enthusiasm were smashed to pieces.' Not the enemy, but 'the cold force of the material' had prevailed.[74] The writer Ernst Jünger, held in high esteem at the Reichsarchiv, made a very similar point. For him the fighting during First Ypres marked the demise of the individual and the triumph of technology. Nevertheless, Jünger conceded that Langemarck—irrelevant in terms of military history—had its place in the 'history of ideas'.[75] Jünger's point might go some way to explain why the official history did not undermine the Langemarck myth in the long run. The myth was so deeply entrenched in German society that no historical facts could override its transcendental truth.

Soldiers, gasping for breath, had not managed to intone 'Deutschland, Deutschland über alles' in the midst of battle—but they had sung it in their hearts! So said a regimental history compiled 'with use of the official material from the Reichsarchiv', as stated in the subtitle. The book covers not only First Ypres but also the Second Battle: 'Promptly at six o'clock the gas cylinders are opened and the wind drives the chlorine gas in in thick, greenish clouds towards the enemy; an unforgettable, curious sight.' The regiment storms forward, one reads, in a 'cheerful, jolly' mood. 'The success of the assault surpassed all expectations.' There is no hint of shame or guilt, only 'pride', in this account of 22 April 1915, the day when modern chemical warfare began.[76] The Reichsarchiv's own assessment was less upbeat. The volume on military operations in 1915, published in 1932, concludes that the new weapon passed its test, but that the army command failed to exploit the tactical advantage. The published text is a much toned-down version of an earlier draft. In it the operational aim was identified bluntly as 'the extermination of the enemy'.[77] The wording rang alarm bells with Fritz Haber. The Nobel Laureate, who had been instrumental in developing the gas weapon, urged the official historians to weigh their words carefully. And so they did. Performing legal acrobatics, they argued that the German use of poison gas respected both the letter and the spirit of international law. The official history even alleged that 'The introduction of the gas weapon did not contradict the laws of humanity either', for bullets proved more lethal than gas and almost all gas victims made a full recovery.[78]

Controversy was also stirred up in 1933, at least in diplomatic circles, by the publication of the latest volume of the French official history. The British Embassy in Paris and the Foreign Office were very concerned by the portrayal of the British at Second Ypres, among a host of other points, and noted the protests of the Canadian government at the depiction of its corps in the fighting.[79] Ypres was also the focus of the first volume of the Canadian official history, which finally appeared in 1938. Much bitterness had been caused in Canada by the rumours put about by the former minister of militia, Sir Sam Hughes, that General Sir Arthur Currie, commander of the Canadian Corps from 1917, had been profligate with his men's lives and often took flawed decisions. A. F. Duguid, the Canadian official historian, had already entered into extensive correspondence with his British counterpart in the 1920s over comments about the performance of Canadian units during the drafting stages of the first volume of *Military Operations: France and Belgium, 1915*. This made a definitive Canadian statement all the more pressing. However, Duguid proved extremely slow in completing a Canadian volume capable of addressing all of these controversies. In the meantime, many other commentators had gone into print leaving the Canadian government concerned that the official record might leave little impression on popular perceptions. Such fears appear to have been unfounded, for on publication reviewers infused the work with a dual purpose as both history and memorial, expressing relief on behalf of veterans, their families, and the relatives of the bereaved that a fitting tribute had been delivered in the detail of the research and coverage. Duguid's volume was warmly received because of its perceived impartiality, but it was actually a strategy of avoiding controversy rather than dealing with it head-on, which ensured that the men of the Canadian Corps could continue to be revered for their actions at Saint-Julien in spring 1915 and unseemly debate about the nature of their leadership minimized.[80]

Although the gas attacks remained a dreadful chapter in the military history of the Ypres salient, by the 1930s it was largely overshadowed in the anglophone world by a growing controversy about Passchendaele. Basil Liddell Hart's 1930 book, *The Real War,* provided a condemnation of British generalship, with Third Ypres highlighted as the nadir. Republished in 1934 as *A History of the World War,* Liddell Hart's persuasive work played a significant role in establishing a new orthodoxy about the battle. Third Ypres was unequivocally declared 'a synonym for military failure—a name black-bordered in the records of the British Army'. Particularly devastating was the infamous anecdote that a staff officer (said by many to have been Launcelot Kiggell, Haig's chief of staff) was alleged to have visited the front and broken down in tears sobbing 'Good God, did we really send men to fight in that?'[81] This story became a touchstone for all who wished to depict higher ranking officers as utterly out of touch with those who actually fought the war.

The original title, *The Real War,* is somewhat misleading. The book offers a strategical critique rather than an exploration of the 'real' experience of soldiers under fire. The latter was the approach taken by Werner Beumelburg in his 1928 popular history of Third Ypres. Commissioned by the Reichsarchiv and aimed at the general reader, *Flandern 1917* seeks 'to psychologically explore the characteristic experience of the Flanders Battle [the name under which Third Ypres was known in Germany] in order to convey an emotional insight into the enormous struggle'.[82] This marked a radical departure from traditional operational studies and came close to what one would call today a history of emotions. Despite the occasional reference to military strategy, *Flandern 1917* is principally narrated from the soldier's point of view. By profession a writer rather than a historian, Beumelburg deploys an arsenal of literary techniques to engross the reader: battle scenes are written in the present tense, the narrative is interspersed with dialogues and spiced up with metaphorical language ('the screaming battle').[83] One chapter follows a character named Müller—the Everyman of the war of attrition. What becomes apparent from Beumelburg's account is that the traditional notion of a great battle—as a decisive encounter—had lost its meaning. Even though he pronounces Third Flanders 'a great victory', Beumelburg suggests that the true outcome was something much more significant: 'the making of a new type of soldier', that is, the battle-hardened *Frontschwein* (front hog), driven by a sense of absolute loyalty towards his comrades.[84]

* * * * *

Forgotten today, Beumelburg was at one time the most published author of war books in Germany. His career prospered after Hitler's accession to power in 1933. Although a loyal supporter of the Third Reich, Nazi ideology had little impact on his writings. Rather, he continued writing in the nationalist vein developed during the Weimar years. However, Hitler became Beumelburg's new Everyman: 'Among the combatants of Langemarck in October and November 1914 was the war volunteer Adolf Hitler.'[85] Hitler himself had realized how valuable a tool references to Langemarck were. In his trial for high treason after the failed 1923 putsch, Hitler invoked the dead of Langemarck to challenge the prosecution's case: 'There rise again 350,000 17-, 18-, 19-year-old boys who once in 1914 went out and who with the "Deutschlandlied" on their lips marched into death in Flanders. They will rise again as the accuser.'[86] Sentenced to a lenient term, Hitler used his time behind bars to compose *Mein Kampf*, including the following passage about his baptism of fire in Flanders in autumn 1914: 'And from the distance the strains of a song reached our ears, coming closer and closer, leaping from company to company, and just as Death plunged a busy hand into our ranks, the song reached us too and we passed it along: *Deutschland, Deutschland über alles, über alles in der Welt.*' Hitler sought to inherit the mantle of the dead of 1914 and, at the same time, pass himself off as a hard-bitten soldier who fought over the same 'sacred soil' again in 1917. Furthermore, Hitler states that it was 'on the front south of Ypres' in October 1918 that he was temporarily blinded in a gas attack (although it has been argued that his blindness was psychosomatic). Recuperating in hospital, Hitler learned about the revolution in Berlin and, allegedly, made his fateful decision to go into politics.[87] The fighting in Flanders is a recurring theme in *Mein Kampf*, and it was in the years following its publication in 1925–7 that Hitler's war service (which he had actually spent in the relative comfort of regimental headquarters) began to assume centre stage in Nazi propaganda.[88]

The Nazi Party fashioned itself as the political embodiment of 'youth'. This claim was not completely unfounded since its membership was significantly younger than that of any other political party in the Weimar Republic. The Nazis made particular advances among university students, usurping the leadership of the German Students' Association in 1931. The Nazis' rise to power in 1933 enabled the official students' representatives to intensify their commemorative efforts. Thus they introduced the 'Langemarck Sacrifice'—a levy imposed on all university students.[89] In addition, they brought out the *Langemarckbuch* (Book of Langemarck) as an 'intellectual memorial'. The book reiterates that there was 'a "Langemarck"... at all fronts of the great war'. Distinguishing between Langemarck and 'Langemarck', between the battle and the idea, the book asserts: 'That we lost near Langemarck will always be irreparable. That we won "Langemarck" is our proudest victory.'[90] In other words, 'Langemarck' transcended conventional notions of victory and defeat—an idea that was hardly new. In fact, during the Third Reich the Langemarck myth was to evolve along established lines; its core remained stable, and even its inherent ambiguities and dissonances were left unresolved. What changed, though, was agency: Langemarck became a state-sponsored myth. In a society where voluntary associations (such as the Stahlhelm Students' Circle 'Langemarck') were 'synchronized' (that is, dissolved or swallowed up), party and state assumed the role of guardians of the myth.

The *Langemarckbuch* reiterated the students' claim to the 'priesthood'. In practice, however, a serious rival emerged in the form of the Hitler Youth. Initially, it was local Hitler Youth branches that embraced the cultural memory of Langemarck as their own. In Thuringia, for example, the Hitler Youth organized a 'memory march' in an effort to recapture the experience of 1914; and in Hanover the Hitler Youth annexed a youth hostel already named 'Langemarck' from the Christian boy scouts.[91] The national leadership took longer to realize the potential of the myth, especially as a vehicle to integrate bourgeois youths into its organization. In November 1934 they took over the Langemarck Donation (including its administrative apparatus) from the German Students' Association, and from 1935 onwards Langemarck became a central plank of the Hitler Youth's strategy: it commissioned a Langemarck cantata, staged the largest ever Langemarck rally in Berlin, and established a leadership academy which not only bore Langemarck in its name, but also functioned as a reliquary for souvenirs brought back from Flanders.[92] The Hitler Youth reiterated that Langemarck stood for 'the sacrifices [made] at all fronts' and they even included the 'martyrs' of the Nazi movement in this community of the dead.[93] Langemarck had always been a symbol of both youth and students, but now the emphasis shifted decidedly towards the former. This led to friction with the students' leadership, which had no intention of giving up its claim to the myth. This episode is typical of administrative chaos and internal rivalries in the Third Reich. Hitler proved himself a 'weak dictator' in intervening personally in the conflict between the Hitler Youth and student leadership in February 1937, confirming the prerogative of the students but still allowing the dispute to rumble on well into the Second World War.[94]

Hitler assumed the role of high priest of the cult of Langemarck during the 1936 Olympics. All interwar games had incorporated an element of war commemoration but these had been low-key affairs

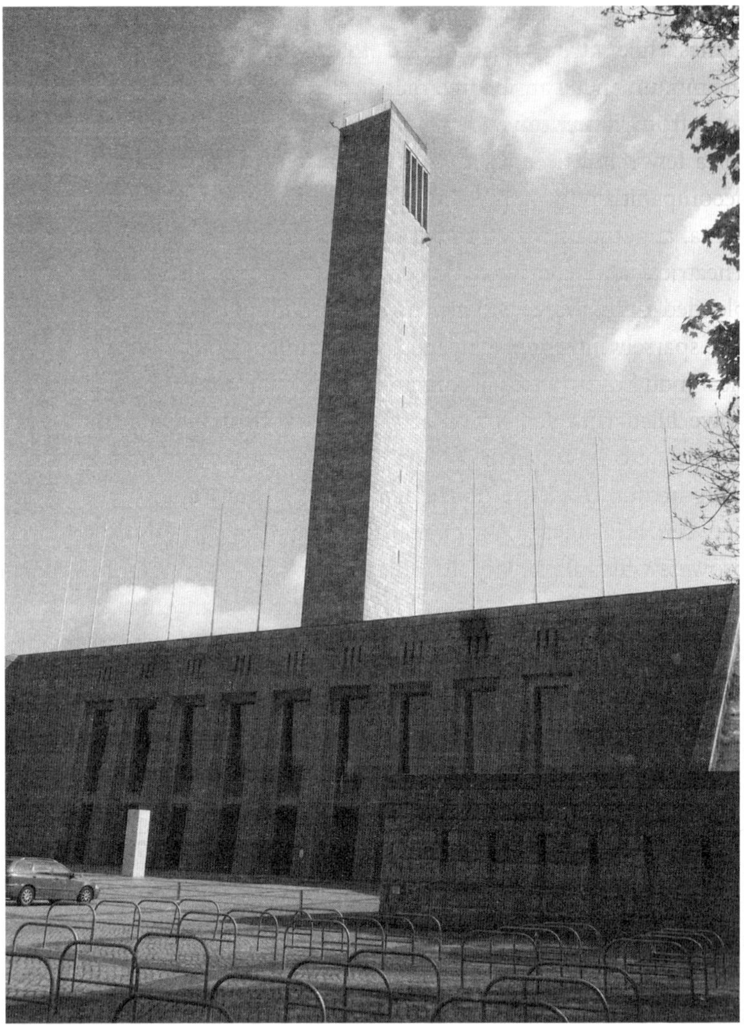

Figure 23. Langemarck Hall in the bell tower of the Olympic stadium in Berlin built in 1936. Photograph, April 2014.

compared to the Berlin Olympics. Arriving at the stadium to open the games, Hitler first inspected the assembled athletes before retreating to the monumental Langemarck Hall in the bell tower. There he switched roles from Führer to veteran and back again. He remained in the hall for a few minutes in silent communion with the spirts of the dead, accompanied only by his minister of war. Only then did he enter the arena, announced by a trumpet fanfare, and declare the games open. Theatrical and understated at the same time, Hitler's performance blended the private with the public, contemplation with spectacle. The sparsely furnished Langemarck Hall, built in the style of neoclassical modernism, featured seventy-six regimental flags and a symbolic grave filled with soil from Langemarck cemetery. According to its architect, Werner March, the 'sanctuary' gave stony expression to 'the faith in our revived German nation'.[95] It created a liminal space between life and death where athletics merged with war, sporting prowess with soldierly valour. A similarly grand Langemarck Memorial Site was envisaged at Hanover. Local student representatives were the driving force behind the scheme. It was an initiative fraught with difficulties right from the start: the municipal authorities dragged their heels, the minister of the interior refused permission for a nationwide fundraising campaign, and the organizers proved utterly incompetent. The low point was a supposed mass rally on 1 August 1939 that was sparsely attended, because the organizers had not taken into account that the date coincided with the holiday season.[96]

The Langemarck myth was a propaganda gold mine—and a pitfall. The Nazis' mastery of the dark art of propaganda is undisputed among historians. Less well known are the propaganda blunders committed by the regime. Whenever Langemarck was concerned, the Nazis were prone to get into a muddle. At Hanover the main problem was the lack of coordination and conviction; in other cases they stumbled over the ambiguities inherent in the myth. Consider the book *Langemarck 1914* by Wilhelm Dreysse, a disabled war veteran and staunch believer in Nazism. It was first published in October 1934 to coincide with the twentieth anniversary of the battle. Keen for his work to have impact, the author travelled from his home in Bonn to the Gestapo headquarters in Berlin in order to hand-deliver a copy for the perusal of Reinhard Heydrich. In his covering letter Dreysse alluded to a 'Masonic plot' (in which he even implicated his own publishers) to conceal the truth about Langemarck. He alleged that the publishers had suppressed the subtitle, 'To the youths who always have to bleed and die for the mistakes of the old generation'.[97] The hysterical letter was merely acknowledged and the book shelved in the Gestapo's library. Around the same time the Nazis' news service endorsed the newly published title and a string of positive reviews began to appear.[98] Nobody seemed to realize the explosive potential of the book until former officers who recognized themselves in the text stepped forward. They were outraged by the criticism levied against the officer corps' failure in leadership. Dreysse, now smelling a 'Catholic' conspiracy behind the attacks on his book, went on the offensive with a pamphlet entitled 'Controversy over Langemarck'. He overplayed his hand. Rather than vindicating Dreysse's account, the censor now re-examined the original and retracted its previous recommendation.[99]

Inexplicably, the book remained in print for four more years. It was the fourth edition, published before Christmas 1938, that sparked a full investigation during which another issue emerged: the infringement of Hitler's copyright. Dreysse had reproduced both a 1914 painting of Wytschaete and a long Hitler quotation without permission—thus dragging the Führer into his feud with the officers of the imperial army. There followed a flurry of letters between the Ministry of Propaganda, the party's central office, Hitler Youth leaders, and army officers. At first, the book remained on sale but reprints were banned. Finally, Gestapo officers got round to reading the book that had been gathering dust in their library. They concluded that in its portrayal of NCOs in particular the book came close to the hated *All Quiet on the Western Front*. In September 1939 the Gestapo seized all remainders; they were pulped five months later.[100] This story is not merely illustrative of administrative jumble in the Third Reich, it is also indicative of the Nazis' problem with managing an older myth full of ambiguities. 'Langemarck' enshrined a story of heroic failure. Dreysse was not the first person who wanted to 'correct' the myth. However, his search for the culprits clashed with the regime's desire for a rapprochement with the army and the old elites, and as Germany was mobilizing for a new war, they had no time for an embittered veteran settling old scores.

Popular histories of Langemarck proved a propaganda minefield.[101] An infinitely more successful form of propaganda was the naming of roads. Many Langemarck streets had been created during the Weimar years; after 1933 their number increased exponentially. This was to a large extent a (sub)urban phenomenon, concentrated in housing estates on the outskirts of growing cities. In Breslau, Freiburg, and Stuttgart, Langemarck or Ypres streets sprung up as part of 'war

Figure 24. Street sign for Langemarckstraße in Freiburg's 'heroes' quarter' opened in 1934. Photograph, August 2014.

quarters' dedicated to battles and generals. While Stuttgart's Ypernstrasse (wedged between Flandernstrasse and Kemmelstrasse) was just one of thirteen streets named after campaigns of the Great War, in Freiburg's 'heroes' quarter' Langemarck was given pride of place.[102]

Mayors used the politics of street naming to gain a foothold in milieux considered oppositional. The cult of Langemarck became intimately linked to the provision of affordable housing for working families. Yet the Nazis deployed the Langemarck myth in order to penetrate a diverse range of social strata. In Augsburg, Habsburgerstrasse, originally laid out in 1916, became Langemarckstrasse in an effort to overwrite any residual sympathies for the multi-ethnic Habsburg Empire. In staunchly Catholic Münster, Nazi student leaders demanded that Windthorststrasse gave way to a new Langemarckstrasse (not realizing that the road had actually been named after a former mayor rather than his famous namesake, Ludwig Windthorst, leader of the Centre Party and Bismarck's nemesis); Pius Avenue was also on their list.[103] Langemarck streets also replaced sites of memory connected to the Weimar Republic, for instance Rathenaustrasse in Essen and Stresemannplatz in Recklinghausen. In Bonn, Peace Street—named in the aftermath of the London Conference of 1924—became Langemarckstrasse.[104] The renaming of existing roads was not merely an administrative act, but often embedded in a public ritual of taking down old street signs and replacing them with new ones.[105] Local mayors were usually the driving force behind the ideological reorganization of urban spaces. However, the national students' leadership tried to muscle in with a nationwide campaign launched on Langemarck Day 1937. Yet local authorities rarely welcomed such interference. Mannheim, whose streets are laid out in a grid pattern without names, refused to acquiesce; Jena retorted that the proposal to change the name of Princes' Moat (Fürstengraben) into Langemarck Trench was 'undignified'.[106]

'Crecy, Agincourt, Cadiz, Blenheim, Gibraltar, Inkermann, Ypres' were names that 'rang musically' in British ears, and Britons, Evelyn Waugh quipped,

> had never fallen to the habit of naming streets after their feats of arms; that was suitable enough for the short-lived and purely professional triumphs of the French, but to put those great manifestations of divine rectitude which were the victories of England to the use, for their postal addresses, of milliners and chiropodists, would have been a basement to which even the radicals had not stooped.[107]

Such a 'basement' was precisely what the Nazis intended. The veneration of Langemarck was to spread from the lecture theatres into the public squares; it was to become a lived memory, not simply a ritualized legacy. Langemarck began to leave its mark on the paraphernalia of everyday life in cities: business cards, roadmaps, directories (sometimes with a brief explanatory note).[108] People waited at bus stops called Langemarckstrasse or Flandernstrasse, and the names of these stops were shouted out on public transport. In addition, schools and student hostels bore the name of the famous battle. Here cultural memory blended with everyday life.

The effort to create an organic form of commemoration, fusing the sacred with the everyday, culminated in the establishment of the *Langemarckstudium* (Langemarck Studies) and, through it, the creation of a new elite who would carry on the torch of remembrance. The *Langemarckstudium* was to pave the way for gifted but underprivileged young men to attend university. The idea of opening tertiary education to the children of working-class families was not new; the Nazis simply implemented—with great fanfare, to be sure—a scheme dating back to the Weimar Republic. The beginnings were very modest, with a total of twenty-two students commencing studies at Heidelberg and Königsberg in autumn 1934. The title *Langemarckstudium* was formally adopted in 1938 when the programme expanded to Hanover and Stuttgart. It was a misnomer, for this was neither a proper *Studium* (a course of studies leading to a degree), nor were the students enrolled at university. The scheme was rather a preparatory programme designed to increase access to higher education on the basis of National Socialist 'selection'. Talent alone was not enough; students also had to fulfil racial and political criteria. The organizers of the *Langemarckstudium* started a publicity campaign which implied that universities would become 'places of education for the entire *Volksgemeinschaft*. The university becomes the people's school'.[109] This led to friction with the Ministry of Education which warned against raising unrealistic expectations. Rather than a vehicle of social mobility transforming class structures, the *Langemarckstudium* was to remain the preserve of a select group, a male racial elite of no more than 1,000 men.[110]

The Reich Student Leadership stated that the title *Langemarckstudium* 'reminds us daily of the sacrifice of those heroic youths who went singing to their deaths. They died for a new Reich of a socialist order. Langemarck is, therefore, not only a memory of a military event but first and foremost a political mandate.' The programme's director added that Langemarck was the ur-moment during which the '*Volksgemeinschaft* of the coming Reich' became apparent. History and German were the two core subjects taught, but lessons also included English, geography, maths, and sciences. Questions in the exams tested the usual knowledge, but the students' answers were expected to exhibit a National Socialist slant. Interestingly, commemorative ritual played a minor role in the education of Langemarck students, perhaps because the entire programme represented 'the living memorial... to the heroes of Langemarck'.[111]

* * * * *

The Second World War gave the *Langemarckstudium* a new lease of life. Numbers tripled and the organizers stepped up their propaganda. Moreover, the commemorative dimension of the programme became more explicit, as alumni killed in the Second World War were given a place in the Nazi pantheon next to their 1914 forebears.[112] However, the programme director emphasized that war enthusiasm was a thing of the past; calmness and determination were the order of the day.[113] Wartime propaganda justified the precious resources channelled into the programme by comparing it to an 'intellectual armament factory'. Moreover, students were told that they stood 'in the front line... just like our comrades on the Eastern Front'.[114] The new cohort included the war-disabled, soldiers with leave of absence from the Wehrmacht, and pro-German students from occupied Belgium, the Netherlands, and Scandinavia. In particular, Flemings were invited to join the pan-Germanic *Volks-Gemeenschap* created in the name of Langemarck during the Second World War.[115]

On the eve of the Second World War the restoration of Ypres had been almost complete. 'The last traces of the bombardment of Ypres during the last War will soon have disappeared', reported *The Times* in March 1940.[116] But the age of reconstruction, epitomized in the optimistic rebuilding of the town centre, was over. Britain declared war on Germany in September 1939, an act which placed the British Settlement at Ypres in a liminal state. Leo Murphy of the Ypres Salient War Museum began packing up his collection and relocated to Brighton in autumn 1939.[117] Other expatriates stayed put. Yet, with the Nazi invasion of May 1940 and the rapid collapse of the defending forces, evacuation became an urgent issue. The IWGC prepared a plan which was put into action on 18 May. It was the start of a harrowing journey of uncertainty and fear which ended on 23 May when the majority were evacuated from Calais. 'Here the dead possessed the ground,' the *New York Times* commented on 2 June 1940, 'but last week the fiercely living no longer could keep what the quiet dead had held. Ypres fell to the German Army after twenty-six years.'[118] Fighting occurred near Ypres and British units caused some minor damage to the Menin Gate by destroying its causeway over the moat. Having failed to carry out similar demolition work on all other access routes, the action was pointless in the extreme. Convinced the British people wanted reassurance about the condition of the memorials, IWGC Vice Chairman Fabian Ware circulated information to the press as well as broadcasting on the BBC during the Armistice Day observations of 1940.[119]

Dixmude, Langemarck, Ypres, Kemmel—'What a proud list of names *in one day*!', exclaimed Joseph Goebbels.[120] For once, reality surpassed propaganda. Hitler had seemingly reversed the ignominious defeat of 1918 and finally captured the 'holy soil' almost without any bloodshed.[121] 'General Bloodless' was at the peak of his popularity, and Ypres was the most significant stop on the road to Paris. Hitler's return to the place where he had allegedly received his baptism of fire was a carefully staged affair captured by his photography tsar, Heinrich Hoffmann.[122] Ypres stood no longer for defeat and stalemate but for blitzkrieg and victory. Revealing the symbolic significance of the Menin Gate, Hitler himself inspected it on 1 and 26 June. Not all German soldiers were magnanimous in victory; they destroyed the French gas memorial at Steenstraat, erased the inscriptions ('Here the invader was brought to a standstill') from almost all Demarcation Stones, and some painted swastikas on the Menin Gate.

The Menin Gate had become a site of contested memories on the eve of the Second World War. In the late 1930s groups of German veterans and the Hitler Youth increased their visibility during the Last Post, causing some disquiet as wreaths with Nazi insignia were left and the Hitler salute rendered during the ceremony. When wreaths were stolen in March 1939, the German government complained officially

Figure 25. Hitler visiting the Langemarck war cemetery. Photograph by Heinrich Hoffmann, June 1940.

to the Belgian authorities. A few weeks later, French veterans brought a sackful of Verdun soil to the gate and buried it on the rampart lawns on the southern side of the memorial.[123] The symbolism was intense. The hole was dug into Belgian soil made British through sanguinary sacrifice; it was then conjoined with the equally sacred soil of Verdun underlining the solidarity of Belgium, Britain, and France, and the legacy left to the three nations by the actions of their soldiers. It was against this backdrop that the Nazis intensified their symbolic presence in the salient following the Fall of France in 1940. With the bugles silent during the war, Langemarck cemetery—now looked after by the Hitler Youth—became a focal point of commemorative rituals.[124]

The prism of Ypres provided a vital lens for understanding and contextualizing the new conflict. 'Second Langemarck' made possible a reunion of the living and the dead. It was also an imagined meeting between different generations. A German soldier newspaper recounted how veterans of the first battle of Langemarck shared their war memories with participants of the new campaign.[125] Something similar occurred in Britain. The nascent Home Guard, it has been argued, resembled an 'enormous memory club' where ex-servicemen commanded special authority.[126] In addition, Dover, as the new symbol of British stoicism, was christened 'Hellfire Corner' in reference to the notorious Hellfire Corner on the Menin Road which the British imperial armies had defended unflinchingly between 1914 and 1918.[127] These were the preliminaries to the Blitz proper. When news of the bombing of Coventry broke in November 1940, initially comparisons with Ypres were made to convey a sense of utter devastation. However, soon it transpired that the Second World War was a very different conflict, and Coventry itself became a cultural reference point for what war could do to a city. 'Coventration' soon entered the English vocabulary as an unprecedented act of brutality that conventional language could not adequately capture.[128]

In Britain Ypres began to fade from the national consciousness after 1940. The Ypres League collapsed and Ypres Day observance ceased. One reason was that the new war generated new symbols such as

Coventry. More importantly, though, memories of the Western Front had little purchase in a war without a western front. Ypres represented a potential embarrassment in the period between Dunkirk and D-Day. Ypres was not forgotten, but its remembrance was held in abeyance until September 1944 when the city was liberated by the Allies. Yet, in some minds, the strategic bombing campaign against Germany was something akin to a western front. Bomber Command was charged with reducing Germans to submission without the need for a land campaign. Air power 'means no more Passchendaeles', suggested the *Daily Express* in December 1943.[129]

In Germany the cult of Langemarck continued during the Second World War. While the core of the myth remained unchanged, the lessons of Langemarck were applied to increasingly diverse contexts. In October 1941 the Reichsarchiv's successor, the Kriegsgeschichtliche Forschungsanstalt (War Historical Research Institute), received instructions to prepare a brief popular account of the battle for a Japanese audience. Japan had joined with the Axis powers in the Tripartite Pact in the previous autumn, and now the Japanese ambassador showed great interest in the story of young men plunging into certain death. The official historian did not disappoint his client; he unashamedly revived the old tale that dated back to the army communiqué of November 1914—despite the fact that this version had been effectively debunked by the 1929 official history.[130] In the course of the Second World War, Langemarck transmuted from an idealistic image to be admired into a practical lesson to be emulated. In a last-ditch effort to rally morale during the final days of the Battle of Stalingrad, Hermann Göring invoked the memory of Langemarck.[131] The legacy of Langemarck became further implicated in the racist war on the Eastern Front when Flemish volunteers were assigned to the newly formed SS-Sturmbrigade 'Langemarck' in May 1943 (which was expanded into the SS-Grenadier-Division 'Langemarck' in October 1944). For the foreign volunteers, Langemarck was a place name, not a symbol. It was ill-suited as a symbol to rally support among Flemish nationalists, many of whom harboured pan-Dutch (rather than pan-Germanic) aspirations, and in the end the SS was forced to quell a rebellion among the Flemish contingent. Langemarck might have had little resonance for the individual SS volunteer, but in the name of Langemarck, the symbol of collective belonging, the organization committed war crimes, notably against 'partisans', in the east.[132]

* * * * *

The Second World War represented a pivotal moment for the memory of the First. The blitzkrieg in the west had ended the commemorative battles for Langemarck that had begun in 1928. During this time, Germans had staked their claim to a landscape to the north-east of the 'British' city of Ypres—a promise that was fulfilled with the invasion of France in May 1940. The intersecting memories of the two world wars are a subject that historians have barely begun to research. While the story of Ypres was put on ice in Britain between 1940 and 1944, ready to be revived at a later stage, Langemarck became contaminated by its association with Nazism, war, and genocide. How this impacted on the search for a 'usable past' after the Second World War is the subject of Chapter 6.[133]

6

Ieper in Peace, 1944–2014

On 6 September 1944 the Polish 1st Armoured Division liberated Ypres. Within hours of the last German soldier being driven out of the city, the Last Post was played under the Menin Gate again. The resumption of the commemorative ritual after a lapse of four years was widely reported. The Canadian press even revived the standard rhetorical flourishes about the city: 'This is historic ground, this town of Ypres, and the villages around. It is rich with the blood and sacrifice of British and Canadian soldiers and Australians, too.'[1] Since then not a single day has gone by without the Last Post being sounded; the 20,000th ceremony in 1988 and the 25,000th in 2001 were special occasions that entered into the annals of the city.[2] But this impression of continuity is deceptive. Ypres in the aftermath of the Second World War was no longer the unrivalled site of war commemoration that it had been between 1918 and 1940. The Somme, Vimy Ridge, and Gallipoli, which provided alternative prisms through which to view the conflict, gained in prominence, sometimes overshadowing the erstwhile 'Holy Ground of British Arms'; and at Coventry a dynamic hub of war remembrance, centred around the legacy of an even greater conflict, emerged. Besides, Ypres was no more. The town to which battlefield tourists returned from the 1960s had changed its name to Ieper. Along with the name change came a change in agency as the local authorities showed greater determination to shape the public culture of war remembrance. Langemar*ck*, too, was a thing of the past, replaced by Langemar*k*. The new spelling (in German) was not simply a matter of orthography. Langemarck had represented both an idea and a site; Langemark, by contrast, was a mere place name. After 1944 the Langemarck myth was never invoked again. Similarly, the myth of the Yser front, cultivated by Flemish nationalists during the interwar years and during the Nazi occupation (when the Yser Pilgrimages had brought together German military and Flemish nationalists), became highly problematic—so polarizing in fact that one night in 1946 'unknown' persons blew up the Yser Tower at Dixmude.

* * * * *

Taking possession again of the war cemeteries in and around Ypres in late 1944, the IWGC could not but marvel that the memorials and graves were generally in a fair condition. Even though the Wehrmacht had treated the law of war with contempt, especially in eastern Europe, it had—much to the surprise of contemporary observers—not defaced the British imperial cemeteries in Belgium.[3] To be sure, the results of horticultural neglect represented a formidable challenge, but in time all cemeteries were restored to their former splendour. The Ypres salient was spared the kind of topographical remodelling that happened at the Somme in the 1960s.[4] The changes that did occur were subtle. Soldiers killed during the retreat to Dunkirk in 1940 found a final resting place in Flanders fields, the memory of their sacrifice blending neatly into the existing commemorative landscape. In the course of time the rupture of 1940–4 became barely visible. Yet the people who tended the graves represented a new generation. The ex-serviceman/gardener was a dying species. In fact, the whole British 'colony' was all but extinct. Although some returned, the atomization caused by the conflict proved irreversible. Eton Memorial School never reopened its gates, and the number of regular worshippers at St George's church declined dramatically. Nevertheless, the Belgian law that had established the British Settlement in 1931 was never repealed. Arguably, Ypres and the salient became a, if not the, cultural bastion of empire in the age of decolonization. Through the medium of memory the British Empire continued to exist long after imperial

Figure 26. Menin Gate memorial. Postage stamp, 1967.

rule itself had been abolished.[5] True, the term 'imperial' was dropped in 1960 when it became the Commonwealth War Graves Commission (CWGC), but this did not change the fact that dead had fallen, and were commemorated, as soldiers of the Empire. For decades roads in Flanders remained dotted with markers signposting the cemeteries of the *Imperial* War Graves Commission for there seemed to be no urgency to replace the old enamel plaques with new ones.

By a decree of 10 November 1944—the fortieth anniversary of the Battle of Langemarck—the work of the Official German War Graves Service in Belgium was suspended. Over the next decade the fallen soldiers of the Great War were left in limbo. The legal situation was unclear, and while the Belgians were soon keen to conclude a new treaty so as to pass the responsibility (and cost) back to the Germans, the West German authorities dragged their heels—after all, they faced the monumental task of burying the dead of the second global conflict to engulf the nation in a generation. In an attempt to force the issue, Belgium began to refuse entry to the tiny group of German battlefield pilgrims before shutting access to all German cemeteries in 1952.[6] Eventually, in 1954 the governments of West Germany and Belgium reached a new agreement, and the Volksbund assumed responsibility for the care of all German war graves on Belgian soil. It embarked immediately on a massive programme of reorganizing and redeveloping the cemeteries inherited from the Official German War Graves Service.

Between 1955 and 1957 over 134,000 soldiers were exhumed from 270 different sites to be reinterred in four concentration cemeteries at Langemark, Hooglede, Menen, and Vladslo. All other cemeteries were dissolved. These drastic measures represented, in the chilling bureaucratic language of the 1950s, the 'final solution' of the war graves question.[7]

All unidentified soldiers were transferred to a mass grave at Langemark. Barely larger than the size of a tennis court, this so-called 'comrades' grave' now contained the mortal remains of 25,000 men. The choice of a 'big word' notwithstanding, no attempt whatsoever was made to eulogize over camaraderie in war and death. Langemark's new message was religious not political in tone. 'I have called you by name, you are mine' (Isaiah 43:1), reads the inscription on the grave. Also the severe appearance of the cemetery was softened. A sculptural group of four stylized soldiers with helmets in hand mourning the dead were added, as was a high cross and a number of smaller crosses made of basaltic lava. Langemark was redesigned to such an extent that the label 'First World War cemetery' is highly inaccurate. It is important to recognize that this is a post-*Second* World War cemetery containing the graves of soldiers of the First World War. The Langemarck myth about the self-sacrifice of German youth in 1914, about a military defeat turned into a moral victory, that had underpinned the original design, had evaporated into thin air in the aftermath of the Reich's unconditional surrender. The 'students' cemetery' of Langemar*ck* became the 'soldiers' cemetery' at Langemar*k*. A tiny variation in the name's ending signified a big change in meaning. Ostensibly, this alteration reflected merely the new official spelling of the town's name. More crucially, it signalled a departure from the Langemarck myth that no longer had any purchase. On the one hand, the myth was tainted by association with Nazism and genocidal war; on the other, the whole notion of 'heroism' had become anathema in the second post-war era.[8] 'From monuments to traces' is how one scholar has summed up the transformation of German commemorative culture.[9] The traces remained visible at Langemark. The cemetery's motto,

'Germany must live, even if we must die', was not erased but the inscription was subtly amended with the addition of 'Heinrich Lersch, 1914'. Adding the name of the poet and the date of writing was a pragmatic solution that alluded to the historical context and suggested an implicit distancing from the original sentiment.[10]

Tyne Cot's status as the largest British imperial war cemetery in the world remained unchallenged after 1945. By contrast, Langemark was surpassed in size by Lommel, the biggest German war cemetery in Western Europe. Opened in 1959, it contains the graves of 39,000 soldiers of the Second World War. Thus a separate topography of remembrance emerged in eastern Belgium just at the moment when cemeteries in Flanders were being dissolved. The creation of four concentration cemeteries at Langemark, Hooglede, Menen, and Vladslo was a highly rational decision, and the Volksbund reckoned that it would not cause much emotional pain. A public outcry was not expected, given 'the waning interest' of families. Hence the Volksbund proceeded with the 'destruction of personal grave markers'.[11] But the dead were not entirely forgotten. One Otto Kösler was deeply anguished that his brother had been reinterred in a new location and, moreover, that he had not been informed. He demanded to know what had happened to the gravestone and the zinc coffin that were after all his property.[12] Kösler engaged in an extensive correspondence with both the Volksbund and the Foreign Office. Perhaps it was the anguish shining through letters like these that made the Volksbund propose the erection of memorials at the sites of former cemeteries, an idea flatly rejected by the Belgian authorities.[13]

'Deeply distressed' by the Volksbund's plans to abandon the cemetery at Esen near Dixmude, Hans Kollwitz wrote a letter of protest to its secretary general. As the executor of Käthe Kollwitz's will and the brother of Peter, who was buried at Esen, he was doubly affected by the proposals. The Volksbund reassured Hans Kollwitz that the *Grieving Parents* sculpture and Peter would be reunited in their new location at Vladslo (about 4 miles to the north of Esen). In truth, though, the ensemble at Vladslo bears only superficial resemblance to the original one. The gap between the figures of the father and the mother is significantly reduced and the two sculptures are positioned at the end rather than the entrance of the cemetery. Hans Kollwitz grudgingly accepted the new arrangements. What sweetened the pill for him was the promise that replicas of the two figures were to be placed in a war ruin in Cologne. This project enjoyed the backing of the president of the Federal Republic. Ten years after the end of the Second World War West Germany still had no official 'national' war memorial; the *Grieving Parents* were to fill this void. In the early years of the Federal Republic, as one historian has remarked, 'there was no public sphere of death as there had been in the Weimar Republic'.[14] The Cologne figures—the mother was carved by a young Joseph Beuys—were not exact copies but enlarged versions made of a different material. Placed in a church burnt out during the bombing of Cologne, the figures assumed a completely new meaning in their new context. Images of Flanders lingered on, but they were overwritten by a new narrative of national suffering and universal sadness. Unveiling the memorial in 1959, President Heuss referred to the 'murderous battles' of autumn 1914, but also to the destruction of the model of the *Grieving Parents* in the 'firestorm of Berlin'.[15] He praised the figures as the embodiment of sorrow and grief—grief not only for the dead (of the last war) but also for the divided nation. In a more nuanced speech, Cologne's mayor acknowledged the transmutation of Käthe Kollwitz's design from a memorial to an individual to a collective symbol. The Cologne memorial, he stressed, remembered 'all dead . . . The dead of Cologne, the dead of the nations of the world.'[16] He also spoke of German 'guilt', although in the vaguest of terms; but perhaps it was not necessary to be more explicit since everybody knew what nobody wanted to know.

* * * * *

In its immediate aftermath the Second World War naturally enough became the focus of public interest in contemporary history, pushing the earlier conflict to one side. The military history of the Great War petered out to a trickle, but where kept alive it was in studies of the Passchendaele campaign. In the anglophone world, a brilliantly readable account of that battle, published in 1958, played a major role in the revival of interest in the conflict. Yet that was preceded by the first significant post-1945 study in the publication of the latest volume in the British official history which focused on Passchendaele. Subjected to a torturous series of revisions and rewrites during the mid-1940s in which General Sir Hubert Gough accused G. C. Wynne, Edmonds's junior collaborator, of weighting the case against him (when, in fact, that was very much the intention of Edmonds himself), the book finally reached publication in late 1948. This only occurred after much byzantine discussion in which Edmonds achieved a volte-face, blaming the whole affair on Wynne and sympathizing with Gough. Coming so soon after the end of the second great global conflict, and with the British public utterly distracted by the pressures of post-war austerity, the work made little impact on the popular consciousness; public debate about it was restricted to correspondence in the elite press. It was a fact acknowledged by the *Times Literary Supplement* which noted that, had it 'appeared twenty years ago... it would have aroused the widest interest and might have created what is called a "sensation"'.[17]

Like its British counterpart, the German official history of the First World War was unfinished business; yet the release of the final two instalments of the series in 1956 made no impression on the German reading public either. Originally completed by the Kriegsgeschichtliche Forschungsanstalt (the successor of the Reichsarchiv) in 1942 and 1944 respectively, only a small number of copies had been produced for official use during the Second World War. The volume dealing with military operations in summer and autumn 1917 stresses that the 'fire storm' of Passchendaele—a term that now had a wholly different resonance—surpassed all previous battles including Verdun and the Somme. Moreover, it declares the outcome 'a great German defensive victory'.[18] Likewise, the volume covering 1918 emphasizes German successes at Mount Kemmel, thereby implicitly corroborating the legend of a victorious army 'stabbed in the back' that had poisoned the political culture of the Weimar Republic.[19] However, the political and historiographical battles of old had lost their power to polarize. Moreover, publication was a deliberately low-key affair. In fact, the two volumes were not formally published but merely reprinted under the aegis of the Federal Archives (Bundesarchiv). These massive tomes in Gothic typescript were never supposed to fly off the shelves, but to gather dust in reference libraries where they could be consulted by an increasingly small group of German military historians.

Only in Britain could the military history of the Great War still cause a stir in the world of history publishing. A true sensation was finally delivered in 1958 with *In Flanders Fields: The 1917 Campaign* written by an American Second World War veteran, Leon Wolff. Wolff's book had a perfect curtain-raiser in the form of a debate, seemingly dispassionate and scholarly, but clearly driven by deep-seated emotions, in the pages of *The Spectator*. Initiated by an article entitled 'The Campaign in the Mud' by John Terraine, who was rapidly emerging as a major opponent of those who condemned the war and the British military establishment as little short of criminals, he argued that context had been lost over the battle, creating deep misunderstandings of its intentions and progress. Unsurprisingly, Basil Liddell Hart, the self-proclaimed doyen of military history, responded with vigour, resulting in a flurry of correspondence. It was into this journalistic battle of words and opinions that Wolff's book was published.[20]

For his part, Wolff turned the story of Passchendaele into a Greek tragedy in which the stupidity and hubris of generals and politicians collided with the forces of nature in the appallingly wet summer and autumn of 1917. Whereas in the 1920s, accounts of Ypres often implied the martyrdom of a generation in spiritual terms, Wolff deployed it as a bitter waste of men thrown into conditions wilfully ignored by high command. Emphasizing the massive gap between those directing the battle and those fighting it, he capitalized on Liddell Hart's letter to *The Spectator* earlier in 1958, identifying Launcelot Kiggell as the officer who allegedly broke down in tears when he finally saw the forward zone, including it as a perfect illumination of the war of ironies, follies, and miseries. Wolff allowed no room for ambiguity about his views, damning the battle as self-evident stupidity: 'There has never been any argument about the worthlessness of the few miles of muddy ground captured.'[21] Reviewing it for the *Times Literary Supplement,* Cyril Falls, a former infantry officer and member of the official history team, adopted a regretful tone that Wolff had used his skills to pursue so unbalanced an argument. However, Falls did concede that the necessity of a second global war and the way in which it was fought seemed to prove that the first was indeed a monumental disaster and incompetently managed.[22] Harsher conclusions were reached by other readers. *The Economist*'s reviewer deemed Passchendaele 'a crime born of the conceit of dull men' and the *Daily Mail* judged the campaign 'the war at its most hellish'.[23]

The interwar voice of dissent about the conflict now became the dominant orthodoxy summed up in Alan Clark's assertion on behalf of his generation that 'the First [World War] is as remote as the Crimea, its cause and personnel obscure and disreputable'.[24] A. J. P. Taylor was among those angry men of the late fifties and early sixties. In his highly influential 1963 *The First World War: An Illustrated History,* he underlined strongly the negative judgements of the Passchendaele campaign, damning it as the nadir of a meaningless experience: 'Third Ypres was the blindest slaughter of a blind war.'[25] Given that Taylor campaigned in his spare time for nuclear disarmament, one wonders to what extent his thinking about futility in the First World War was shaped by the MAD (Mutually Assured Destruction) scenario of another seemingly unwinnable conflict, the Cold War. Taylor's radicalism was not universally shared in military history publishing, however. John Swettenham provided a quiet celebration of (Canadian) achievements in the First World War in his *To Seize the Victory,* published to coincide with the fiftieth anniversary of the Second Battle of Ypres. Yet even he could find little to redeem Third Ypres, calling it a 'barren victory'.[26] Thus, in popular history publishing, Passchendaele had become the yardstick of futility against which to judge the war in its entirety.

* * * * *

Rituals of remembrance continued to keep the memory of Ypres alive in Britain. Ypres Day was not restored after 1945, but Armistice Day and the poppy appeal were. In Coventry and other blitzed cities Flanders poppies were now planted in memory of servicemen, civil defence members, and civilians 'who gave their lives' in both world wars.[27] As a result, the poppy's association with Flanders fields diminished somewhat, although it never disappeared completely. In addition to the annual rites of commemoration, there was the observation of key dates, which became even stronger as the veterans began their prolonged demographic decline. The fiftieth anniversary of the outbreak of the First World War saw its profile in British popular culture increase significantly. At the same time, it also reprised the idea that Ypres was the quintessence of the conflict. This was seen in the premiere of *Hamp,* John Wilson's play (inspired by a novel by J. L. Hodson) about a young and inarticulate working-class soldier executed for desertion during Third Ypres, in August 1964. It provides a highly revealing insight as to how the conflict was perceived by the fiftieth anniversary of its outbreak. The precise chronology had become irrelevant. Consideration of the fact that the actual anniversary being observed was August 1914—long before the huge slaughters of the trench stalemates, particularly that of Passchendaele—was immaterial and not even conceived. The war had become synonymous with mud, blood, shell shock, and Ypres.

While the memory of Ypres had evolved in unison across the British Empire in the interwar years, distinct national patterns became apparent around the time of the fiftieth anniversary. The imperial rhetoric of Ypres, and the Great War generally, had, if not entirely collapsed, certainly lost its appeal in the former Dominions. In Australia Ypres was almost completely lost to popular culture fifty years after the Battle of Passchendaele. Study of the Australian press for the autumn of 1967 turned up one article and that was about *King and Country*, the film version of *Hamp*. As other historians have shown, this period coincided with a general downturn in the profile of Anzac Day and war veterans in Australian culture, but was also the tipping point for a revival of interest in which Gallipoli would become the sole focus of attention for many years.[28] A similar, albeit less radical, trend was discernible in Canada. Although the Second Battle of Ypres retained its profile, Vimy Ridge—which in the twenties and thirties, prior to the unveiling of the memorial in 1936, had been at best the *primus inter pares* of Canadian war commemoration—became the dominant image of Canada's Great War.

In West Germany Langemarck—once a name pregnant with meaning—ceased to evoke cultural memories, notably among young people. A survey among 118 army conscripts born in 1945 and 1946 revealed that, fifty years on, only eight respondents had even heard of the once famous battle; for the rest Langemarck meant nothing. For the pollster this was due to the cumulative effect of years of 'mental demilitarization'.[29] Shaped by the legacy of Nazi violence and the horrors of the Second World War, the political culture of the Federal Republic was inadvertently a vehicle of forgetting the Great War. The new political climate also had a profound impact on veterans' associations, the principal custodians of the memory of the First World War post-1945. On the eve of the fiftieth anniversary, the Grünes Korps of Langemarck veterans pronounced the war futile and the patriotic fervour of old incomprehensible; the overriding image was of a world that had long since passed. Their only solace was that, fifty years on, Flanders had become a symbol of world peace, international reconciliation, and European unity.[30] This shift in attitudes among organized veterans is astounding. At Ypres German veterans-turned-pacifists found congenial partners. A reception was held in their honour in the town hall in 1964. The ceremonies that marked the fiftieth anniversary of the outbreak of war in Ypres reveal a concerted effort by the city authorities to Europeanize the image of Ypres and the salient, and to find new meaning in joint commemorations with many partners over the summer and autumn of 1964.[31] These included a Franco-Belgian day of remembrance which highlighted France's role in the defence of the Yser and the First Battle of Ypres. There was not the slightest hint of anti-British sentiment, but there was the political will to shed the Anglocentric image of Ypres as 'Holy Ground of British Arms' fashioned a generation earlier. The brotherly embrace of European neighbours came together with a war of words with Brussels. Notably, the Belgian broadcaster Belgisch Radio-en Televisieomroep (BRT) stood accused of snubbing Ypres by giving insufficient airtime to the events held there in 1964.[32]

The mayor and tourist office used the fiftieth anniversary to create a new image for their city—so much so that by the end of the commemorative cycle the city was believed to be a contender for the Nobel Peace Prize.[33] Once a byword for death and destruction, Ypres became a symbol of world peace and European unity. In order to achieve this aim, municipal leaders sought to forge a strategic alliance with another iconic war-torn city. In November 1967 Benjamin Britten's *War Requiem* was performed in the finally restored St Martin's Cathedral to mark the fiftieth anniversary of the Third Battle of Ypres.[34] Originally composed for the consecration of the new Coventry Cathedral in 1962, the requiem juxtaposed the liturgical text of the Latin requiem mass with the war poetry of Wilfred Owen, at that time still a relatively obscure war poet and not the household name he has become since. Ypres seemed keen to align itself with the pacifist message of the *War Requiem* and, more generally, with Coventry's growing reputation as a 'peace city'. This represents a striking reversal of the respective standing of the two cities. Back in November 1940 British commentators had found it necessary to conjure up images of war-torn Ypres in order to make sense of the scene of devastation at Coventry, but by 1967 the Midlands city had matured into an international hub of war commemoration in its own right and a model to be emulated.

The 1967 performance of the *War Requiem* was deemed so poignant that it was decided to repeat it the following year, this time in

Dortmund's Westfallenhalle under the auspices of the President of the Federal Republic and the King of the Belgians. The political aim was to use the event to strengthen the embryonic twinning between the regions of West Flanders and Westphalia. The German press was taken by Owen's supposedly 'timeless' words, the emotional depth of Britten's music, and the overall message of reconciliation across national divides.[35] It was implicit that the First World War was only understandable through the experience of the Second, and, moreover, that political lessons had to be learned from the two conflicts. This went very much against the grain of British commemorative culture which tended to represent the First World War on its own terms, effectively decoupling the intersecting memories of the two world wars. However, British observers would no doubt have subscribed to the organizers' claim that 'the Third Battle of Ypres was synonymous with the fighting and the carnage at the Western Front throughout the whole of the First World War'.[36] Clearly, the reduction of the Western Front, or even the war, to a single campaign was not exclusively a British phenomenon.

* * * * *

The fiftieth anniversary marked the moment when television as the new medium of memory came into its own. Radio-Télévision Belge (RTB) broadcast over four years a 118-episode documentary, while French television produced *Trente ans d'histoire* (1964), with the intention of fostering Franco-German reconciliation (albeit in a Gaullist vein).[37] Perhaps the most successful of all was the monumental British *Great War* series. First broadcast between May and November 1964 on BBC2, very much the subordinate channel, it quickly picked up such a large audience that it was transferred to BBC1 for a repeat run before the series was even complete on its sister channel. Regularly reaching viewing figures of 18 to 20 million, the series was a phenomenon and made a similar impact in Australia and Canada. The Passchendaele episode, entitled 'Surely We Have Perished'—a line from Wilfred

Owen's poem 'Mental Cases'—was written by John Terraine. However, it was atypical of Terraine's approach as it did not follow a generally 'revisionist' line about Field Marshal Douglas Haig. Punctuated with far more poetry than many other episodes, it shows the hand of the producer, Tony Essex, who had been a little unsure about the lack of human touch in the earlier episode about the Somme. As such, it appealed to the popular conception of the battle far more closely and found an appreciative and sympathetic audience. Michael Peacock, the director of programmes for BBC2, was stunned by the episode. In a note to Essex he deemed it 'the most moving and terrifying so far. Its emotional impact surpassed even the Verdun and Somme programmes. The use of quotation to underline the horror of the mud and the sense of despair and futility which hung over the armies created a testament of overwhelming power.'[38] Evidently, a canon of Great War literature had arrived which was *the* experience of the entire conflict and it had found its perfect expression in the Battle of Passchendaele.

Somewhat ironically given its nature, the episode brought to the boil a simmering row between the production team and Basil Liddell Hart, appointed adviser to the series by the BBC's senior management. Liddell Hart had become increasingly angry at the tone adopted by Terraine and Correlli Barnett, both of whom he disagreed with on the fundamentals of the British conduct of the war. Convinced that he had been ignored over the Somme episode, he took extreme umbrage at not being sent the script of 'Surely We Have Perished', taking it as a deliberate oversight so as to sideline his views. Although that may well have been part of the intention, Liddell Hart showed himself utterly ignorant of the hand-to-mouth nature of the production of the series in which some episodes were completed only hours before their scheduled broadcast slot. Deciding to make a public stand, he wrote some typically waspish letters to *The Times* announcing his decision to have nothing further to do with the series.[39]

* * * * *

After all the media hype generated by the fiftieth anniversary cycle, the silence of memory seemed to have permeated the 1970s and early 1980s. In Ypres itself the events held in summer 1974 were extremely low-key compared to 1964. Commemorations in the city intensified somewhat in the run-up to 11 November 1978, only to fade away again in 1984.[40] Yet significant developments during this decade and a half occurred in a different realm of memory, and without a blaze of publicity, in the relatively quiet world of history publishing. In contrast to the sensational revisionism of the 1960s, the new trend aimed not to turn conventional wisdom about the war on its head, but to add nuance by giving a voice to ordinary soldiers and their experiences through the emerging techniques and technologies of oral history. In 1971 Martin Middlebrook's *The First Day on the Somme* appeared, which proved a phenomenal and enduring success, inspiring a host of others to deploy the same approach. Chief among these was Lyn Macdonald who commenced her series of books on the conflict in 1978 with *They Called it Passchendaele,* which was released with obvious deliberation in November to coincide with the sixtieth anniversary of the Armistice.[41] Taking its title from Siegfried Sassoon's bitterly ironic poem 'Memorial Tablet', Macdonald deployed a novelist's eye of detail, anecdote, and atmosphere and produced a highly readable—and unashamedly Anglocentric—account of the battle. At the same time, her ability to lift phrases and idioms from the *Ypres Times* and other such publications of the interwar period gave her work an almost nostalgic yearning for a past age dominated by the noble fellowship of the trenches. It certainly provided a distinct antidote to John Terraine's *The Road to Passchendaele: A Study in Inevitability* published the previous year, thus meeting the actual anniversary. The 'inevitability' element is never explained, just accepted as an implicit given, in a study which claims an Olympian overview by giving the reader the lightest of guiding touches as s/he proceeds through a selection of documents. Clearly believing that he was telling the objective truth, Terraine made almost no self-analytical comment about his methodology or process of editing, and as a result *The Road to Passchendaele* was, and is, the densest and arguably the least successful of all his works.[42] Judging by the general lack of comment in the press about it, and how infrequently it is cited by others, the book has failed to have the impact Terraine desired. Instead, the Macdonald–Middlebrook approach was very definitely the one the general public found more inspiring and persuasive.

While Middlebrook's later work on Bomber Command received some attention in West Germany, his First World War books went by and large unnoticed; and Macdonald was all but unknown to German readers. It was not that home-grown authors filled this gap in the non-fiction market, for there was none. The First World War—the interwar epithet *der grosse Krieg* all but forgotten—simply vanished from publishers' lists. Even though oral history and the history workshop movement made rapid advances in West Germany, the *Alltagsgeschichte* (history of the everyday) of the First World War remained an unwritten chapter for another twenty years. In another way, too, German history publishing was lagging twenty years behind. The phase of historical 'revisionism', beginning with Wolff's *In Flanders Fields,* that had been a gift to British publishers and bookshops in the 1960s, had bypassed West Germany. To be sure, Fritz Fischer's 1961 study of German war aims, *Der Griff nach der Weltmacht* (The Grab for World Power), sparked a controversy. However, at the heart of the debate was not the First World War as such, but the continuities between Imperial Germany and the Third Reich.[43] Revisionist history aimed at a general readership arrived eventually in West Germany in the form of two books about the Battle of Langemarck published in 1981 and 1986 respectively. In Helmut Kopetzky's ironically titled *In den Tod—Hurra!* (Forward to Death—Hurrah!) the war is portrayed as both absurd and criminal. Written in the present tense and in the style of a collage, this unconventional work draws heavily on diaries, soldiers' letters, and interviews; that is, 'ego-documents' which the historical establishment had almost completely ignored. Kopetzky's digressions into the politics of memory in the interwar years were also thought-provoking, showing that a history of Langemarck could not stop with the events of autumn 1914.[44] Brought out by a far Left publisher widely suspected of being financed by the East German communists, the book was very much preaching to the converted.

Another title which appeared in 1986, Karl Unruh's *Langemarck*, achieved a broader and more lasting impact. Penned by a veteran of the Second World War, this work seeks systematically to unmask the Langemarck myth that had originated in the famous army communiqué of 11 November 1914. Yet Unruh was no follower of Roland Barthes; his understanding of a 'myth' lacked the subtlety of post-structuralist French philosophy. For Unruh the Langemarck myth was not a 'mode of signification', but a plain untruth. Thus he shows that the celebrated 'young regiments' were not made up exclusively or predominantly of students, that soldiers were inadequately trained and equipped, that they could not have sung the 'Deutschlandlied' during the assault, that in short the whole episode—the formative experience of an (imagined) generation—amounted to an unmitigated and unacknowledged disaster.[45] None of this was actually new. In fact, the evidence marshalled by Unruh, largely derived from some forty regimental histories, had been in the public domain for decades. What is more, a critical discourse about the Langemarck myth had been a staple of left-wing journalism in the late 1920s, although neither the author himself nor the reviewers seemed aware of this. Walter Görlitz, writing in *Die Welt*, called the book 'harrowing, disturbing and not so easily superseded', while the *Studentenkurier* credited Unruh with the 'correction of a national myth'.[46] In fairness it has to be said that no author before Unruh had demolished the Langemarck myth as comprehensively as he did, and the book has remained a standard work for historians, both popular and academic, to this day.[47]

* * * * *

While television broke through as the new commemorative medium of choice at the time of the fiftieth anniversary, a considerable amount of energy was invested in revitalizing the most traditional of commemorative forms, the war memorial, during the 1960s and 1970s. Significantly, in Belgium and France, as well as in Germany, these efforts concentrated on First World War monuments intentionally destroyed during or in the aftermath of the Second World War: the gas memorial of Steenstraat, the Yser Tower in Dixmude, and the Langemarck Hall at Berlin's Olympic stadium. The Steenstraat memorial dedicated to the victims of gas warfare was one of the very few monuments blown up by the Wehrmacht. In 1961 a new monument, dominated by a 20-metre-high cross, was unveiled on the site of the one levelled in 1941. The unveiling took place at a time when France was engaged in a bloody colonial war in Algeria and, at the same time, in a rapprochement with her former arch-enemy, Germany. This was no coincidence. One historian has argued that post-war European integration was built on the twin pillars of remembering war and forgetting colonial violence.[48] Remarkably, reports in the French press barely touched on either the actual event commemorated or the destruction of the original monument. Instead, the unveiling provided an opportunity to celebrate the newly found spirit of European unity and reconciliation. 'We want to construct with our former enemies a peaceful Europe', declared the French minister for veterans, Raymond Triboulet, at Steenstraat.[49] Not the massive cross but a 'petite lampe de la fraternité' appeared the main feature of the memorial, and *Le Figaro* stressed that identical lamps were to be found at Les Invalides, the memorial to the Unknown Jewish Martyr in Paris, and, in due course, in a cathedral in Germany.[50] Thus the new memorial entered into communication with other sites of memory dedicated to the Second World War.

Multiple layers of memory also underpinned the second Yser Tower erected on the battlefield of the Flemish lowland in the post-war period. The Mecca of Flemish separatism during the interwar era, it had become for many Belgians a symbol of treason and collaboration in the Second World War, a memorial of shame. The tower was dynamited by 'unknown' persons in 1946. Initially, the blame was placed on left-wing anti-fascist resistance fighters, but today historians assume that the perpetrators were members of the army and/or right-wing resistance loyal to the Belgian state.[51] In any case, no one was ever charged, a fact that encouraged rumours of a judicial conspiracy to protect the culprits. In 1950 rubble from the tower was used to construct the new Pax gate, and although it was ostensibly dedicated to the idea of 'peace', this building did nothing to pacify Flemish firebrands. Over the next few years the Flemish press revived bitter memories of the interwar period, comparing the attack on the tower to the destruction of *Heldenhuldezerkjes,* the headstones of Flemish soldiers killed in the Great War, by the Belgian authorities in the 1920s.[52] Radical Flemish nationalism saw a revival in the second half of the 1950s during which time the annual Yser Pilgrimage became once again the largest regular political demonstration in Belgium, attracting tens of thousands of 'pilgrims'. On the occasion of the 1965 pilgrimage an even taller Yser Tower (84 metres in height) was inaugurated. As one commentator has put it, war memorials erected

Figure 27. Twenty-fifth Yser Pilgrimage. Postage stamp, 1952.

Figure 28. Yser Tower at Dixmude. Postage stamp, 1963.

after the Second World War 'impress us with their enormity…, not with their profundity'; the Yser Tower illustrates this perfectly.[53] The new tower provided a focal point not only for the Flemish movement but increasingly for neo-fascists from all over Europe, too, who converged on Dixmude during the 1970s.[54] This unsavoury alliance appalled moderate Flemish nationalists and contributed to the eventual decline of the annual Yser Pilgrimage in the 1980s.

Arguably, the most political of all war memorials was the Langemarck Hall, Hitler's semi-private shrine dedicated to the cult of Langemarck, situated in Berlin's Olympic complex. In 1947 British troops blew up the (by then unstable) bell tower which housed the memorial hall. To be sure, this was a health-and-safety measure rather than an attempt to eradicate Nazism. Although the Allied Control Council had ordered the removal of all physical traces of militarism and Nazism by

1 January 1947, it remained open to interpretation whether or not the directive applied to war memorials. The British occupation authorities tended to take a lenient stance, willing to draw a distinction between sites of memory and sites of ideology. Even so, it remains a puzzle that the Langemarck Hall, of all memorials, was not completely demolished. It survived in a ruined state until 1960 when the West Berlin authorities instructed the original architect to oversee the reconstruction of the bell tower and memorial hall. Completed in 1962, the hall did not attract much attention until 1979 when an external organization suggested converting it into an international memorial to Olympic athletes killed in war.[55] This initiative alerted the West German Ministry of Defence to the existence of the hall. Keen to invent 'traditions' for the post-war army, yet anxious to avoid anything that reeked of militarism, the ministry ordered staff officers to investigate the potential of the Langemarck Hall. Their verdict was unequivocal: Langemarck 'is certainly not a *traditionswürdig* [tradition-worthy] event'.[56]

Significantly, the report focused on the events of 1914 rather than the memorial of 1936. The experts seemed well versed in the history of the First World War, but oblivious to the purpose and use of the hall in the Third Reich. This aspect of the hall's history was never completely forgotten, though. The influential news magazine *Der Spiegel* decried it from time to time as an example of Nazi architecture.[57] Nevertheless, the Langemarck Hall was not subjected to a major overhaul until the 2006 FIFA World Cup, held in Germany, when the German Historical Museum installed an illuminating exhibition about both the edifice's past and the Langemarck myth.[58] Why the Langemarck Hall had fallen off the radar during a period of intense *Vergangenheitsbewältigung* (coming to terms with the past) is difficult to explain. Location might have played a role; the hall was situated on the fringes of the Olympic complex on the outskirts of West Berlin. The 1980s and 1990s saw a number of often heated disputes over streets, barracks, and schools named 'Langemarck' in various German towns, yet the forgotten Langemarck Hall represented an anomaly in the commemorative culture of this period.

Figure 29. Bus stop at Langemarckplatz in Koblenz named during 1930s. Photograph, August 2015.

The British continued to use existing memorials to remember the battles of Ypres after the Second World War. No major new structures were added to the commemorative landscapes either at home or abroad until the 1990s. Since then a reinvigoration in memorialization of the war has combined with an increasing popular desire to mark 'traumatic' experiences of many different types. An overt component of this drive has been the creation of new monuments that address either controversial topics or include those deemed marginalized. Both are aimed at integration and engagement with, and immersion in, a common narrative, albeit one that has become considerably more complex through the addition of new elements. This trend has been seen in Ypres with a number of memorial projects which have particularly aimed at foregrounding positive (internationalist) lessons and/or neglected (colonial) narratives.

The most impressive of all new monuments is the Island of Ireland Peace Park at Messines opened on 11 November 1998. Thirty-two metres in height, representing each county of Ireland, the memorial takes the form of a round tower, a typical construction in early medieval Ireland, and from its commanding position provides a splendid view of the surrounding countryside. The gestation and unveiling of the memorial was a highly politicized process which commenced with a pilgrimage to the Western Front by members of the nationalist and unionist parties of the Republic and Northern Ireland, known as the Journey of Reconciliation. From this arose the decision to mark the contribution of the whole of Ireland to the Great

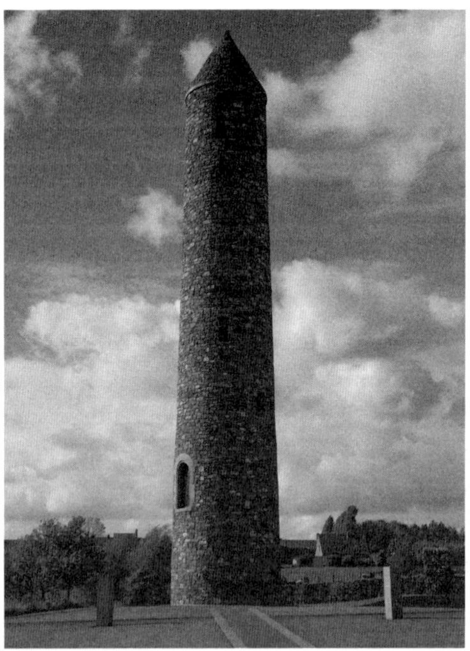

Figure 30. Island of Ireland Peace Park at Messines opened in November 1998. Photograph, May 2014.

War. The symbolism of the Wytschaete area, some 5 miles south of Ypres, so deeply ingrained in pan-Irish culture in the 1920s, as the place where the 16th Irish and 36th Ulster Divisions had attacked side by side in the Battle of Messines in June 1917, was a natural focus; although in this instance, a site on the edge of the ridge a few miles from Wytschaete was selected due to its prominent position and ease of access from the main road to Ypres. Unveiled by the Queen and the President of the Republic of Ireland, in the presence of the King and Queen of the Belgians, the memorial was a statement about reconciliation and perfectly consistent with the post-war image of Ypres as a peace city. Although the idea of Irish togetherness had been part of the interwar discourse on commemoration, this memorial marked a quantitative and qualitative leap forward. Seemingly more reflective, more inclusive and complex than the 'simple' earlier national and imperial memorials, the inclusivity was reductionist insofar as it did little to address the complex issues behind the Great War and conflict more generally. Instead, it replaced them with an ahistorical aura of peace and understanding.[59]

Intimately linked with the Island of Ireland Peace Park is the nearby Messines Peace Village Hostel. Partly funded by the European Union, the hostel is home to the Flanders Peace Fields project which brings groups of young people from across the world to visit the sites as well as engaging in sporting and other activities designed to foster understanding and harmony. An integral part of this 'let's-all-be-friends' project is a granite memorial to the so-called Christmas truce of 1914. It features a football, and visitors regularly decorate the memorial with club scarfs and other soccer paraphernalia in allusion to the purported football friendly in no man's land on Christmas Day 1914. Despite historical research having deconstructed the simplistic idea of fraternizations between British and German soldiers, in popular culture the Christmas truce has become a reassuring symbol of common humanity in the midst of the barbarity of war.[60]

Arguably more in tune with the martial spirit of earlier commemorations is the Indian memorial erected on the ramparts close to the south portico of the Menin Gate. Public interest in the Indian presence in the Ypres salient had significantly increased by the time the memorial was inaugurated in March 2011 (and replacing an earlier version erected in 2002), largely because the Indian Corps had included combat troops—unlike the barely commemorated Chinese Labour Corps.[61] Moreover, the fact that brave Indian contingents had suffered appalling losses in the notorious German chlorine gas attack of 1915 made them even more worthy of commemoration. The new memorial is formed of a plinth supporting Indian heraldic lions and surrounded by Indian national symbols. Bearing the simple inscription 'India in Flanders Fields 1914–1918', it has echoes of Herbert Baker's majestic Neuve Chapelle memorial to the Indian Corps dedicated in 1927.[62] At the same time, the decision to erect a 'mini Neuve Chapelle' reveals the centrality of Ypres for the modern visitor to the Western Front. Its unveiling on the anniversary of the Battle of Neuve Chapelle underlines this switched focus: Ypres is again, after a brief interlude during the 1970s and early 1980s, *the* proxy location for the entire front for British and Commonwealth visitors.[63]

* * * * *

What came first, the memorials or the visitors, is impossible to determine. The proliferation of new memorials (and museums) in the Ypres salient, especially since the 1990s, has coincided with the influx of a new generation of battlefield tourists. As during the first wave of 'battlefield pilgrimages' in the interwar period, the disposable income and leisure time of anglophone visitors have fuelled this development, whereas visitors from other countries have been less visible and less well catered for. However, in the immediate aftermath of the Second World War few foresaw the eventual revival of battlefield tourism. Even so, despite the easily understood fall-away in profile of the Great War in the 1940s and 1950s, it never quite disappeared, and Ypres, although much quieter, remained a focus for British and Commonwealth, particularly Canadian, travellers.

To be sure, Ypres the place name ceased to exist in 1951 when, at least officially, it became Ieper. 'Ypres' was the French spelling and, as such, a thorn in the side of some Flemish nationalists. The correct spelling, a controversial issue for some time before the Great War, preoccupied the city council in 1936 and 1951. The fact that there were at least four widely used variations of the Flemish spelling complicated things further. In 1936 and again in 1951 the mayor and city councillors expressed the same pragmatic reservations about Flemishizing the city's name: the war had turned Ypres into an international brand name and ditching it would have a detrimental effect on tourism.[64] Economics trumped politics. Yet a Royal Commission on names and dialects would have none of it, but before its guidelines could be fully implemented in 1939 the Second World War had broken out and the issue was shelved. In 1949 a new law on place names was passed, and still the local politicians did not budge until the Ministry of the Interior put its foot down in 1951. Strangely, the fact that Ypres was an English tongue-twister was never mentioned. Back in 1919 an American newspaper had suggested that the right way to pronounce the city's name was 'to make the noise a swallow makes just before sunrise'.[65] Regardless of what Belgian authorities decreed in 1951, to thousands of anglophone veterans Ypres/Ieper remained simply 'Wipers'.

Post-Second World War Ieper benefited from a highly developed tourist infrastructure, including a large number of hotels and cafés with a long track-record in catering for anglophone visitors and their tastes. With the huge expansion in car-ownership and the advent of the modern roll-on, roll-off car ferry in the 1960s, and the addition of Le Shuttle tunnel service in 1994, allowing passengers to drive their own cars on to the Channel Tunnel train, the ability of British tourists to visit the old battlefields was transformed with visitor numbers soaring. Overnight stays in hotels increased from 3,561 in 1959 to 36,555 in 1992 and 124,043 in 2005, even though car-based day trips became the norm.[66] In addition, the introduction of the cut-price ticket for long-haul flights also increased significantly the number of visitors from the former Dominions of the British Empire. While Gallipoli became a hotspot for Australian backpackers, the Western Front saw increasing numbers of visitors from down under, too. The crucial difference is that a dawn service in the Dardanelles was typically tacked on to a package holiday, whereas journeys to the European battlefields tended to be studious, reflective undertakings.[67] The steep resurgence in battlefield tourism (the more noble term 'pilgrimage' having gone out of use) in the 1990s did not come out of the blue, but had been gathering momentum for some time. This phenomenon was apparent by the 1970s as revealed in *The Times* which identified the swelling tide of visitors, perceiving the war as an antique curiosity for the modern generation:

> For the present generation, the Ypres salient, Mons, 'Plugstreet Wood', Passchendaele and other battle landmarks are as remote as La Haye Sainte and Quatre Bras. But thousands of visitors, young and old, come out on a tour of the battlefields and war cemeteries of the Somme and Flanders every year, many from as far afield as Australia, Canada, and South Africa along with a dwindling band of ancient veterans.[68]

By the sixtieth anniversary another renaissance had occurred in the form of the tourist guidebook to the old Western Front. For the first time since the 1930s, publishers brought out a new generation of travel guides. Like popular military history, the writing of guidebooks was no longer a predominantly male domain. The crucial work in this field first appeared in August 1976: *Before Endeavours Fade* by Rose Coombs, then a member of staff at the Imperial War Museum. With its evocative title, employing the initials BEF and invoking the spectre of oblivion, Coombs's book provided a comprehensive guide to the Western Front. Although British interest was shifting towards the Somme, as shown by the publication date, Ypres remained the anchoring point, as revealed in the foreword provided by Alfred Caenepeel, the founder of the war museum in the Cloth Hall in 1972 and for many years vice chairman of the Last Post committee. Due to the book's strict north–south geographical path across the former frontline, Ypres dominated the early chapters, acting as a gateway to the Western

Front, as it still does some thirteen revised editions later.[69] A welter of guidebooks have been produced since, with the focus on more and more refined areas of ground and themes, as exemplified by the 'Battleground Europe' series produced by the populist military publisher Pen and Sword.[70] The effect of these works has resurrected the microgeographies of the salient and also ensured that those returning as pilgrims, informed by the vast range of family history now accessible via the Internet, can visit the exact places where their relatives fought and died. New guidebooks to the Western Front are proliferating, and the digital age of satellite navigation and instant mobile Internet connections means that a visitor can gain additional information easily and continually.

A significant feature of the tourism boom to the old Western Front and Ieper from the 1990s onwards has been the translation of newspaper reportage about it to the travel section in addition to the general news columns. Such a development reveals the extent to which visiting battlefields has now become a general component of a wider tourism package. The coverage also implies that many have become ignorant of the Western Front sites over the years, lacking the knowledge of previous generations. By the same token, it may also reveal the unfamiliarity of travel correspondents 'discovering' these locations for the first time themselves and sharing these revelations with their readers. Such pieces have become standards of broadsheet Saturday and Sunday supplements across Britain and the Commonwealth. Typically, the pieces point out the main memorials, the beautifully maintained cemeteries combined with a sense of awe that local people are still so respectful about the dead. Of course, nowhere is this more strongly exemplified than in the Last Post ceremony at the Menin Gate. Amidst all this are comments on the quality of food and drink, hotels, and transport links.[71] By contrast, a visitor to the Somme will find its nodal town of Albert still underdeveloped in terms of tourist infrastructure and its main memorial at Thiepval some distance from the town with no cheery bars and cafés within easy reach. Moreover, the classical flourishes of Blomfield's Menin

Gate are far more appealing to most visitors, used as they are to similar styles dominating civic buildings and the like in their home towns and cities, whereas Thiepval is a rigorous architectural examination paper, demanding intense concentration and study before it reveals its messages and meanings.

Since its formal opening in November 1972, the war museum in the Cloth Hall has served as a gateway to the former salient; numerous battlefield tourists have started their journey back in time from there. The original museum concept focused almost exclusively on the materiel of war, with copious displays of guns and uniforms, though steering well away from a fetishization of weapons.[72] However, the curators refrained from contextualizing the exhibits, instead preferring to let the objects speak for themselves. In this respect, the Herinneringsmuseum (remembrance museum) was no different from other such institutions around the world that functioned as quasi-reliquaries. Yet, in the long term, the curatorial minimalism proved unattractive, if not inaccessible, to museum visitors with little knowledge of the war. Following an initial overhaul of the permanent exhibition in the 1980s, a completely redesigned and much expanded museum opened its doors in 1998. Inspired by the cultural history of warfare—a field of research that was beginning to take off in university history departments in Western Europe and North America—the newly named 'In Flanders Fields Museum' gave much room to the human stories behind the objects.

The new permanent exhibition appealed to the senses and worked on the visitors' emotions, too, for instance, by recreating the sounds and smoke of an artillery barrage.[73] Furthermore, the museum's name invoked an important collective memory and invited (anglophone) visitors to bring their cultural baggage with them. While this was in line with similar strategies employed at the Imperial War Museum (which until 2014 boasted a pseudo-realistic 'trench experience'), the In Flanders Fields Museum was lagging behind the museological trend towards a stylized and deliberately remote representation of war (as developed at the Historial de la Grande Guerre in Péronne at the

Somme in 1992). Hence, in the run-up to the centenary, the museum was given yet another revamp, with the aim of striking a balance between facts and emotions, cognitive and sensory stimuli, original objects and multimedia installations. Attached to the museum is a vibrant research centre that houses historical documents and scholarly works, collaborates with universities, and, above all, strengthens self-reflective examination about the museum and its practices.[74] Naturally, even the museum's latest incarnation will not (and does not aim to) satisfy everybody; critics might say that it treats Ypres as a place fought over, without explaining why, and that it contains scant reference to the war as one of Belgian national self-defence and none to the strategic significance of the area. Such omissions are a reflection of its long-standing mission: reinvented several times between 1972 and 2012, the In Flanders Fields Museum has stayed true to its pacifist message, namely that the war was an aberration, never to be repeated.

As many people now visit Flanders with relatively little knowledge, a simplified salient trail (for motorists) has emerged which places emphasis on certain key sites, leading to a very heavy footfall at Sanctuary Wood museum with its heavily restored trenches, Hooge Crater (for its cemetery and private museum), Hill 60, Tyne Cot cemetery, the German cemetery at Langemark, Poelcapelle and Essex Farm cemeteries (because of the presence of two schoolboys among the dead), the Island of Ireland memorial, and Hyde Park (Royal Berks) Corner cemetery and memorial at Ploegsteert ('Plugstreet'). These can be seen as part of a circuit before heading back into Ypres for refreshment and the Last Post ceremony, which has grown significantly in length since the 1980s due to the number of parties laying wreaths. Aware of the pressure this places on parts of the local infrastructure and the very partial understanding it can lead to, the In Flanders Fields Museum is now keen to promote alternative trails, encouraging the visitor to slow down by walking or cycling and studying the landscape more closely. Similarly, the installation of a new visitor centre dedicated to the history of military medicine at Lijssenthoek cemetery, near Poperinghe, in 2012 aimed to rebalance the picture. Built on a site close to where four massive field hospitals had stood during the war, the visitor centre aims to redress the image of the salient as one enormous mass grave by highlighting the care wounded soldiers received during and after the war.[75]

This rise of visitors has also had a significant effect on local economies outside Ieper itself. Consider the southern sector of the former salient. At Ploegsteert an architecturally striking, semi-underground visitor centre was inaugurated in 2013.[76] Constructed with a significant contribution from the Australian government, the 'Plugstreet 14–18 Experience' reflects the increasing number of antipodean tourists, as does the recent addition of an orientation table and information boards at the nearby New Zealand memorial at Messines. What is more, l'Auberge café-restaurant next to Berks Corner cemetery introduced a summertime Last Post ceremony in 1999 and offered guided walking tours around the local war sites. The same dynamics of commemoration, tourism, and musealization are at work in other parts of the Ypres salient, too. At Hooge a museum-cum-café opened in the old chateau chapel in 1994. Ten years later Zonnebeke saw the opening of a local authority-run museum dedicated to the Battle of Passchendaele. These ventures are far from original, however, being a renaissance of the interwar activities, with the businesses at Sanctuary Wood and Hill 60 providing the elements of continuity.

At Tyne Cot the number of visitors was starting to cause difficulties with parking and facilities. Responding to this problem of parking congestion, in September 2002 the West Flanders regional government declared Tyne Cot a protected monument, and this led to the erection of a new visitors' centre and car park. The centre focuses on three themes: firstly, the history of the site and the evolution of the cemetery; secondly, the architectural and horticultural nature of the cemetery; and thirdly, those who lost their lives in the vicinity. There are 100 individual photographs, representing one man for each day of the battle. Costing 1.5 million Euros and co-financed by the European Union, Tourism Flanders, the Province of West Flanders, Zonnebeke Council, and the generous gift of land from the Depuydt-Camerlynck family, the scheme came under the wider aegis of the 'War and Peace in the Westhoek' project instigated in 2002 to better coordinate, signpost, and make accessible the various war sites and museums in the region in a clear reflection of tourism's value to the local economy. A further reflection of its status was the fact that it was opened by Elizabeth II and Albert II of the Belgians on 12 July 2007 as an integral part of the ninetieth anniversary commemorations of Third Ypres.[77]

With numbers reaching deluge proportions by the first decade of the twenty-first century, signs of discontent began to emerge at the perceived shift in atmosphere. Extracurricular tours of the salient became an integral part of history lessons in secondary schools, but a growing number of teachers voiced their concerns. One reflected that 'there seems a growing trend of forcing emotion on pupils … my main worry is the potential for trivialising and demeaning the whole experience'.[78] Individual travellers came under renewed scrutiny, too. A 2003 article in *The Times* tackled the downside of this reawakening of interest in the salient. After listing the huge increase in hotel rooms, souvenir shops, and cafés and bars catering for British tastes, it went on to recount the problems. One British man who did not want to be named, but somewhat ironically was involved 'in the war industry', bemoaned the fact that 'it's tourism, not remembrance now. All that's missing is the jugglers and the fire-eaters. This town is living off the war.' He went on to condemn the fact that clapping had become common at the end of the Last Post ceremony, as if it was a performance. Flashlights and shutter noises accompany the ceremony as many a visitor now sees and feels through the camera lens. Ted Smith, the author of a series of guidebooks to the salient, said 'It's gone 100 per cent for tourism. There's museums popped up all over the place, but they are collections of battlefield rubbish just in it for the money. It's an industry with a lot of cowboys.' Peter Slosse, head of the Ieper tourist office, was clearly aware of the sensitivities and called it a 'daily concern for us. We definitely don't want to be a theme park. Everything we do is done out of respect for the dead—it must always be about remembering.' Pitting tourism against remembrance, the phoney against the authentic, was hardly new. In effect, the argument has returned to the position at the end of the Great War and the early twenties regarding spiritual ownership: who has the right to interpret and instruct the visitor and how should the visitor behave?[79] Dismissing it as 'dark tourism' is an easy exercise, taken up with some zeal often by the same newspapers that lured readers (of the travel section) there in the first place. Recent sociological research, however, suggests that journeys for voyeuristic or ghoulish reasons are negligible, and that the majority of travellers have a genuine interest in military history and/or feel a personal connection to the war dead.[80] This connection might be feeble, but then fictive kinship has always been an undercurrent of war commemoration.

With the passing away of the veterans during the 1970s, the presence of German visitors in and around Ieper declined dramatically—precisely at the moment when British battlefield tourism started to pick up again.[81] Most German veterans went to their graves with their war stories, and only a negligible number of families toured the battlefields in the hope of recapturing something of the war experiences of real or fictive kin. To be sure, the West German media continued to monitor new developments in the salient, especially those considered shocking. Thus in 1972 'Das Erste', the first German television channel, reported about a macabre 'peace museum' at Wytschaete displaying excavated sculls, while newspapers were incensed about the prospective sale of the 'blood-drenched Hill 60'.[82] Yet by the 1980s battlefield tourism had become an altogether marginal phenomenon, perhaps with the exception of Verdun which was the site of a public display of reconciliation between President François Mitterrand and Chancellor Helmut Kohl in autumn 1984. The powerful image of these two political heavyweights holding hands over the graves of the war dead cemented the notion that Verdun was the quintessential symbol of the madness that was the First World War.[83] In contrast, Flanders—the mere mention of the name could still send shock waves through the generation of survivors in the 1950s[84]—faded from German collective memory and largely disappeared from tourist itineraries.

It was not so much that Ypres was forgotten per se in Germany. Rather, it seems, Germans did not feel the same emotional connection to the war dead and the landscape that middle-aged or older Britons did. Visiting the cemeteries appeared at best a ghoulish, at worst a politically dangerous, activity. Helmut Kopetzky's critical history of the Langemarck myth suggested that the war cemetery had deteriorated into a meeting ground of German neo-Nazis.[85] Vladslo was different, though, attracting primarily devotees of art rather than battlefield tourists. The end of the Cold War, and thus the post-war period, had no impact in this field. What is often called the 'memory boom' of the 1990s—with its focus on the Second World War and the Holocaust—did nothing to restore the place of Ypres in the popular consciousness. The fact that the war cemeteries at Langemark and Vladslo registered increasing numbers of visitors around the turn of the century did not indicate a new trend.[86] The cemeteries had by that time passed out of the realm of family memory into that of national heritage. Although we lack precise figures, there can be no doubt that the sombre multimedia visitor centre opened next to Langemark cemetery in 2006 (designed, incidentally, by the same architectural firm responsible for the one at Tyne Cot in 2007) has attracted vastly more anglophone than German visitors.[87] Significantly, a visit to Ieper and the war cemeteries never became part of the wider tourism package in Germany. A travel agent's advertisement placed in a local newspaper in the run-up to the centenary in 2014 is rather revealing: 'Lively, picturesque Flanders' was the theme of the four-day round tour, which included stops at Antwerp, Bruges, and Ghent—with Ieper given a wide berth.[88]

* * * * *

Nothing illustrates the trajectories of British and German representations of Ypres in recent years better than the field of popular culture and commerce. Commemoration is not only a sacred act but also a commodity, resulting in products such as the video game *Dire Heroes: Gas Attack at Ypres* (for the younger generation) or the lager beer 'Passchendaele' (for the middle-aged and upwards).[89] As with so many products that can be purchased in Ypres, the producers and retailers make an overt association between consumption and purchase as an act of remembrance in itself. Nowhere is this delicate balancing act more clearly seen than on the labels of each bottle of 'Passchendaele' (a beer very much more attuned to the Anglo-Saxon palate than traditional Belgian brews), for they request that 'when opening a bottle of Passchendaele please hold a minute of silence to commemorate those who fell on the battlefield'. There have also been cases where retailers arguably overstepped the bounds of decency. In 1998 a local butcher planned to launch an 'In Flanders Fields pâté', until the In Flanders Fields Museum intervened, convincing him that such a product would be tasteless. And then there was the case of a bar named 'IeperEat' (pronounced like 'Ypérite') that opened opposite the In Flanders Fields Museum in 2017—100 years after mustard gas or *ypérite* had been used for the first time in the salient.[90]

Paradoxically, trivialization and domestication of war often go hand in hand with sacralization. With the renaissance of the sense that the Great War battlefields were sacred ground, imparting valuable spiritual experiences about the soul of a nation, it was perhaps inevitable that sport, and sports' celebrities, would make the association. Fuelled by the money pouring in, thanks to increasingly lucrative television contracts, sport has been turned into a reified product by those responsible for marketing it. Given the ever-expanding reach of the Anzac story into contemporary Australian life, it was hardly surprising that the Australian cricket team visited Gallipoli on its way to England for the 2001 Ashes tour. Presented as a moment of poignant revelation for young men who somehow managed to ingest the very essence of their nation through the visit, the England team followed a similar path in 2009, visiting Ypres. Few commentators believed that there could be anything even vaguely odd or disconcerting about either highly stage-managed event. However, former England cricketer-turned-journalist

Mike Atherton could not help injecting a moment of wry humour—an immensely rare commodity in the contemporary conception of anything to do with commemoration of the conflict—when he noted that Ypres was 'an odd choice, there being no better example in history of lions being led by lambs. Let us hope it was a history lesson that Strauss [the England captain] did not take to heart.'[91]

By 2008 and the ninetieth anniversary of the Armistice, with the veterans now reduced to a tiny number, another generation seemed prepared to reinstate Passchendaele as some sort of ghostly figure haunting the imagination. The Canadian director Paul Gross's film *Passchendaele* commenced production in the autumn of 2007, starting a publicity trail tied in with the anniversary of the battle's end. Released in October 2008 in time to bed down for the Armistice commemorations, it achieved mixed reviews and was internationally not a commercial success, partly due to its unevenness as a film, which made it neither a war epic nor a romantic melodrama. It flopped at the box office in Germany where the distributor had altered the main title to *Das Feld der Ehre* (The Field of Honour), rightly suspecting that Passchendaele would not mean anything to German audiences. In Canada, however, the film met with a very strong initial reception from cinemagoers and it aroused much media comment, ensuring that the battle was widely discussed.[92] Helping to buttress this profile was the release of the album *Every Light Must Fade,* in December 2008, by the Alberta-based band F&M. A collection of reflective, occasionally dark, original ballads, it includes 'Passchendaele 1917', which is by far the longest and most meditative piece on the album. A further indication of the deep footprint Ypres has left on Canadian popular culture is the fact that an Ontario 'doom metal' band called itself Woods of Ypres. It is even more remarkable an indicator given the fact that the band is not ostensibly interested in the conflict and has not recorded a song making any kind of direct reference to Flanders

It seems a remote prospect that the German national team will ever make a detour to Flanders on route to a football tournament, that German songwriters will have anything to say about Langemarck, or that references to the battle will ever be used to market German beer. German commemorative culture, exceedingly and self-consciously earnest, has proved resistant to commodification. But cultural habitus is only part of the explanation. More importantly, it is a reflection of the divergent commemorative paths that Britons and Germans followed in the post-war period. In contrast to other historians who have identified the 1960s and 1990s as crucial phases in the evolution of the cultural memory of the Great War, we argue that the relatively quiet 1970s and early 1980s marked a pivotal period. To be sure, in Britain the fiftieth anniversary of the Great War refocused attention on the conflict and its survivors, and it saw a change in expression with many more people willing to openly condemn the war as futile.[93] Yet the same trend, albeit less pronounced, could be detected in 1960s West Germany. Moreover, this was also the last time when Germans, and Belgians, attempted to imbue the commemoration of the Great War with new meaning by Europeanizing its legacy. The fiftieth anniversary was a dynamic period, buzzing with commemorative activities. From a comparative perspective, though, it was during the 1970s and 1980s that national peculiarities in the remembrance of war became apparent. The French, having erected an impressive memorial at Steenstraat in 1961, lost interest in the salient, seemingly content to concentrate on Verdun. During the 1980s the annual Yser Pilgrimage of Flemish nationalists sank into obscurity. Yet this period saw also a slow revival in British battlefield tourism, a renaissance of the guidebook genre, and the emergence of a popular history focused on the ordeal of ordinary soldiers in the anglophone world. These trends had no equivalent in West Germany. After *c*.1970 it appears that fewer and fewer Germans felt a personal connection with the dead of the Great War or a spiritual bond with an imagined landscape around Ypres. Memory faded into history, and Ypres ceased to function as a gateway to the First World War. The 'memory boom' of the 1990s with its emphasis on traumatic memory did little to rekindle interest in the First World War in Germany, where it remained firmly fixed on the legacy of the Holocaust. In Britain and its former

Dominions, too, a notion of trauma underscored the 'memory boom'. However, in contrast to the relative lack of German interest in the battle, in the British context traumatic memory seemed to refer back to the Ur-trauma of the twentieth century: mud, blood, shell shock—and Ypres.[94]

7

Conclusion

Wipers at the Centenary

On 12 February 2016, exactly 100 years to the day since it was first published, the *Wipers Times* was relaunched as the *Fritz Times* by the German publisher of the broadsheet *Die Welt*. Just like the world's most famous 'trench journal', its modern-day successor aimed to provide comic relief; it ridiculed, amongst others, the dress sense of the British clubbers during cold winter nights, the footballing skills of the England team, and the royal family for the size of their ears as well as for being German in the first place. The *Fritz Times* reinserted a bit of jocularity into German commemorative culture, a trait that had essentially disappeared since the left-wing press had poked fun at the Langemarck myth during the Weimar years. Yet underneath the light-hearted humour was a more serious appeal to the British reader of the *Fritz Times*: 'Today we need you for a successful European Union. And that is why we are printing this edition. Then you can have your newspaper back.'[1] Subsequent events suggest that this message did not get through, despite the conservative press giving the *Fritz Times* an unreserved thumbs-up. The *Daily Telegraph* applauded their German counterparts for their mastery of British humour, conceding that '"The Hun" has the last word'.[2]

Occasional jabs at their local rivals, Messrs. Hun and Co., had been a recurring theme of the original *Wipers Times* published in twenty-three issues between February 1916 and December 1918. The story of this soldier newspaper—from inauspicious beginnings in a casemate under the old ramparts of Ypres to eventual rise to media stardom in the early twenty-first century—encapsulates many of the themes running through this book. Moreover, it is illustrative of the varied trajectory of the cultural memory of the war in the twentieth century and beyond. Only for a few months in 1916 was the *Wipers Times* in fact produced in 'Wipers' itself and actually entitled *Wipers Times*. When the newspaper's unit, 12th Battalion Sherwood Foresters, were redeployed elsewhere along the Western Front, it changed its name accordingly: *'New Church' Times, Kemmel Times, Somme-Times, B.E.F. Times,* and in November and December 1918 *Better Times*. But only the title *Wipers Times* stuck, impressing the soldiers' slang name of the Flemish city on the anglophone imagination.

As early as March 1916 the *Nottingham Evening Post* speculated that the *Wipers Times* might retain 'value in future years', and in July 1917 *The Tatler* stated the case for 'preserving this priceless paper for posterity'.[3] They need not have worried. The first (partial) facsimile edition, 'as a permanent record of the gaiety of the soldier', appeared shortly before Christmas 1917.[4] The timing is illuminating. Even though the war was not yet over (in fact, preparations for the facsimile reproduction must have begun during the Third Battle of Ypres), 1917 marks a crucial year for the formation of the post-war memory of the conflict, for that was the year of the founding of both the IWGC (later responsible for the construction of the Menin Gate) and the Imperial War Museum (now the home of Paul Nash's paintings of the Ypres salient).

To be sure, the long-term success of the *Wipers Times* as a vector of memory was in no way preordained. The *Times Literary Supplement* noted in November 1917 that its contents were 'essentially esoteric; the terms used are cryptic and technical, and personal allusions abound'.[5] Edmund Blunden, reviewing the 1930 (complete) facsimile edition of the *Famous Wartime Trench Magazine* (as the edition was subtitled) in the same journal, made a similar point. The *Wipers Times* was steeped in the soldiers' idiom and 'the details are too local and momentary to be grasped, especially under their humorous disguises'. The trademark humour, the newspaper's chief selling point, was also potentially undermining its usefulness as a memory aid: 'Nobody now, except old initiates, will quite catch the point of "Cage Hotels Limited" or "The Zillebeke Fishing and Exploration Co., Ltd."'[6] Here, though, Blunden was mistaken. As we have seen, the interwar years saw a renewal of the microgeographies that had emerged during the war, and specific places in the Ypres salient retained their symbolic power and recognition. Thus, spoof advertisements for building plots on Hill 60 (managed by estate agents Bosch & Co.), sporting news from the Sanctuary Wood golf course (with some tricky holes), or letters to the editor complaining about potholes in the Menin Road would have made any battlefield tourist (and the vast majority who had never been to Ypres) chuckle.[7]

British and Dominion armies created between 100 and 200 distinct titles, but only the *Wipers Times* has become a household name—much to the annoyance of some editors of other soldier newspapers. Writing to *The Observer* in 1930, the former editor of the *Lead Swinger* complained that the *Wipers Times* was given undue attention, that it had been by no means the first trench journal, and that 'future historians' in particular must not be misled by the excitement created by the reissue of the *Wipers Times*.[8] So, how can one explain the newspaper's long-enduring success? Three reasons stand out.

Firstly, the *Wipers Times* benefited from its association with what was, until the 1960s at least, the principal site of memory of the war on the Western Front. Ypres had emerged as the 'Holy Ground of British Arms' from the war and retained this accolade until the Second World War. The *Wipers Times,* in turn, contributed to the process of maintaining the wartime microgeographies of the Ypres salient. In short, Ypres and the *Wipers Times* amplified each other's significance.

Secondly, the *Wipers Times* cultivated a peculiar brand of absurd but jocular humour which contemporary reviewers described variously as 'defiant irreverence' and 'irreverent reverence'.[9] Steering well away from outright subversion ensured that the newspaper did not fall foul of the censor or the military command (Field Marshal Lord Plumer even wrote the foreword for the 1930 reprint).[10] Humour (out of the soldier's mouth) did nothing to undermine the hallowed aura of Ypres; the two could be tightly intertwined. The *Wipers Times*'s sense of humour is a long way from the biting satire of circumstances and acid irony that, according to Paul Fussell, became the signature of the war.[11] Interestingly, though, Fussell's seminal book, *The Great War and Modern Memory*, appeared in 1975, two years after the first post-1945 facsimile of the *Wipers Times* had appeared. Reviewing the 1973 edition of the *Wipers Times*, *The Economist* noted aptly 'low key, generalised irony which never turns into bitter satire'.[12]

Thirdly, the *Wipers Times* was a journalist's newspaper par excellence, despite the fact that its editor, Captain F. J. Roberts, had no background in journalism. 'Have you ever sat in a trench in the middle of a battle and corrected proofs?', asked *The Tatler*.[13] Such a degree of journalistic commitment commanded professional respect. What is more, the format of the *Wipers Times* had a strong appeal to fellow journalists. Complete with correspondence column, serial story, fashion page, golf notes, and classified advertisements, it parodied features of the home press—and the press loved it. The mass media of the early twentieth century were in constant dialogue with one another.[14] Journalists appreciated how the *Wipers Times* not only poked fun at the war but held up a mirror to their trade, too. Again, Captain Roberts's treatment of the civilian press was satirical without being disrespectful. Just as the *Wipers Times* reflected on the mainstream press, newspapers and magazines in their turn carried articles about the phenomenon of trench journalism in general and the *Wipers Times* in particular. The final analysis of 'The Journalism of the Trenches' appeared in *The Times* in December 1939; it suggested that the *Wipers Times* had set (too) 'high [a] standard for their successor of to-day'.[15]

During the Second World War, the *Wipers Times*—like all mementoes of Ypres—became an embarrassing reminder of the absence of a western front until the Normandy landings. Save for one reminiscence in the local newspaper of the Sherwood Foresters—the *Nottingham Evening Post*—in July 1944, the *Wipers Times* disappeared from the print media's radar for the duration of the conflict and its aftermath.

It was not until 1973 that the *Wipers Times* was republished again. By then the Somme had come to dominate the cultural memory as the war's most ironic battle, although no one bar a few experts had ever heard of the *Somme Times* (the title under which the *Wipers Times* appeared in July 1916). The new pre-eminence of the Somme and 1 July in the commemorative calendar notwithstanding, the *Wipers Times*, just as Ypres itself, re-emerged as a significant site of memory during the 1980s. While the 1973 facsimile had been produced by a small firm, a heavyweight in publishing, Macmillan, brought out a reprint in 1988.[16] Around this time the mass media rediscovered their old love, and a string of radio and television programmes about the *Wipers Times* were broadcast between 1987 and 2013, culminating in the eponymous television drama written by *Private Eye* editor Ian Hislop and starring ex-Python Michael Palin on BBC2 in September 2013.

Television critics widely welcomed the BBC production as an antidote to the expected solemnities of the centenary.[17] An underlying theme of the mass media's engagement with the *Wipers Times* in the run-up to the centenary was the 'forgotten' humour of the soldier newspapers: 'We are all familiar with the First World War of blood and mud, of lions led by donkeys, the futility, the boredom and the slaughters. Less well remembered, however, is the pitch-black humour of the trenches,' claimed *The Times* in November 2007.[18] The rediscovery of 'forgotten' voices of the war—and, even better, the unmasking of commemorative 'taboos'—were the new stock-in-trade of post-Cold War commemorations, and even a publication as famous and widely available as the *Wipers Times* now appeared in need of rescue from oblivion.[19]

The *Wipers Times* is now a teaching resource in schools, the title of a West End play, the name of a Belgian beer as well as of other merchandise.[20] The original 'trench journal' has multiplied and transmuted into other media. Our book is a contribution to a new type of 'media' history or rather 'mediation' history.[21] Unlike normal media history which focuses on the historicization of forms of mass communication (the press, broadcasting, the Internet), our approach is more encompassing. The media explored here range from newspaper articles and television programmes to feature films, battle paintings, history books, war memorials, commemorative rituals, battlefield tourism and consumer products. They operate in multiple registers, from the discursive to the visual, performative, material, and spatial. We have charted how the interplay of a host of media fashioned images of Ypres, and how the battles of Ypres in turn generated new forms of media representation. The experience and memory of war became inseparable from the act of mediation. Ernst Jünger—like many soldiers, an avid newspaper reader—noted in his wartime diary and post-war memoir how he was thrown into battle in Flanders in August 1917 knowing about it from the press, and the thrill it gave him to read about his unit's exploits in the newspapers.[22] Jünger's own powerful representation of 'Langemarck' in 1917 was suspended in a web of signification created by other media; his 'experience' of war was filtered through army communiqués and the press. Any attempt to distil the 'real' war and the 'authentic' experience from its representations is ultimately a futile exercise; medium and message are inextricably interwoven.[23]

Much recent historical research into the history of the Great War aims to 'go beyond' the Western Front, arguing that it was for a reason that contemporaries coined the term '*world* war'. The 'Greater War' is the programmatic title of an innovative series of books which contends that the conflict had 'a greater territorial reach than the well-published struggle on the Western Front'.[24] New research that explores how the First World War touched the entire planet is to be highly welcomed. But the binary opposition between global war on the one hand and the Western Front on the other requires unpicking. People from five continents converged on Ypres between 1914 and 1918; various nations have mapped their memories on to the city and the salient since then. The First World War turned the city of Ypres and its environs into a transnational site of experience and memory, a global and local place. Fittingly, an image of the ruined Cloth Hall adorns the cover of *First World War Studies,* a new journal launched in 2010 that aims to free the field of geographic constraints.[25] It is indeed difficult to think of a more poignant symbol of the global conflict that was the Great War.

NOTES

Preface

1. See e.g. Manfred Hettling and Jörg Echternkamp (eds.), *Gefallenendenken im globalen Vergleich: Nationale Tradition, politische Legitimation und Individualisierung der Erinnerung* (Munich, 2013); Santanu Das (ed.), *Race, Empire and First World War Writing* (Cambridge, 2011).
2. Henry Reed, 'Lessons of War', in Jon Stallworthy (ed.), *The Oxford Book of War Poetry* (Oxford, 1984), 254–7.
3. See e.g. Hew Strachan, *The First World War in Africa* (Oxford, 2004); Eugene Rogan, *The Fall of the Ottomans: The Great War in the Middle East, 1914–1920* (London, 2015); Michelle Moyd, 'Centring a Sideshow: Local Experiences of the First World War in Africa', *First World War Studies* 7 (2016), 111–30.
4. Dominiek Dendooven and Piet Chielens (eds.), *World War I: Five Continents in Flanders* (Tielt, 2008).
5. Henri Lefebvre's *The Production of Space*, trans. Donald Nicholson-Smith (Malden, MA, 1991) is paradigmatic.
6. Pierre Nora, 'Between Memory and History: *Les Lieux de Mémoire*', *Representations* 26 (1989), 7–24. An overview of the field is provided in David Lowenthal, *The Past is a Foreign Country—Revisited* (Cambridge, 2015). For the ever-expanding historiography of material culture and the First World War, see Nicholas J. Saunders and Paul Cornish (eds.), *Contested Objects: Material Memories of the Great War* (London, 2009).
7. Michael Williams, *Ivor Novello: Screen Idol* (London, 2003); see also Michael Hammond and Michael Williams (eds.), *British Silent Cinema and the Great War* (Basingstoke, 2011).
8. The literature on the nature of memory, remembrance, and politics is now extensive. For good overviews, see Jay Winter and Emmanuel Sivan (eds.), *War and Remembrance in the Twentieth Century* (Cambridge, 1999); T[imothy] G. Ashplant et al. (eds.), *The Politics of War Memory and Commemoration* (London, 2000).
9. See e.g. George L. Mosse, *Fallen Soldiers: Reshaping the Memory of the World Wars* (Oxford, 1990) and Mosse, 'National Cemeteries and National Revival: The Cult of the Fallen Soldiers in Germany', *Journal of Contemporary History* 14 (1979), 1–20. For a different interpretation, see Benjamin Ziemann, *Contested Commemorations: Republican War Veterans and Weimar Political Culture* (Cambridge, 2013).

10. See the important works by Bernd Hüppauf, 'Langemarck, Verdun and the Myth of a *New Man* in Germany after the First World War', *War & Society* 6/2 (1988), 70–103; and Jay W. Baird, *To Die for Germany: Heroes in the Nazi Pantheon* (Bloomington, IN, 1990).
11. See e.g. Adrian Gregory, *The Silence of Memory: Armistice Day 1919–1946* (Oxford, 1994); Alex King, *Memorials of the Great War in Britain: The Symbolism and Politics of Remembrance* (Oxford, 1998); K[en] S. Inglis, *Sacred Places: War Memorials in the Australian Landscape* (Melbourne, 1998); Daniel J. Sherman, *The Construction of Memory in Interwar France* (Chicago, 1999); Gerhard Schneider, '*... nicht umsonst gefallen*'? *Kriegerdenkmäler und Kriegstotenkult in Hannover* (Hanover, 1991); Reinhart Koselleck and Michael Jeismann (eds.), *Der politische Totenkult: Kriegerdenkmäler in der Moderne* (Munich, 1994).
12. Johan Meire, *De stilte van de Salient: De Herinnering aan de Eerste Wereldoorlog rond Ieper* (Tielt, 2003) offers an anthropological study. On the cultural significance of paths and tracks, see Robert Macfarlane, *The Old Ways: A Journey on Foot* (London, 2012).

Chapter 1

1. For the sake of clarity and convenience, the dates of the battles given in this section are those according to the Historical Section (Military Branch) Committee for Imperial Defence. As the Preface makes clear, this imposes a framework that was not necessarily shared by the other combatants, whether allied or enemy.

Chapter 2

1. Hartmut Berghoff et al. (eds.), *The Making of Modern Tourism: The Cultural History of the British Experience, 1600–2000* (Basingstoke, 2002).
2. Muriel V. Searle, *Down the Line to Dover: A Pictorial History of Kent's Boat Train Line* (Tunbridge Wells, 1984), 48, 116.
3. Thomas Nipperdey, *Deutsche Geschichte 1866–1918*, i. *Arbeitswelt und Bürgergeist* (Munich, 1990), 176–81.
4. Quoted in Jack Simmons, 'Railways, Hotels, and Tourism in Great Britain, 1839–1914', *Journal of Contemporary History* 19 (1984), 216.
5. *Daily Mail*, 8 and 23 August 1899; see also Marc Constandt, *Een eeuw vakantie: 100 jaar toerisme in West-Vlaanderen* (Tielt, 1986), 20–8.
6. *Illustrated London News*, 12 May 1906.
7. *Manchester Guardian*, 4 October 1907.
8. See e.g. *Hartlepool Mail*, 4 May 1898; *Derby Mercury*, 11 May 1898.
9. *The Cyclists' Continental Companion: A Road Book of Belgium, Germany, France, Holland, Switzerland, Italy* (London, 1899), 6.

10. *Morning Post*, 3 August 1897.
11. *Manchester Guardian*, 29 June 1897.
12. Percy Fitzgerald, *A Day's Tour: A Journey through France and Belgium* (London, 1887), 55.
13. Rudy Koshar, '"What Ought to be Seen": Tourists' Guidebooks and National Identities in Modern Germany and Europe', *Journal of Contemporary History* 33 (1998), 323–40.
14. Karl Baedeker, *Belgien und Holland nebst dem Großherzogtum Luxemburg: Handbuch für Reisende* (25th edn., Leipzig, 1914), 213–17.
15. K[arl] Baedeker, *Belgium and Holland: Handbook for Travellers* (4th edn., London, 1875); Baedeker, *Belgique et Hollande y compris le Luxembourg: Manuel du voyageur* (17th edn., Leipzig, 1901).
16. Karl Baedeker, *Belgium and Holland Including the Grand-Duchy of Luxembourg: Handbook for Travellers* (11th edn., London, 1894), 29–31.
17. *Cook's Tourists' Handbook for Belgium, Including the Ardennes: With Map and Plan* (London, 1896), 53; *Ward, Lock and Co.'s Guide to Belgium, Including the Ardennes and Luxemburg* (5th edn., London, 1906), 40.
18. H. T. Luks, *Belgien und Holland: Praktisches Handbuch für Reisende* (Grieben Reise-Bibliothek 22; Berlin, 1891), 92–3.
19. *Ypres: Guide illustré du touriste à Ypres et aux environs* ([2nd edn.,] Ypres, 1909).
20. *Manchester Guardian*, 26 June 1902, 19 June 1911, 9 July 1914; *Manchester Courier*, 2 July 1913; *Newcastle Journal*, 17 July 1914.
21. See Baedeker, *Belgium and Holland* (1894), 26; *Cook's Tourists' Handbook*, 53; *Ward, Lock and Co.'s Guide*, 40.
22. *Hull Daily Mail*, 24 June 1912.
23. See also Mark Derez, 'A Belgian Salient for Reconstruction: People and *Patrie*, Landscape and Memory', in Peter H. Liddle (ed.), *Passchendaele in Perspective: The Third Battle of Ypres* (London, 1997), 437–58.
24. Baedeker, *Belgien und Holland*, 213–17.
25. Paul Vidal de La Blache, *États et nations de L'Europe: Autour de la France* (Paris, 1891), 212. For similar comments, see *La Croix*, 17 December 190; *Le Figaro: Supplément littéraire du dimanche*, 6 February 1909.
26. Fitzgerald, *Day's Tour*, 53–4.
27. *Western Times*, 8 July 1901.
28. T. Francis Bumpus, *The Cathedrals and Churches of Belgium* (London, 1909), 117.
29. *Morning Post*, 7 February 1898.
30. *Lloyd's Weekly Newspaper*, 5 March 1899.
31. Laurence Binyon and William Strang, *Western Flanders: A Medley of Things Seen, Considered and Imagined* (London, 1899), *Dundee Courier*, 5 November 1906.
32. G. W. T. Omond and A. Forestier, *Bruges and West Flanders: Painted by A. Forestier; Described by G. W. T. Omond* (London, 1906).
33. *La Justice*, 15 December 1884; *L'Aurore*, 31 May 1913.
34. *Gloucester Journal*, 19 November 1910.

35. *Berwickshire News and General Advertiser*, 26 March 1907.
36. Henry d'Ideville, *Lettres flamandes: Cassel, Bergues Saint-Winoc, Dunkerque, Ypres, Oxelaere* (Paris, 1876), 17–22; Omond, *Bruges and West Flanders*, 95–119; George Wharton Edwards, *Some Old Flemish Towns* (London, 1913), 100–31.
37. Baedeker, *Belgium and Holland* (1894), 29; Baedeker, *Belgique et Hollande*, 200; Baedeker, *Belgien und Holland*, 213.
38. *Western Times*, 8 July 1901.
39. *Berwickshire News and General Advertiser*, 26 March 1907.
40. D'Ideville, *Lettres flamandes*, 17.
41. *Le Figaro: Supplément littéraire du dimanche*, 16 June 1888.
42. Fitzgerald, *Day's Tour*, 55–6.
43. Edwards, *Some Old Flemish Towns*, 111.
44. Luks, *Belgien und Holland*, 92–3.
45. *Manchester Guardian*, 2 March 1899.
46. Binyon and Strang, *Western Flanders*, 44–5.
47. Fitzgerald, *A Day's Tour*, 54.
48. Omond, *Bruges and West Flanders*, 119.
49. Binyon and Strang, *Western Flanders*, 3.
50. Armand Heins and Georges Meunier, *En pays flamand: Croquis et notes* (Ghent, 1892), 6.
51. For the quotations from Binyon and Strang, *Western Flanders*, 4, 6–13, 4, 14–19, 27, 44–5.
52. Geoff Dyer, *The Missing of the Somme* (London, 1994), 7, orig. emphasis.
53. Paul Fussell, *The Great War and Modern Memory* (London, 1975); Samuel Hynes, *A War Imagined: The First World War and English Culture* (London, 1990).
54. Quoted in Mark D. Larabee, 'Baedekers as Casualty: Great War Nationalism and the Fate of Travel Writing', *Journal of the History of Ideas* 71 (2010), 475.

Chapter 3

1. *Daily Mail*, 4 March 1915.
2. *Daily Mail*, 5, 8, and 9 March 1915.
3. *The Times*, 6 December 1914.
4. *Daily Mail*, 30 November 1914.
5. *Daily Mail*, 22 May 1915.
6. *Sydney Morning Herald*, 13 January 1915.
7. Published in Canadian War Records Office, *Canada in Khaki: A Tribute to the Officers and Men Now Serving in the Canadian Expeditionary Force* (London, 1917), 37.
8. *Sydney Morning Herald*, 14 November 1914.
9. *Dundee Evening Telegraph*, 6 June 1915.
10. *The Times*, 6 December 1914.
11. Sue Malvern, 'War Tourisms: "Englishness", Art, and the First World War', *Oxford Art Journal* 24 (2001), 45–66.

12. BArch, R 8034-II/7600, fo. 138: *Berliner Tageblatt*, 14 December 1914.
13. *Daily Express*, 7 November 1914; *Manchester Guardian*, 26 November 1914.
14. *Daily Mail*, 19 December 1914.
15. *Daily Mail*, 20 May 1915.
16. *Daily Express*, 27 October 1914.
17. *Midlands Advertiser*, 18 December 1914; *Daily Mail*, 30 November 1914.
18. *Toronto Star*, 28 June 1916.
19. See advertisement in *Daily Mail*, 22 April 1916.
20. *War Illustrated*, 5 December 1914.
21. *The Times*, 5 May 1915. For other examples, see *Aberdeen Journal*, 22 May 1915; *Dundee Courier*, 24 April and 25 May 1915; *Exeter and Plymouth Gazette*, 10 August 1915.
22. *Le Matin*, 24 April 1915.
23. *Journal des débats politiques et littéraires*, 26 April 1915.
24. *The Times*, 29 April 1915.
25. *The Times*, 13 July 1915.
26. *Vossische Zeitung*, 23 April 1915.
27. BArch, R 8034-II/7605, fo. 78: *Kölnische Zeitung*, 1 June 1915.
28. *The Times*, 3 July 1915; *Illustrated London News*, 21 August 1915.
29. *Le Matin*, 18 November and 17 December 1915, 14 October 1916.
30. Charles Le Goffic, *Dixmude: Un chapitre de l'histoire des fusiliers marins (7 Octobre–10 Novembre 1914)* (Paris, 1915), 1; see also J[ean] Pinguet, *Trois étapes de la brigade des marins: La Marne–Gand–Dixmude* (Paris, 1918).
31. *Le Matin*, 26 April 1915.
32. *Journal des débats politiques et littéraires*, 26 April 1915.
33. *Schwäbischer Merkur*, 11 November 1914.
34. See in general David Welch, *Germany and Propaganda in World War I: Pacifism, Mobilization and Total War* (London, 2014).
35. Roger Chickering, *Imperial Germany and the Great War, 1914–1918* (3rd edn., Cambridge, 2014), 49.
36. BArch, R 8034-II/7590, fo. 3: *Frankfurter Zeitung*, 12 November 1914.
37. Jeffrey Verhey, *The Spirit of 1914: Militarism, Myth, and Mobilization in Germany* (Cambridge, 2000).
38. Gerd Krumeich, 'Langemarck', in Étienne François and Hagen Schulze (eds.), *Deutsche Erinnerungsorte*, iii (Munich, 2001), 296–7.
39. *Münsterländische Volkszeitung*, 14 November 1914.
40. *Die Woche* 16 (1914), 1897.
41. Quoted in Holger Afflerbach, *Falkenhayn: Politisches Denken und Handeln im Kaiserreich* (Munich, 1994), 195.
42. Bernd Ulrich, *Die Augenzeugen: Deutsche Feldpostbriefe in Kriegs- und Nachkriegszeit 1914–1933* (Essen, 1997), 129.
43. BArch-SAPMO, NY 4402/2: Theodor Leipart, *An meinen toten Sohn Ernst Alexander Leipart als 17 jähriger Kriegsfreiwilliger gefallen am 9. Dezember 1914 bei*

Ypern (Berlin, 1915); cf. Michael Roper, *The Secret Battle: Emotional Survival in the Great War* (Manchester, 2009).

44. Olaf Heinemann, *Der Tag von Langemarck: Geschichten von draußen und daheim* (Leipzig, 1915), 11–33.
45. *Der Krieg 1914/15 in Wort und Bild* 1 (1916), 339.
46. Using Wytschaete as an example, thirty-five different mentions can be found in *The Times, Daily Mail, Daily Mirror,* and *Illustrated London News* between 1915 and 1917.
47. *Daily Mail,* 2 March 1915.
48. *The Times,* 22 December 1917.
49. For examples, see *Freeman's Journal,* 20 August 1896, 1 and 23 August 1904, 23 September 1904, 20 September 1906, 9 May 1908; *Donegal News,* 30 September 1905; *Westmeath Examiner,* 27 June 1903, which carries Thomas Davis's poem, 'Clare's Dragoons'.
50. Patrick Nolan, *The Irish Dames of Ypres: Being a History of the Royal Irish Abbey of Ypres* (Dublin, 1908).
51. R[ichard] Barry O'Brien (ed.), *The Irish Nuns of Ypres: An Episode of the War,* introd. John Redmond (London, 1915).
52. *Freeman's Journal,* 4 February 1916.
53. *Irish Independent,* 9 June 1917.
54. *Irish Examiner,* 8 June 1917.
55. *Skibbereen Eagle,* 9 June 1917.
56. See Clair Wills, *Dublin 1916: The Siege of the GPO* (London, 2009), 86, 103–5; *Irish Times,* 20 December 1923.
57. See Jonathan F. Vance, *Death So Noble: Memory, Meaning, and the First World War* (Vancouver, 1997), 24.
58. For details on the Crucified Canadian and McCrae and his poem, see Suzanne Evans, *Mothers of Heroes, Mothers of Martyrs: World War I and the Politics of Grief* (Montreal, 2007), 53; Vance, *Death So Noble,* 198–200.
59. *Toronto Star,* 1 and 3 May 1915.
60. *Manchester Guardian,* 29 October 1917.
61. *Manchester Guardian,* 7 November 1917.
62. *New Zealand Herald,* 17 October 1917.
63. *Farmer and Settler,* 28 September 1917; *Barrier Miner,* 2 November 1917.
64. See e.g. BArch, R 8034-II/7599, fo. 115: *Kölnische Volkszeitung,* 20 November 1914; and fo. 116: *B.Z. am Mittag,* 20 November 1914.
65. *The Times,* 13 July 1915; *Toronto Star,* 5 May 1915.
66. *The Times,* 13 November, 2 and 16 December 1914.
67. *The Times,* 2 November 1916.
68. *The Times,* 8, 24, and 31 October 1917.
69. *The Times,* 8 June 1917.
70. *The Times,* 8 October 1917.
71. *Manchester Guardian,* 7 November 1917; *Daily Mail,* 8 November 1917.

72. *The Times*, 8 November 1917.
73. *Daily Mail*, 29 April 1918.
74. Hugh B. C. Pollard, *The Story of Ypres* (London, 1917), 68.
75. Pollard, *Story of Ypres*, frontispiece.
76. Dyer, *Missing*, 6.
77. John Oxenham, *High Altars: The Battle-Fields of France and Flanders as I Saw Them* (London, 1918), 37–44.
78. Wilson McNair, *Blood and Iron: Impressions from the Front in France and Flanders* (London, 1918), 254.
79. G. Valentine Williams, *With Our Army in France and Flanders* (London, 1915), 110.
80. Pollard, *Story of Ypres*, 14.
81. Joseph E. Morris, *Belgium* (Beautiful Europe; London, 1915), 10. For a similar example of a rapidly altered reissue, see George Wharton Edwards, *Vanished Towers and Chimes of Flanders* (Philadelphia, 1916), 65–82.
82. C. J. Magrath, *Ypres–Yper: A Few Notes on Its History before the War* (London, [1918]), 3.
83. Magrath, *Ypres*, 16–39.
84. BArch, R 8034-II/7601, fos. 143–5: *Kreuz-Zeitung*, 11 January 1915.
85. BArch, R 8034-II/7600, fo. 193: *Deutsche Zeitung*, 22 December 1914.
86. BArch, R 8034-II/7600, fo. 33: *Vossische Zeitung*, 2 December 1914.
87. Max Beckmann, *Briefe im Kriege*, ed. Minna Tube (Munich, 1984), 71.
88. *Kriegslieder des XV. Korps 1914–1915 von den Vogesen bis Ypern* (Berlin, 1915), 77.
89. Carl Zuckmayer, *A Part of Myself* (London, 1970), 157.
90. [Percy] Wyndham Lewis, *Blasting and Bombardiering* (London, 1937), 160–1.
91. *Der Krieg 1914/15 in Wort und Bild* 1 (1916), 224–5, 233.
92. Maria Tippett, *Art at the Service of War: Canada, Art and the Great War* (Toronto, 1984), 26–30.
93. *The Western Front: Drawings by Muirhead Bone* (London, 1917), 10–11.
94. *Western Front*, pl. II.
95. Dyer, *Missing*, 120.
96. *Western Front*, pl. V.
97. *Western Front*, pl. III.
98. *Western Front*, pl. IV.
99. *Daily Express*, 11 February 1916.
100. Quoted in Richard Cork, *A Bitter Truth: Avant-Garde Art and the Great War* (New Haven, 1994), 200.
101. Quoted in Cork, *A Bitter Truth*, 198.
102. For differing interpretations of Nash's sense of mission, see Cork, *Bitter Truth*, 196–203 and Sue Malvern, *Modern Art, Britain and the Great War: Witnessing, Testimony and Remembrance* (New Haven, 2004), 31.
103. See Malvern, *Modern Art*, 35.
104. McNair, *Blood and Iron*, 306.
105. Quoted in Cork, *Bitter Truth*, 198.

106. *The Spectator*, 2 August 1918.
107. HStAS, J 150/119 Nr. 7: Severin Rüttgers, 'Ÿpern/Einst und jetzt', *Beilage zur Kriegszeitung der 4. Armee* 60, 9 July 1917; Willy Norbert, 'Ypern—die "ewige Stadt"', *Velhagen & Klasings Monatshefte* 30 (1915–16), 522–35.
108. Alfred Baudrillart, *La Guerre allemande et la catholicisme* (Paris, 1915), 7, 8, 21.
109. *Le Monde illustré*, 24 November 1917.
110. *Illustrated London News*, 5 December 1914.
111. *Illustrated London News*, 16 January and 28 August 1915.
112. *Daily Mirror*, 27 August 1917.
113. *Illustrated London News*, 2 December 1916.
114. *Daily Mirror*, 18 February 1918.
115. *Daily Mirror*, 5 October 1917.
116. *Daily Mirror*, 13 October 1917.
117. *Daily Mirror*, 16 October 1917.
118. *Daily Mirror*, 17 December 1917.
119. Bruce Bairnsfather, *Bullets & Billets* (London, 1916), 177, 183.
120. Frederic Coleman, *From Mons to Ypres with French: A Personal Narrative* (London, 1916); Ernest W. Hamilton, *The First Seven Divisions: Being a Detailed Account of the Fighting from Mons to Ypres* (London, 1916); Henry Beckles Willson, *In the Ypres Salient: The Story of a Fortnight's Canadian Fighting, June 2–16, 1916* (London, 1916).
121. HStAS, M 1/11 Bü 165, fos. 7–12: *Schwäbischer Merkur*, 3 November–3 December 1917.
122. Alexander Watson, *Enduring the Great War: Combat, Morale and Collapse in the German and British Armies, 1914–1918* (Cambridge, 2008), 168–72.
123. Stefan Goebel, *The Great War and Medieval Memory: War, Remembrance and Medievalism in Britain and Germany, 1914–1940* (Cambridge, 2007), 161–3.
124. *Schwäbische Kunde aus dem großen Krieg*, ii, ed. Hauptmann d. Res. Schmückle im Auftrag des Königl. Württ. Kriegsministeriums (Stuttgart, 1918), 74, 120, 125.
125. [Otto Schwink], *Ypres, 1914: An Official Account Published by Order of the German General Staff* (London, 1919), 83.
126. Markus Pöhlmann, *Kriegsgeschichte und Geschichtspolitik: Der Erste Weltkrieg. Die amtliche deutsche Militärgeschichtsschreibung 1914–1956* (Paderborn, 2002), 50–7, 195.

Chapter 4

1. For the full details behind this complex history, see Dominiek Dendooven, *The Menin Gate and the Last Post: Ypres as Holy Ground* (Koksijde, 2001).
2. TNA, CAB 24/106/45: Winston S. Churchill, Preservation of the Cloth Hall and Cathedral at Ypres, 26 May 1920.
3. Henry Beckles Willson, *Ypres: The Holy Ground of British Arms* (Bruges, 1920), p. xiii.

4. For details of the reconstruction of Ypres, see Meire, *De stilte*, 109–35.
5. *New York Times*, 20 June 1919.
6. *Daily Mail*, 25 June 1919.
7. *Church Times*, 27 June 1919.
8. For an account of the royal tour, see Frank Fox, *The King's Pilgrimage* (London, 1922).
9. CWGC, 03/1348129: Prince Maurice of Battenberg file, correspondence, 6 July 1920.
10. *Ypres Times* 2/8 (1925), 221.
11. PA AA, R 96018: Walther Rathenau, memorandum, 16 July 1919; *Mitteilungen des Referates Wiederaufbau der zerstörten Gebiete Belgiens und Nordfrankreichs* 86 (1919), 32.
12. *Vossische Zeitung*, 23 November 1924.
13. Beckles Willson, *Ypres*, 1.
14. *The Times*, 29 July 1922.
15. *The Times*, 6 June, 5 August, and 3 October 1919.
16. *Ypres and the Battles of Ypres* (Illustrated Michelin Guides to the Battle-Fields 1914–18; Clermont-Ferrand, 1919), 69.
17. *Ward, Lock and Co.'s Handbook to Belgium and the Battlefields* (7th edn., London, 1921), 48–65, 80–4.
18. Grand Quartier général, *Aux champs de gloire: Le Front belge de l'Yser*, illus. Urbain Wernaers (Brussels, 1921).
19. BArch, R 8034-II/7605, fo. 43: *Berliner Lokal-Anzeiger*, 22 May 1915.
20. BArch, R 8034-II/8864, fo. 113: *Neue Presse* [?], 28 September 1920.
21. W. Kretzschmar, *Deutsche Heldenfriedhöfe in Belgien und Frankreich* (2nd edn., Pößneck, 1928), 9.
22. *Die leichte Artillerie* 4/4 (1927), 28; see also *Divisions-Zeitung der ehemaligen 46. Reserve-Division* 3/16 (1926), 3.
23. PA AA, R 47826: Johannes Lenzen to Auswärtiges Amt, 13 September 1926.
24. For a broader history of this process, see David W. Lloyd, *Battlefield Tourism: Pilgrimage and the Commemoration of the Great War in Britain, Australia and Canada, 1919–1939* (Oxford, 1998).
25. *The Times*, 31 July 1922, emphasis added.
26. *Ypres Times* 1/4 (1922), 112–13.
27. *Ypres Times* 1/1 (1921), 1–2.
28. *Daily Graphic*, 25 July 1927.
29. *Daily Express*, 25 July 1927; *The Times*, 23 July 1927.
30. C. J. Magrath, 'Life in Ypres, 1914–1918', in *The Pilgrim's Guide to the Ypres Salient* (London, [1920]), 1.
31. *The Times*, 18 December 1925.
32. Quoted extensively in British and French newspapers. For examples, see *Daily Express, Daily Mail, The Times, Le Figaro, Le Matin*, and *Le Temps*, 25 July 1927.
33. Pathé Gazette 1419, 28 July 1927.

34. *Ypres Times* 3/8 (1927), 223.
35. *Townsville Daily Bulletin*, 26 July 1927.
36. *Daily Express*, 25 July 1927.
37. *Berliner Tageblatt*, 16 September 1928.
38. TNA, WO 32/5879: Church Army Scheme for Permanent National Memorial at Ypres, 1919; CWGC, WG 360/4, Pt. 1: Ypres Memorial Church and School, 1924–5; *Church Times*, 17 October 1919, 25 August 1927; *The Times*, 18 December 1925.
39. For a good example of Irish press coverage of the event, see *Irish Examiner*, 12 July 1924.
40. See Jason Myers, *The Great War and Memory in Irish Culture, 1918–2010* (Palo Alto, CA, 2013), 158–9.
41. LAC, RG 38, vol. 419: Meetings of the Canadian Battlefields Memorials Committee, 1920–54; Canadian Battlefield Memorials Commission, *Canadian Battlefield Memorials* (Ottawa, 1929).
42. *Evening Standard*, 14 August 1923.
43. LAC, RG 38, vol. 419: 7th Meeting, 19 January 1923. National Archives of Australia, A6006, 1921/3/15: Proposed Australian Memorial at Jerusalem and Imperial Memorial at Ypres, 1921; A11804, 1922/169: Ypres: Imperial Memorial, 1920–3; A461, K370/1/15: War Memorials: Menin Gate, Ypres, 1920–36.
44. CWGC, SDC 56: New Zealand Memorials, 1922.
45. BArch, R 8034-II/7609, fos. 110–11: *Frankfurter Zeitung*, 4 December 1915; see Mosse, *Fallen Soldiers*, 43, 113.
46. BArch, R 8034-II/7605, fos. 75–7: *Deutsche Tageszeitung*, 31 May 1915.
47. BArch, R 8034-II/7614, fo. 3: *Vossische Zeitung*, 6 September 1917.
48. *Kriegsgräberfürsorge* 2/3 (1922), 30; 2/5 (1922), 52.
49. Susanne Brandt, *Vom Kriegsschauplatz zum Gedächtnisraum: Die Westfront 1914–1940* (Baden-Baden, 2000).
50. PA AA, R 47824: Deutsche Gesandtschaft Brüssel to Auswärtiges Amt, 6 January 1925.
51. PA AA, R 47824: Direktor des Zentralnachweiseamts to Auswärtiges Amt, 23 October 1925; Auswärtiges Amt to Reichsfinanzministerium, 31 October 1925.
52. PA AA, R 47824: Architekt Höger, Bericht zu meiner 1. Besichtigungsreise, 25 May 1927; Architekt Tischler to Kanzler Hirschfeld, 14 June 1927.
53. TNA, WO 32/5569: Report of Inspection of Sites, 12 July 1919.
54. Robert Wohl, *The Generation of 1914* (London, 1980), 42–84.
55. Uwe-K. Ketelsen, '"Die Jugend von Langemarck": Ein poetisch-politisches Motiv der Zwischenkriegszeit', in Thomas Koebner et al. (eds.), *'Mit uns zieht die neue Zeit': Der Mythos der Jugend* (Frankfurt am Main, 1985), 68–96; Detlev J. K. Peukert, *The Weimar Republic: The Crisis of Classical Modernity* (London, 1993), 7–9, 89–95.

56. Friedrich Kreppel, 'Nie wieder Langemarck!' [1923], in Werner Kindt (ed.), *Grundschriften der deutschen Jugendbewegung* (Düsseldorf, 1963), 436–7; see also Ziemann, *Contested Commemorations*, 54–9.
57. Jay W. Baird, *Hitler's War Poets: Literature and Politics in the Third Reich* (Cambridge, 2008), 50–2.
58. Mark Connelly, 'The Ypres League and the Commemoration of the Ypres Salient, 1914–1940', *War in History* 16 (2009), 51–76.
59. See *The Times*, 16 December 1917.
60. See CWGC, WG 1308, pts 1–3: Ypres League correspondence, 17 November 1920, 7 and 10 May 1924.
61. See *La Revue du Touring-club de France* 37/391 (June 1927), 109, 119; *Ypres Times* 1/9 (1923), 226–7.
62. *Daily Express*, 22 July 1927.
63. John Buchan, *Nelson's History of the War* (London, 1921–2), i. 368.
64. Buchan, *Nelson's History*, ii. 52.
65. Buchan, *Nelson's History*, iii. 601–2.
66. Buchan, *Nelson's History*, iii. 592–603.
67. *Saturday Review*, 17 June 1922.
68. *Sunday Times*, 1 March 1925.
69. *TLS*, 29 September 1927.
70. J. E. Edmonds and G. C. Wynne, *Military Operations: France and Belgium, 1915* [ii] (History of the Great War: London, 1927), 306–7. For the controversy over French's memoirs, see Richard Holmes, 'Sir John French and Lord Kitchener', in Brian Bond (ed.), *The First World War and British Military History* (Oxford, 1991), 113–39.
71. See review in *TLS*, 9 April 1925.
72. Service historique de la Défense, 2M23: Méthodes et règles à suivre pour le travail historique: document de redaction pour 'Les Armées françaises dans la Grande Guerre', n.d.; [Pierre-Alexis] Ronarc'h, *Souvenirs de la guerre (août 1914–septembre 1915)* (Paris, 1921).
73. *Mercure de France*, 15 August 1921.
74. *La Nouvelle Revue* (November 1921), 285.
75. Erich Otto Volkmann, *Der Große Krieg 1914–1918: Kurzgefaßte Darstellung auf Grund der amtlichen Quellen des Reichsarchivs* (5th edn., Berlin, [1924]), 183.
76. *Courier Journal*, 30 November 1919.
77. [Paul] von Hindenburg, *Out of My Life*, trans. F. A. Holt (London, 1920), 288.
78. Erich von Falkenhayn, *Die Oberste Heeresleitung 1914–1916 in ihren wichtigsten Entschließungen* (Berlin, 1920), 23–6.
79. Wilhelm Schreiner, *Der Tod von Ypern. Schicksal in Flandern* (7th edn., Herborn, [1927]), 244.
80. Werner Beumelburg, *Ypern 1914* (Schlachten des Weltkrieges 10; Oldenburg, 1925), 5, 9; see Pöhlmann, *Kriegsgeschichte*, 195.

81. Thomas Mann, *Der Zauberberg: Roman*, ed. Michael Neumann (Große kommentierte Frankfurter Ausgabe 5; Frankfurt am Main, 2002), 1081–5; trans. adapted from H. T. Lowe-Porter in *The Magic Mountain* (London, 1927), 896–9.
82. Franz Herwig, 'Neue Romane', *Hochland* 22/1 (1924–5), 693; see Herbert Lehnert, 'Langemarck—historisch und symbolisch', *Orbis Litterarum* 42 (1987), 286–8.
83. See e.g. editorial in *The Times*, 29 July 1922.
84. *Toronto Star*, 22 April 1919.
85. *Toronto Star*, 25 April 1921.
86. *Toronto Star*, 23 April 1923.
87. *Sydney Morning Herald*, 22 September 1919.
88. See examples in *Daily Mail*, 10 November 1923; *Daily Mirror*, 7 November 1925; *Sunday Times*, 31 October 1926.
89. See Robert J. Lamb, *James Kerr-Lawson: A Canadian Abroad* (Windsor, WO, 1983), 27–8.
90. *Colour Magazine* 9/2 (1919), 39–40.
91. Canadian War Records Office, *Art & War: Canadian War Memorials*, introd. P. G. Konody (London, [1919]), pl. XVII.
92. Quoted in Cork, *A Bitter Truth*, 223.
93. See *The Gate of Eternal Memories: 'Menin Gate at Midnight' (or 'The Ghosts of Menin Gate'). The Story of Captain Will Longstaff's Great Allegorical Painting* (Melbourne, [*c.*1929]).
94. For full details, see F[reddy] Hubrechtsen, *Het Panorama van de IJzerslag, 1921* (Brussels, 1993); 'Het IJzerpanorama' <http://www.wereldoorlog1418.nl/ijzerpanorama/index.html> [accessed 25 September 2015].
95. Pöhlmann, *Kriegsgeschichte*, 214.
96. *Der Weltkrieg im Bild: Frontaufnahmen aus den Archiven der Entente*, introd. Werner Beumelburg (Munich, [*c.*1926]).
97. Medienzentrum für Westfalen, Bildarchiv, Begleitheft MZA 534: Wilhelm Schulz, 'Ypern 1914: Die deutsche Jugend in der Schlacht von Ypern im Oktober und November 1914', Vaterländischer Lichtbilderverlag, [*c.*1925].
98. *Daily News*, 18 July 1927.
99. *Cape Times*, 24 August 1926.
100. Mark Connelly, *Celluloid War Memorials: The British Instructional Films Company and the Memory of the Great War* (Exeter, 2016).
101. See *In Flanders Fields Museum Jaarboek* (2013), 132–4.

Chapter 5

1. *The Scotsman*, 29 April 1932; Philip Longworth, *The Unending Vigil: A History of the Commonwealth War Graves Commission 1917–1984* (London, 1985), 105.
2. *The Times*, 13 August 1928.

3. *Los Angeles Times*, 9 August 1928; see also Thomas Dixon, *Weeping Britannia: Portrait of a Nation in Tears* (Oxford, 2015).
4. *The Times*, 9 August 1928.
5. Maxim Ziese and Hermann Ziese-Beringer, *Das unsichtbare Denkmal: Heute an der Westfront* (Berlin, [1930]), 63.
6. See e.g. Graham Seton Hutchison, *Pilgrimage* (London, 1935).
7. PA AA, R 47830: Generalkonsulat Antwerpen to Bayerischer Kriegerbund, 24 September 1929.
8. Ziemann, *Contested Commemorations*, 154–8.
9. *Der Stahlhelm-Student* 4/1–2 (1932–3), 12.
10. Quoted in Wolfgang Löhr, 'Langemar(c)k und der Kartellverband katholischer deutscher Studentenvereine', in Marc Zirlewagen (ed.), *'Wir siegen oder fallen': Deutsche Studenten im Ersten Weltkrieg* (Cologne, 2008), 403.
11. *Ypres Times* 5/7 (1931), 200, and 7/3 (1934), 70–2; *The Scotsman*, 4 August 1933.
12. PA AA, R 47828: Grieben-Verlag to Auswärtiges Amt, 20 September 1927; see also Marjolein Kinsbergen, 'Memory Wars? Nationalisme en de herdenking van de Eerste Wereldoorlog in Duitse, Britse en Franse reisgidsen tijdens het interbellum', *Handelingen van het Genootschap vor Geschiedenis to Brugge* 151 (2014), 195–222.
13. Karl Baedeker, *Belgien und Luxemburg: Handbuch für Reisende* (26th edn., Leipzig, 1930), 235; *Belgium and Luxemburg* [*sic*]: *Handbook for Travellers* (16th edn., Leipzig, 1931), 51.
14. Toc H, *Over There: A Little Guide for Pilgrims to Ypres, the Salient, and Talbot House, Poperinghe* (London, 1935), 14–16.
15. R. Buckinx, *Ypres et ses environs: Petit guide du touriste / Ypres and Its Surroundings: A Little Guide for the Tourist* (Ypres, n.d.); compare his *Ypern und die deutschen Kriegerfriedhöfe: Führer mit Karte*, trans. V. de Byser (Langemarck, [*c.*1931]).
16. R. H. Mottram, *Journey to the Western Front: Twenty Years After* (London, 1936), 74.
17. Nicholas J. Saunders, *Killing Time: Archaeology and the First World War* ([2nd edn.,] Stroud, 2010), 31–63.
18. *Rheinisch-Westfälische Zeitung*, 14 February 1929; *Berliner Lokal-Anzeiger*, 6 February 1929.
19. PA AA, R 47828: von Rohrscheidt to Konsul Kraske, 15 September 1927.
20. *Berliner Tageblatt*, 16 September and 9 October 1928; *Deutsche Allgemeine Zeitung*, 13 October 1928.
21. PA AA, R 47829: Auswärtiges Amt to Theodor Einert, 22 September 1928; Auswärtiges Amt to Franz Meister, 20 November 1928.
22. Antoine Prost, 'The Dead', in Jay Winter (ed.), *The Cambridge History of the First World War*, iii. *Civil Society* (Cambridge, 2014), 581.
23. PA AA, R 47834: Gesandtschaft Brüssel, Studentenfeier auf Friedhof Langemarck, 11 September 1928; *Der Tag*, 18 August 1928.
24. BArch, R 129/68: Vorstand der Deutschen Studentenschaft to Einzelstudentenschaften, 18 October 1928.

25. *Deutsche Zeitung*, 24 April 1929.
26. PA AA, R 47834: Robert Tischler and Christoph Hacker, Deutscher Soldatenfriedhof Langemarck, 7 March 1930; see also Brandt, *Kriegsschauplatz*, 192–207; Anette Freytag and Thomas Van Driessche, 'Die Deutschen Soldatenfriedhöfe des Ersten Weltkriegs in Flandern', *Relicta* 7 (2011), 163–228.
27. PA AA, R 47852: Direktor des Zentralnachweiseamts für Kriegsverluste und Kriegergräber to Auswärtiges Amt, 14 June 1932.
28. Mosse, *Fallen Soldiers*, 84–92; see also Thomas W. Laqueur, *The Work of the Dead: A Cultural History of Mortal Remains* (Princeton, 2015), 447–88.
29. *Kriegsgräberfürsorge* 16/5 (1936), 71.
30. *Der Stahlhelm-Student* 3/1–2 (1931–2), 51.
31. BArch, R 129/963: Hans-Georg Moka to Studentenschaft der TH Dresden, 28 June 1932; R 129/962: Langemarck-Spende to Angehörige der deutschen Soldaten, n.d.; [Josef Magnus Wehner], *Langemarck: Ein Vermächtnis* (Munich, 1932), 10.
32. Hans Kollwitz (ed.), *The Diary and Letters of Kaethe* [*sic*] *Kollwitz*, trans. Richard and Clara Winston (Evanston, IL, 1988), 63.
33. Claudia Siebrecht, *The Aesthetics of Loss: German Women's Art of the First World War* (Oxford, 2013), 3; Regina Schulte, 'Käthe Kollwitz's Sacrifice', *History Workshop Journal* 41 (1996), 214.
34. PA AA, R 47827: Reichsminister von Keudell to Käthe Kollwitz, 6 July 1927.
35. *De Poperinghenaar*, 31 August 1930; see also Bruno De Wever, 'Diksmuide: de Ijzertoren. Strijd om de helden von de Oorlog', in Jo Tollebeek et al. (eds.), *België: Een parcours van herinnering*, ii. *Plaatsen van tweedracht, crisis en nostalgie* (Amsterdam, 2008), 60–71.
36. BArch, NS 38/2032: Programm der Langemarck-Fahrt der westlichen Hochschulen, 10–13 November 1932; *Berliner illustrierte Nachtausgabe*, 9 July 1932; see also Sophie de Schaepdrijver, 'Occupation, Propaganda and the Idea of Belgium', in Aviel Roshwald and Richard Stites (eds.), *European Culture in the Great War: The Arts, Entertainment, and Propaganda, 1914–1918* (Cambridge, 1999), 281–92.
37. Archives nationales, F21/7058/F: Belgique Steenstraet: Monument des combattants français et belges victimes de la première émission des gaz asphyxiants, 1928; see also Antoine Prost, *In the Wake of War: 'Les Anciens Combattants' and French Society*, trans. Helen McPhail (Providence, RI, 1992).
38. *Le Figaro*, 29 April 1929; *Le Matin*, 29 April 1929.
39. *Le Matin*, 11 November 1929.
40. See LAC, RG 25, vol. 1496: R. J. Ralston to O. D. Skelton, 18 April 1928, on the denominational issue.
41. *Daily Mirror*, 6 April 1931.
42. *The Scotsman*, 25 October 1929; *The Times*, 5 February 1931; see also Bert Heyvaert, '"A Little Sprig of the Empire": De Britse kolonie in Ieper tijdens het interbellum (1919–1940)', Licentiate diss., University of Leuven, 2002.

43. *Ypres Times* 4/2 (1928), 55.
44. *Ypres Times* 4/7 (1929), 212.
45. TNA, ED 121/30: H. J. R. Murray, Report on Condition of Education, 20 March 1929.
46. Archief van het Koninklijk Paleis / Archives du Palais royal, II A 2/29: De Chinese donation voor de reconstructie van Ieper, August 1919; *Het Ypersch Nieuws*, 30 March 1929.
47. *New York Times*, 16 July 1930; 1 February 1931.
48. *The Observer*, 5 August 1928; *The Scotsman*, 12 March 1932.
49. Edmund Blunden, *Undertones of War* (London, 1965), 306–10.
50. *Manchester Guardian*, 8 August 1939; *Irish Times*, 29 November 1923; *The Scotsman*, 27 February 1932.
51. TNA, BT 31/24723/156080: Company No. 156080: Ypres Garage Ltd, 1919–32; *Western Daily Press*, 13 November 1930; *Toronto Star*, 24 April 1936; *Nottingham Journal*, 8 August 1928.
52. *New York Times*, 21 November 1918.
53. *Derby Daily Telegraph*, 19 July 1923; 13 February 1939.
54. *L'Express du Touquet-Paris-Plage*, 13 July 1935.
55. *Würzburger General-Anzeiger*, 14 November 1928.
56. StdA Bonn, Pr 31/785a: Stadtverordneter Winckel to Oberbürgermeister Falk, 21 October 1931.
57. Hans Schwarz, *Die Wiedergeburt des heroischen Menschen: Eine Langemarck-Rede vor der Greifswalder Studentenschaft am 11. November 1928* (Berlin, 1930), 13–14, 26.
58. Oswald Bumke, *Langemarck: Drei Ansprachen* (Munich, 1929), 5; see also BayHStA, Abt. V, Plakatsammlung: Nr. 16034, 'Geist und Macht', 18 November 1928; Nr. 16079, 'Eine Krisis der Medizin', 13 December 1928.
59. *Vossische Zeitung*, 18 November 1928.
60. *Vorwärts*, 11 and 12 November 1929.
61. *Verhandlungen des Deutschen Reichstags: V. Wahlperiode 1930*, vol. 444. *Stenographische Berichte* (1931), 400 (10th session, 6 December 1930).
62. *Vossische Zeitung*, 16 March 1930; *Augsburger Post*, 18 March 1930; see also Wolfram Pyta, *Hindenburg: Herrschaft zwischen Hohenzollern und Hitler* (Munich, 2009), 545–53.
63. Adrian Gregory, *The Last Great War: British Society and the First World War* (Cambridge, 2008), 252, orig. emphasis; cf. Jay Winter, 'Commemorating War, 1914–1945', in Roger Chickering et al. (eds.), *The Cambridge History of War*, iv. *War and the Modern World* (Cambridge, 2012), 310–26.
64. Dendooven, *Menin Gate*, 113–27.
65. S[idney] N[ewman] Sedgwick, *At the Menin Gate: A Melodrama, and a Parable, Written for the League of Nations Union* (London, [1929]); see also Helen McCarthy, 'The League of Nations, Public Ritual and National Identity in Britain, *c.*1919–1956', *History Workshop Journal* 70 (2010), 108–32.

66. Universitätsarchiv Münster, Best. 4, Nr. 236, fo. 21: Stellv. Kurator to Minister für Wissenschaft, Kunst und Volksbildung, 30 July 1932; see also Frank Reichherzer, *'Alles ist Front!': Wehrwissenschaften in Deutschland und die Bellifizierung der Gesellschaft vom Ersten Weltkrieg bis in den Kalten Krieg* (Paderborn, 2012), 179–85.
67. Hüppauf, 'Langemarck'.
68. BArch, R 72/184: Stahlhelm-Studentenring 'Langemarck', 1928–31; *Der Stahlhelm-Student* 1/1 (1929–30), 1, and 1/5 (1929–30), 2–3.
69. BArch, R 72/172, fos. 35–61: Hans Martin Fritzsche, 'Unsere Ostpreussenstreife 1932', 22 May 1932; see also Goebel, *Great War*, 127–45.
70. Langemarck-Ausschuß (Hochschule und Heer) (ed.), *Langemarck-Gedanken* (Berlin, 1932), 3–4, emphasis added.
71. Löhr, 'Langemar(c)k', 402.
72. Reichsarchiv (ed.), *Der Weltkrieg 1914–1918: Die militärischen Operationen zu Lande* (Berlin, 1925–56), vi. *Der Herbst-Feldzug 1914: Der Abschluß der Operationen im Westen und Osten* (Berlin, 1929), 25; cf. v. *Der Herbst-Feldzug 1914: Im Westen bis zum Stellungskrieg. Im Osten bis zum Rückzug* (Berlin, 1929), 307.
73. *Divisions-Zeitung der ehemaligen 46. Reserve-Division* 3/16 (1926), 8; Ludwig Renn, 'Deutschland, Deutschland über alles', in Kurt Kläber (ed.), *Der Krieg: Das erste Volksbuch vom großen Krieg* (Berlin, 1929), 34–6.
74. George Soldan, *Der Mensch und die Schlacht der Zukunft* (Oldenburg, 1925), 33; see also Jeffrey Herf, *Reactionary Modernism: Technology, Culture, and Politics in Weimar and the Third Reich* (Cambridge, 1984).
75. Ernst Jünger, *Der Arbeiter: Herrschaft und Gestalt* (Hamburg, 1932), 104.
76. Hans Bastanier et al. (eds.), *Geschichte des Großherzoglich-Mecklenburgischen Reserve-Infanterie-Regiments Nr. 214: Unter Benutzung des amtlichen Materials des Reichsarchivs und von Tagebüchern auf Aufzeichnungen vieler Kameraden* (Dessau, 1933), 106–11.
77. BArch-MA, RH 61/726, fo. 41: Fritz Haber to Reichsarchiv, 12 June 1930; see also BArch, N 1022/33, fos. 185–6: Ernst Bauer to Fritz Haber, 20 March 1927.
78. Reichsarchiv (ed.), *Der Weltkrieg 1914–1918: Die militärischen Operationen zu Lande*, viii. *Die Operationen des Jahres 1915: Die Ereignisse im Westen im Frühjahr und Sommer, im Osten vom Frühjahr bis zum Jahresschluß* (Berlin, 1932).
79. TNA, CAB 45/162: Misrepresentation in French Official History of the War, 1933–5.
80. Tim Cook, *Clio's Warriors: Canadian Historians and the Writing of the World Wars* (Vancouver, 2006), 41–92.
81. [Basil] Liddell Hart, *A History of the World War 1914–1918* (London, 1934), 423, 434.
82. [George] Soldan, 'Einführung', in Werner Beumelburg, *Flandern 1917* (Schlachten des Weltkriegs 27; Oldenburg, 1928), 10.
83. Beumelburg, *Flandern*, 126, 135.
84. Beumelburg, *Flandern*, 115, 167.

85. Wener Beumelburg, *Von 1914 bis 1939: Sinn und Erfüllung des Weltkrieges* (Leipzig, 1939), 8; see also Gerd Krumeich, 'Zwischen soldatischem Nationalismus und NS-Ideologie: Werner Beumelburg und die Erzählung des Ersten Weltkriegs', in Wolfram Pyta and Carsten Kretschmann (eds.), *Burgfrieden und Union sacrée: Literarische Deutungen und politische Ordnungsvorstellungen in Deutschland und Frankreich 1914–1933* (Munich, 2011), 295–312.
86. Lothar Gruchmann and Reinhard Weber (eds.), *Der Hitler-Prozess 1924: Wortlaut der Hauptverhandlung vor dem Volksgericht München I*, iv. *19.–25. Verhandlungstag* (Munich, 1999), 1580.
87. Adolf Hitler, *Mein Kampf: Eine kritische Edition*, ed. Christian Hartmann et al. (3rd edn., Munich, 2016), i. 461–2, 547–8; Hitler, *Mein Kampf*, trans. Ralph Manheim (London, 1972).
88. Thomas Weber, *Hitler's First World War: Adolf Hitler, the Men of the List Regiment, and the First World War* (Oxford, 2010), 221, 274.
89. BArch, R 129/1045: Langemarck-Spende to Einzelstudentenschaften, 1 November 1933.
90. Karl August Walther (ed.), *Das Langemarckbuch der deutschen Studentenschaft* (Leipzig, 1933), 8, 211.
91. StdA Hannover, HR 20 Nr. 418: Christliche Pfadfinderschaft to Arbeitsausschuß für die Jugendpflege, 7 March 1934.
92. Arndt Weinrich, *Der Weltkrieg als Erzieher: Jugend zwischen Weimarer Republik und Nationalsozialismus* (Essen, 2013), 267–312; Markus Köster, '"Eine Burg des Glaubens": Ideologie, Architektur und Praxis nationalsozialistischer Jugendbauten am Beispiel der westfälischen HJ-Führerschule Haldem', in Edeltraut Klueting (ed.), *Denkmalpflege und Architektur in Westfalen 1933–1945* (Münster, 1995), 100.
93. Günter Kaufmann (ed.), *Langemarck: Das Opfer der Jugend an allen Fronten* (Stuttgart, 1938), 14, 151–5.
94. BArch, NS 38/2257: Rudolf Heß to G.A. Scheel, 1 February 1937; NS 18/693, fo. 5: [Walter] Tießler to Gaupropagandaleitung Frankfurt, 8 November 1941; see also Weinrich, *Weltkrieg als Erzieher*, 281–9.
95. BArch, R 8034-II/5768: *Nationalsozialistische Landpost*, 7 August 1936.
96. StdA Hannover, HR 13 Nr. 727: Leiter des Arbeitsausschusses to Ehrenausschuß der Langemarck-Gedenkstätte, 5 August 1939; BArch, R 43-II/562b, fo. 60: Chef der Reichskanzlei to Reichsminister des Innern, 14 June 1939.
97. BArch, R 58/900, fos. 143–4: Wilhelm Dreysse to Geheimestaatspolizei-Amt [*sic*] Berlin, 23 October 1934; Wilhelm Dreysse, *Langemarck 1914: Der heldische Opfergang der Deutschen Jugend. Mit einer Kunstbeilage nach einem Aquarell von Adolf Hitler* (Minden, [1934]).
98. BayHStA, Abt. V, Presseausschnittsammlung Nr. 2778: *NSK*, 22 October 1935; *Münchner Zeitung*, 27–8 October 1934.
99. BArch, R 58/900, fo. 200: Reichsstelle zur Förderung des deutschen Schrifttums, Gutachten für Verleger, 21 April 1936.

100. BArch, R 58/900, fos. 235–7: Geheimes Staatspolizeiamt Berlin to Reichsminister für Volksaufklärung und Propaganda, 4 November 1939; fo. 241: Reichssicherheitshauptamt to Stapostelle Bielefeld, 5 February 1940.
101. See Harry Schumann, *Geist von Langemarck: Das Erlebnis von 1914* (Dresden, 1934); *Das Schwarze Korps*, 2 January 1936.
102. StdA Freiburg, C4/XII/29/05: Wilhelm Kotzde-Kottenrodt, Gutachten, 15 June 1934.
103. BArch, NS 38/4146: Gaustudentenführung Westfalen-Nord to Reichsstudentenführung, 26 October 1937; see also Marcus Weidner, '"Wir beantragen...unverzüglich umzubenennen": Die Straßenbenennungspraxis in Westfalen und Lippe im Nationalsozialismus', in Matthias Frese (ed.), *Fragwürdige Ehrungen!? Straßennamen als Instrument von Geschichtspolitik und Erinnerungskultur* (Münster, 2012), 41–98.
104. StdA Bonn, Ok 11: Sitzungsniederschrift, 10 December 1937.
105. *Bremer Zeitung*, 12 November 1937.
106. BArch, NS 38/3819: Oberbürgermeister Jena to Reichsstudentenführer, 11 November 1937; NS 38/4146: Studentenführung der Rheinischen Ingenieursschule to Reichsstudentenführung, 30 October 1937.
107. Evelyn Waugh, *Put Out More Flags* (London, 1943), 25.
108. See *Adreßbuch der Stadt Gelsenkirchen 1939: Zusammengestellt nach amtlichen Unterlagen* (Bochum, 1939), 247.
109. *Görlitzer Zeitung*, 20 December 1939.
110. BArch, R 4901/13898: Reichsminister to [Ulrich] Gmelin, 9 January 1940.
111. *Die Bewegung* 11/15 (November 1943), 7.
112. W. Waidelich, *10 Jahre Langemarck-Studium Königsberg (Pr.): Kriegsrundbrief des Langemarck-Studiums Königsberg (Pr) aus Anlaß seines 10jährigen Bestehens* (Königsberg, 1944).
113. *Der Altherrenbund* 3/7–8 (1941), 1.
114. *Die Bewegung* 11/9 (May 1943), 6.
115. Rijksstudentenverbond (ed.), *Het Langemarck-Studium in Vlaanderen* (Brussels, [1941]), 5.
116. *The Times*, 9 March 1940.
117. *Gazet van Poperinghe*, 17 September 1939.
118. *New York Times*, 2 June 1940.
119. *The Times*, 12 November 1940.
120. Joseph Goebbels, *Die Tagebücher von Joseph Goebbels*, ed. Elke Fröhlich, pt. I: *Aufzeichnungen 1923–1941*, viii. *April–November 1940* (Munich, 1998), 143, emphasis added.
121. Oberkommando der Wehrmacht (ed.), *Sieg über Frankreich: Berichte und Bilder* (Berlin, 1940), 87.
122. Heinrich Hoffmann (ed.), *Mit Hitler im Westen* (Berlin, 1940).
123. Dendooven, *Menin Gate*, 90.

124. *Nachrichtenblatt des Traditionsverbandes des ehem. Reserve-Infanterie-Regiments Nr. 236 (Langemarck-Regiment)* 12/25 (1940), 5–6.
125. *Feldzeitung der Armee an Schelde, Somme und Seine*, 21 December 1940; see also Baird, *To Die for Germany*, 11–12.
126. Dan Todman, *The Great War: Myth and Memory* (London, 2005), 189.
127. Mark Connelly, *We Can Take It! Britain and the Memory of the Second World War* (Harlow, 2004), 147–8.
128. Stefan Goebel, 'Commemorative Cosmopolis: Transnational Networks of Remembrance in Post-War Coventry', in Goebel and Derek Keene (eds.), *Cities into Battlefields: Metropolitan Scenarios, Experiences and Commemorations of Total War* (Farnham, 2011), 163–83.
129. *Daily Express*, 29 December 1943.
130. BArch-MA, RH 61/1276: Wilhelm Dieckmann, 'Der Heldenkampf der deutschen Jugend bei Langemarck', [December 1941].
131. See the memory corpus compiled by Walter Kempowski, *Das Echolot: Ein kollektives Tagebuch. Januar und Februar 1943*, ii. *18. bis 31. Januar 1943* (4th edn., Munich, 1993), 508.
132. BArch-MA, RS 3-27/1, fo. 10: Freiwilligen-Legion Flandern: Kriegstagebuch Nr. 1, November 1941; Bruno De Wever, '"Rebellen" an der Ostfront: Die flämischen Freiwilligen der Legion "Flandern" und der Waffen-SS', *Vierteljahreshefte für Zeitgeschichte* 39 (1991), 589–610.
133. The term is borrowed from Robert G. Moeller, *War Stories: The Search for a Usable Past in the Federal Republic of Germany* (Berkeley and Los Angeles, 2001).

Chapter 6

1. *Toronto Star*, 9 September 1944.
2. Stad Ieper (ed.), *50 jaar Toerisme Ieper: Catalogus tentoonstelling 26 oktober tot 9 november 2008* (Ypres, 2008).
3. *The Scotsman*, 11 September 1944.
4. Paul Gough, 'Sites in the Imagination: The Beaumont Hamel Newfoundland Memorial on the Somme', *Cultural Geographies* 11 (2004), 247.
5. See Bill Schwarz, *Memories of Empire*, i. *The White Man's World* (Oxford, 2011).
6. PA AA, B 10/2235: Trützscher to Botschaft Brüssel, 3 March 1952.
7. VDK, A. 100–899: Endgültige Lösung des Problems der deutschen Soldatengräber 1914/18 in Belgien, 8 December 1956; see also Freytag and Van Driessche, 'Die Deutschen Soldatenfriedhöfe', 189–91.
8. See Jörg Echternkamp, *Soldaten im Nachkrieg. Historische Deutungskonflikte und westdeutsche Demokratisierung 1945–1955* (Munich, 2014), 196.
9. Rudy Koshar, *From Monuments to Traces: Artifacts of German Memory, 1870–1990* (Berkeley and Los Angeles, 2000).

10. VDK, A. 100–899: 'Deutsche Soldatengräber des Ersten Weltkrieges in Flandern', n.d., 3.
11. PA AA, B 92/52: Generalsekretär Markgraf to Auswärtiges Amt, 22 June 1955.
12. PA AA, B 92/52: Otto Kösler to Auswärtiges Amt, 8 August 1955.
13. PA AA, B 92/289: Bundesgeschaftsführer von Hausen to Auswärtiges Amt, 5 December 1961.
14. Michael Geyer, 'The Place of the Second World War in German Memory and History', *New German Critique* 71 (1997), 19.
15. Hannelore Fischer (ed.), *Käthe Kollwitz: Die Trauernden Eltern. Ein Mahnmal für den Frieden* (Cologne, 1999), 157–8.
16. Fischer (ed.), *Käthe Kollwitz*, 156–7.
17. *TLS*, 12 February 1949; see also Andrew Green, *Writing the Great War: Sir James Edmonds and the Official Histories 1915–1948* (London, 2003).
18. Reichsarchiv/Kriegsgeschichtliche Forschungsanstalt des Heeres (ed.), *Der Weltkrieg 1914–1918: Die militärischen Operationen zu Lande* (Berlin, 1925–56), xiii. *Die Kriegführung im Sommer und Herbst 1917. Die Ereignisse außerhalb der Westfront bis November 1918* (Berlin, 1942; repr. Koblenz, 1956), 97–9.
19. Reichsarchiv/Kriegsgeschichtliche Forschungsanstalt des Heeres (ed.), *Der Weltkrieg 1914–1918: Die militärischen Operationen zu Lande*, xiv. *Die Kriegführung an der Westfront im Jahre 1918* (Berlin, 1944; repr. Koblenz, 1956).
20. *The Spectator*, 4 October–27 November 1957, 3 January 1958.
21. Leon Wolff, *In Flanders Fields: The 1917 Campaign* (1958; London, 1960), 208.
22. *TLS*, 27 February 1959.
23. *The Economist*, 21 March 1959; *Daily Mail*, 7 March 1959.
24. Alan Clark, *The Donkeys* (London, 1961), 11.
25. A. J. P. Taylor, *The First World War: An Illustrated History* (London, 1963), 194.
26. John Swettenham, *To Seize Victory: The Canadian Corps in World War I* (Toronto, 1965), 189.
27. *Coventry Evening Telegraph*, 16 November 1957.
28. Alistair Thomson, *Anzac Memories: Living with the Legend* (Melbourne, 1994).
29. VDK, A. 100–899: Friedrich Gerischer, Langemarck in zeitgenössicher und heutiger Sicht [*c.*1966].
30. *Flandern nach 50 Jahren: Erinnerungsfahrt. 'Grünes Korps' Langemarck 1914/1964* (Düsseldorf, 1964).
31. *Het Ypersche Nieuws*, 14 November 1964.
32. Stadsarchief Ieper, TOE/55 (336): Toeristische dienst to BRT, 20 April 1964.
33. *New York Times*, 13 November 1972.
34. In Flanders Fields Museum, Documentatiecentrum, MI 2123: 'War Requiem: St.-Maartenskathedraal Ieper', souvenir programme, 4 November 1967.
35. *Westfälische Rundschau*, 12 November 1968; *Westfälische Nachrichten*, 13 November 1968.
36. Archivamt für Westfalen, Best. 115/562: Übertragung: Paschendale 1917, [1968].

37. Sophie De Schaepdrijver, *Gabrielle Petit: The Death and Life of a Female Spy in the First World War* (London, 2015), 188; Matthias Steinle, 'La Grande Guerre dans la série télévisée *Trente ans d'histoire* (1964): Un projet de réconciliation franco-allemand au sein d'une commémoration gaulliste', in Christian Delporte et al. (eds.), *La Guerre après la guerre: Images et construction des imaginaires de guerre dans l'Europe du XX*[ème] *siècle* (Paris, 2010), 343–65.
38. BBC Written Archives Centre, T/32/1145/1: Michael Peacock to Tony Essex, 21 September 1964.
39. *The Times*, 19 and 21 September, and 5 October 1964; see also Emma Hanna, *The Great War on the Small Screen: Representing the First World War in Contemporary Britain* (Edinburgh, 2009).
40. *Het Wekelijks Nieuws*, 9 August 1974, 17 November 1978, 29 June 1984.
41. Lyn Macdonald, *They Called it Passchendaele: The Story of the Third Battle of Ypres and of the Men Who Fought in It* (London, 1978).
42. John Terraine, *The Road to Passchendaele: The Flanders Offensive of 1917. A Study in Inevitability* (London, 1977).
43. Jay Winter and Antoine Prost, *The Great War in History: Debates and Controversies, 1914 to the Present* (Cambridge, 2005), 47.
44. Helmut Kopetzky, *In den Tod—Hurra! Deutsche Jugend-Regimenter im Ersten Weltkrieg: Ein historischer Tatsachenbericht über Langemarck* (Cologne, 1981).
45. Karl Unruh, *Langemarck: Legende und Wirklichkeit* (Koblenz, 1986); cf. Roland Barthes, *Mythologies*, trans. Annette Lavers and Richard Howard (New York, 2012).
46. *Die Welt*, 18 November 1986; *Studentenkurier* 3 (1987), 19–22.
47. See e.g. Bernd Hüppauf, 'Langemarck-Mythos', in Gerhard Hirschfeld et al. (eds.), *Enzyklopädie Erster Weltkrieg* (2nd edn., Paderborn, 2004), 671–2.
48. Rana Mitter, 'War and Memory since 1945', in Roger Chickering et al. (eds.), *The Cambridge History of War*, iv. *War and the Modern World* (Cambridge, 2012), 557.
49. *La Voix du Nord*, 27 June 1961.
50. *Le Figaro*, 26 June 1961.
51. De Wever, 'Diksmuide'; see also Pieter Lagrou, *The Legacy of Nazi Occupation: Patriotic Memory and Nazi Recovery in Western Europe, 1945–1965* (Cambridge, 2000), 298–300.
52. *Het Wekelijks Nieuws*, 23 August 1952.
53. Richard Bessel and Dirk Schumann, 'Introduction: Violence, Normality, and the Construction of Postwar Europe', in Bessel and Schumann (eds.), *Life after Death: Approaches to a Cultural and Social History of Europe during the 1940s and 1950s* (Cambridge, 2003), 2.
54. See *Eckartbote* 6 (1973), 5.
55. *Kriegsgräberfürsorge* 56/4 (1980), 8.
56. BArch-MA, BW 2/27970, Fü S I 4: Langemarcktafeln im Olympiaglockenturm in Berlin, 28 September 1979; see also Donald Abenheim, *Reforging the Iron Cross: The Search for Tradition in the West German Armed Forces* (Princeton, 1988).

57. *Der Spiegel*, 23 January 1989, 68; 5 April 1993, 62.
58. Rainer Rother (ed.), *Geschichtsort Olympiagelände 1909–1936–2006* (Berlin, 2006).
59. Tom Burke, *The 16th (Irish) and 36th (Ulster) Divisions at the Battle of Wijtschate-Messines Ridge, 7 June 1917: A Battlefield Tour Guide* (Dublin, 2007).
60. See Aribert Reimann, *Der große Krieg der Sprachen: Untersuchungen zur historischen Semantik in Deutschland und England zur Zeit des Ersten Weltkriegs* (Essen, 2000), 186–9; Mark Connelly, *Steady the Buffs! A Regiment, a Region, and the Great War* (Oxford, 2006), 50–1.
61. Dominiek Dendooven, 'Asia in Flanders Fields: A Transnational History of Indians and Chinese on the Western Front, 1914–1920', PhD thesis, Universities of Antwerp and Kent, 2018.
62. Stanley Rice, *Neuve Chapelle: India's Memorial in France, 1914–1918* (London, 1927).
63. Meire, *De stilte*, 351–71.
64. Stadsarchief Ieper, GR 16/16: Verslag van de zitting van de gemeenteraad, 25 May 1951; *Het Ypersch Nieuws*, 13 June 1936.
65. *New York Tribune*, 8 June 1919.
66. Delphine Lauwers, 'Le Saillant d'Ypres entre reconstruction et construction d'un lieu de mémoire: Un long precessus de négociations mémoirelles, de 1914 à nos jours', PhD thesis, European University Institute, 2014, 451.
67. Bruce Scates, *Return to Gallipoli: Walking the Battlefields of the Great War* (Cambridge, 2006), 207.
68. *The Times*, 11 November 1977.
69. Rose E. B. Coombs, *Before Endeavours Fade: A Guide to the Battlefields of the First World War* (13th edn., Old Harlow, 2010).
70. Paul Reed, *Walking the Salient: A Walkers [sic] Guide to the Ypres Salient* (Battleground Europe; Barnsley, 1999).
71. See e.g. *Toronto Star*, 8 April 1995, 5 April 2014; *The Times*, 12 November 1988, 8 November 1997, 11 November 2000.
72. *Het Wekelijks Nieuws*, 10 November 1972.
73. Saunders, *Killing Time*, 184.
74. Susanne Brandt, 'Das "In Flanders Fields Museum" in Ypern', *Geschichte in Wissenschaft und Unterricht* 67 (2016), 471–6; Dominiek Dendooven, 'The Journey Back: On the Nature of Donations to the "In Flanders Fields Museum"', in Nicholas J. Saunders and Paul Cornish (eds.), *Contested Objects: Material Memories of the Great War* (London, 2009), 60–72.
75. *In Flanders Fields Museum Jaarboek* (2013), 114–17.
76. Office du Tourisme de Comines-Warneton, *14–18 Remembrance* (Comines, [2014]).
77. Frank Bostyn et al., *Passchendaele 1917: The Story of the Fallen and Tyne Cot Cemetery* (Barnsley, 2007), 317–20.

78. Cited in John Peter Edwards, 'A War Remembered: Commemoration, Battlefield Tourism and British Collective Memory of the Great War', DPhil thesis, University of Sussex, 2005, 224.
79. *The Times*, 31 October 2003.
80. Jennifer Iles, 'Recalling the Ghosts of War: Performing Tourism on the Battlefields of the Western Front', *Text and Performance Quarterly* 26 (2006), 162–80.
81. Compare the trends outlined in Wiebke Kolbe, 'Trauer und Tourismus: Reisen des Volksbundes Deutsche Kriegsgräberfürsorge 1950–2010', *Zeithistorische Forschungen* 14 (2017), 68–92.
82. PA AA, B 92/530: Dr Fischbacher to Auswärtiges Amt, 29 August 1972; BArch-MA, MSg 2/2860: 'Blutgetränkter Hügel zu verkaufen', unspecified newspaper cutting, [1972].
83. Antoine Prost, 'Verdun', in Pierre Nora (ed.), *Realms of Memory: The Construction of the French Past*, iii. *Symbols*, trans. Arthur Goldhammer (New York, 1998), 393.
84. See Zuckmayer, *Part of Myself*, 157.
85. Kopetzky, *In den Tod*, 13–14.
86. *Frankfurter Allgemeine Zeitung*, 17 November 2001.
87. See Horst Howe et al., *De Duitse begraafplaats in Langemark* (Bruges, 2011), 83.
88. *Westfälische Nachrichten*, 27 May 2014.
89. 'Dire Heroes: Beyond Ypres' <https://boardgamegeek.com/blogger/715> [accessed 29 November 2016].
90. Dominiek Dendooven, personal communication to the authors, 9 January and 12 July 2017.
91. *The Times*, 16 July 2009.
92. *Toronto Star*, 15, 17, 20, and 22 October, 11 and 14 November 2008; 3 February and 3 March 2009.
93. Todman, *Great War*, 141, 221.
94. See Jay Winter, *Remembering War: The Great War between Memory and History in the Twentieth Century* (New Haven, 2006), 44.

Chapter 7

1. *Fritz Times*, 12 February 2016, distributed together with *Die Welt*, 12 February 2016.
2. *Daily Telegraph*, 12 February 2016.
3. *Nottingham Evening Post*, 22 March 1916; *Tatler and Bystander*, 11 July 1917.
4. *Saturday Review*, 8 December 1917.
5. *TLS*, 29 November 1917.
6. *TLS*, 31 July 1930.
7. *Wipers Times*, 12 February 1916.
8. *The Observer*, 3 August 1930.
9. *TLS*, 29 November 1917; *Saturday Review*, 8 December 1917.

10. F. J. Roberts (ed.), *The Wipers Times: Including for the First Time in One Volume a Facsimile Reproduction of the Complete Series of the Famous Wartime Trench Magazine*, foreword Lord Plumer (London, 1930).
11. Fussell, *Great War*, 35. On humour, see Peter Burke et al., 'Forum: Humour', *German History* 33 (2015), 609–23.
12. *The Economist*, 7 July 1973.
13. *Tatler and Bystander*, 12 December 1917.
14. See Siegfried J. Schmidt, 'Medien, Kultur: Medienkultur. Ein konstruktivistisches Gesprächsangebot', in Schmidt (ed.), *Kognition und Gesellschaft: Der Diskurs des Radikalen Konstruktivismus*, ii (Frankfurt am Main, 1992), 425–50.
15. *The Times*, 2 December 1939.
16. Patrick Beaver [ed.], *The Wipers Times: A Complete Facsimile of the Famous World War One Trench Newspaper, Incorporating the 'New Church' Times, the Kemmel Times, the Somme Times, the B.E.F. Times, and the 'Better Times'* (London, 1973; repr. 1988).
17. *Broadcast*, 12 September 2013.
18. *The Times*, 9 November 2007.
19. On the notion of memory 'taboos', see Dietmar Süss, *Death from the Skies: How the British and Germans Survived Bombing in World War II*, trans. Lesley Sharpe and Jeremy Noakes (Oxford, 2014), 518–22.
20. On its use in school teaching, see Mary Brown and Carolyn Massey, 'Teaching "the Lessons of Satire": Using *The Wipers Times* to Build an Enquiry on the First World War', *Teaching History* 155 (2014), 20–8.
21. A useful introduction to the established field, see Martin Conboy and John Steel (eds.), *The Routledge Companion to British Media History* (London, 2015). For new theoretical advances, see Stefan Haas, 'Die kommunikationstheoretische Wende und die Geschichtswissenschaft', in Andreas Schulz and Andreas Wirsching (eds.), *Parlamentarische Kulturen in Europa: Das Parlament als Kommunikationsraum* (Düsseldorf, 2012), 29–43.
22. Ernst Jünger, *Kriegstagebuch 1914–1918*, ed. Helmuth Kiesel (Stuttgart, 2010), 303; *In Stahlgewittern: Historisch-kritische Ausgabe*, ed. Helmuth Kiesel, i (Stuttgart, 2013), 360, 394.
23. Nikolaus Buschmann and Aribert Reimann, 'Die Konstruktion historischer Erfahrung: Neue Wege zu einer Erfahrungsgeschichte des Krieges', in Nikolaus Buschmann and Horst Carl (eds.), *Die Erfahrung des Krieges: Erfahrungsgeschichtliche Perspektiven von der Französischen Revolution bis zum Zweiten Weltkrieg* (Paderborn, 2001), 261–71.
24. Robert Gerwarth and John Horne (eds.), *War in Peace: Paramilitary Violence in Europe after the Great War* (Oxford, 2013), p. i; Robert Gerwarth and Erez Manela (eds.), *Empires at War 1911–1923* (Oxford, 2014).
25. Steven Sabol, 'A Brief Note from the Editor', *First World War Studies* 1 (2010), 1–2.

BIBLIOGRAPHY

Archival Sources

Australia

National Archives of Australia, Canberra
A461, K370/1/15
A2909, AGS6/1/48 pt. 2
A6006, 1921/3/15
A11804, 1922/169

Belgium

Archief van het Koninklijk Paleis / Archives du Palais royal, Brussels
II A 2/29
Stadsarchief Ieper
GR 16/16
TOE/55
In Flanders Fields Museum, Documentatiecentrum, Ieper
MI 2123

Britain

The National Archives (TNA), Kew
BT 31/24723/156080
BT 58/847
CAB 23/37/44
CAB 24/106/45
CAB 45/162
ED 121/30
WO 32/5126
WO 32/5569
WO 32/5853
WO 32/5876
WO 32/5879
WO 32/5892
WO 32/5890

Royal Archives, Windsor
PS/PSO/GU/PS/SV/056080
Commonwealth War Graves Commission Archives (CWGC), Maidenhead
03/1348129
Add 1/1/20
SDC 56
WG 360/4
WG 812/3
WG 1308
BBC Written Archives Centre, Caversham
T/32/1145/1

Canada

Library and Archives Canada (LAC), Ottawa
RG 25, vol. 330
RG 25, vol. 336
RG 25, vol. 1496
RG 25, vol. 1549
RG 38, vol. 419

France

Archives nationales, Paris
F21/7058/F
Service historique de la Défense, Paris
2M23

Germany

Bundesarchiv (BArch), Koblenz
N 1022/33
Bundesarchiv (BArch), Berlin
NS 18/693
NS 38/2032
NS 38/2257
NS 38/3819
NS 38/4146
R 43-II/562b
R 58/900
R 72/172
R 72/184
R 129/68
R 129/962
R 129/963

R 129/1045
R 4901/13898
R 8034-II/5768
R 8034-II/7590
R 8034-II/7599
R 8034-II/7600
R 8034-II/7601
R 8034-II/7605
R 8034-II/7609
R 8034-II/7614
R 8034-II/8864
Bundesarchiv–Stiftung Archiv der Parteien und Massenorganisationen der DDR (BArch-SAPMO), Berlin
NY 4402/2
Bundesarchiv–Militärarchiv (BArch-MA), Freiburg
BW 2/27970
MSg 2/2860
RH 61/726
RH 61/1276
RS 3-27/1
Politisches Archiv des Auswärtigen Amts (PA AA), Berlin
B 10/2235
B 92/52
B 92/289
B 92/530
R 47824
R 47826
R 47827
R 47828
R 47829
R 47830
R 47834
R 47852
R 96018
Bayerisches Hauptstaatsarchiv (BayHStA), Munich
Abt. V, Plakatsammlung
Abt. V, Presseausschnittsammlung
Hauptstaatsarchiv Stuttgart (HStAS)
J 150/119 Nr. 7
M 1/11 Bü 165
Stadtarchiv Bonn
Ok 11
Pr 31/785a

Stadtarchiv Freiburg
C4/XII/29/05
Stadtarchiv Hannover
HR 13 Nr. 727
HR 20 Nr. 418
Archivamt für Westfalen, Landschaftsverband Westfalen-Lippe, Münster
Best. 115/562
Medienzentrum für Westfalen, Landschaftsverband Westfalen Lippe, Münster
Bildarchiv, Begleitheft MZA 534
Universitätsarchiv Münster
Best. 4, Nr. 236
Volksbund Deutsche Kriegsgräberfürsorge Archiv (VDK), Kassel
A. 100–899

Published primary sources

Newspapers and Periodicals

Aberdeen Journal
Der Altherrenbund
Augsburger Post
L'Aurore
Barrier Miner
Beilage zur Kriegszeitung der 4. Armee
Berliner illustrierte Nachtausgabe
Berliner Lokal-Anzeiger
Berliner Tageblatt
Berwickshire News and General Advertiser
Die Bewegung
Bremer Zeitung
Broadcast
B.Z. am Mittag
Cape Times
Church Times
Colour Magazine
Courier Journal
Coventry Evening Telegraph
La Croix
Daily Express
Daily Graphic
Daily Mail
Daily Mirror
Daily News [Perth, WA]

Daily Telegraph
Derby Daily Telegraph
Derby Mercury
Deutsche Allgemeine Zeitung
Deutsche Tageszeitung
Deutsche Zeitung
Divisions-Zeitung der ehemaligen 46. Reserve-Division
Donegal News
Dundee Courier
Dundee Evening Telegraph
Eckartbote
The Economist
Evening Standard
Exeter and Plymouth Gazette
L'Express du Touquet-Paris-Plage
Farmer and Settler
Feldzeitung der Armee an Schelde, Somme und Seine
Le Figaro
Frankfurter Allgemeine Zeitung
Frankfurter Zeitung
Freeman's Journal
Fritz Times
Gazet van Poperinghe
Gloucester Journal
Görlitzer Zeitung
Hartlepool Mail
Hochland
Hull Daily Mail
Illustrated London News
In Flanders Fields Museum Jaarboek
Irish Examiner
Irish Independent
Irish Times
Journal des débats politiques et litteraires
La Justice
Kölnische Volkszeitung
Kölnische Zeitung
Kreuz-Zeitung/Neue Preußische Zeitung
Der Krieg 1914/15 in Wort und Bild
Kriegsgräberfürsorge
Die leichte Artillerie
Lloyd's Weekly Newspaper
Los Angeles Times

Manchester Courier
Manchester Guardian
Manitoba Free Press
Le Matin
Mercure de France
Midlands Advertiser
Mitteilungen des Referates Wiederaufbau der zerstörten Gebiete Belgiens und Nordfrankreichs
Le Monde illustré
Morning Post
Münchner Zeitung
Münsterländische Volkszeitung [Rheine]
Nachrichtenblatt des Traditionsverbandes des ehem. Reserve-Infanterie-Regiments Nr. 236 (Langemarck-Regiment)
Nationalsozialistische Landpost
Newcastle Journal
New York Times
New York Tribune
New Zealand Herald
Nottingham Evening Post
Nottingham Journal
La Nouvelle Revue
The Observer
Ottawa Evening Citizen
De Poperinghenaar
Rheinisch-Westfälische Zeitung
La Revue du Touring-club de France
Saturday Review
Schwäbischer Merkur
Das Schwarze Korps
Scotsman
Skibbereen Eagle
The Spectator
Der Spiegel
Der Stahlhelm-Student
Studentenkurier
Sunday Times
Sydney Morning Herald
Der Tag
Tatler and Bystander
Le Temps
The Times
Times Literary Supplement (TLS)
Toronto [Daily] Star

Townsville Daily Bulletin
Velhagen & Klasings Monatshefte
Verhandlungen des Deutschen Reichstags
La Voix du Nord
Vorwärts
Vossische Zeitung
War Illustrated
Het Wekelijks Nieuws
Die Welt
Western Daily Press
Western Times
Westfälische Nachrichten
Westfälische Rundschau
Westmeath Examiner
Wipers Times
Die Woche
Würzburger General-Anzeiger
Het Ypersche Nieuws
Ypres Times

Books

Adreßbuch der Stadt Gelsenkirchen 1939: Zusammengestellt nach amtlichen Unterlagen (Bochum, 1939).

Baedeker, K[arl], *Belgium and Holland: Handbook for Travellers* (4th edn., London, 1875).

Baedeker, Karl, *Belgium and Holland Including the Grand-Duchy of Luxembourg: Handbook for Travellers* (11th edn., London, 1894).

Baedeker, K[arl], *Belgique et Hollande y compris le Luxembourg: Manuel du voyageur* (17th edn., Leipzig, 1901).

Baedeker, Karl, *Belgien und Holland nebst dem Großherzogtum Luxemburg: Handbuch für Reisende* (25th edn., Leipzig, 1914).

Baedeker, Karl, *Belgien und Luxemburg: Handbuch für Reisende* (26th edn., Leipzig, 1930).

Baedeker, Karl, *Belgium and Luxemburg* [sic]: *Handbook for Travellers* (16th edn., Leipzig, 1931).

Bairnsfather, Bruce, *Bullets & Billets* (London, 1916).

Bastanier, Hans et al. (eds.), *Geschichte des Großherzoglich-Mecklenburgischen Reserve-Infanterie-Regiments Nr. 214: Unter Benutzung des amtlichen Materials des Reichsarchivs und von Tagebüchern auf Aufzeichnungen vieler Kameraden* (Dessau, 1933).

Baudrillart, Alfred, *La Guerre allemande et la catholicisme* (Paris, 1915).

Beaver, Patrick [ed.], *The Wipers Times: A Complete Facsimile of the Famous World War One Trench Newspaper, Incorporating the 'New Church' Times, the Kemmel Times, the Somme Times, the B.E.F. Times, and the 'Better Times'* (London, 1973; repr. 1988).

Beckles Willson, Henry, *In the Ypres Salient: The Story of a Fortnight's Canadian Fighting, June 2–16, 1916* (London, 1916).

Beckles Willson, Henry, *Ypres: The Holy Ground of British Arms* (Bruges, 1920).

Beckmann, Max, *Briefe im Kriege*, ed. Minna Tube (Munich, 1984).

Beumelburg, Werner, *Ypern 1914* (Schlachten des Weltkrieges 10; Oldenburg, 1925).

Beumelburg, Werner, *Flandern 1917* (Schlachten des Weltkrieges 27; Oldenburg, 1928).

Beumelburg, Werner, *Von 1914 bis 1939: Sinn und Erfüllung des Weltkrieges* (Leipzig, 1939).

Binding, Rudolf G., *Deutsche Jugend vor den Toten des Krieges* (Frankfurt am Main, 1933).

Binyon, Laurence, and Strang, William, *Western Flanders: A Medley of Things Seen, Considered and Imagined* (London, 1899).

Bird, Will R., *Thirteen Years After: The Story of the Old Front Revisited* (Toronto, 1932).

Blunden, Edmund, *Undertones of War* (London, 1965).

Buchan, John, *Nelson's History of the War*, 4 vols. (London, 1921–2).

Buckinx, R., *Ypres et ses environs: Petit guide du touriste / Ypres and Its Surroundings: A Little Guide for the Tourist* (Ypres, n.d.).

Buckinx, R., *Ypern und die deutschen Kriegerfriedhöfe: Führer mit Karte*, trans. V. de Byser (Langemarck, [c.1931]).

Bumke, Oswald, *Langemarck: Drei Ansprachen* (Munich, 1929).

Bumpus, T. Francis, *The Cathedrals and Churches of Belgium* (London, 1909).

Burke, Tom, *The 16th (Irish) and 36th (Ulster) Divisions at the Battle of Wijtschate-Messines Ridge, 7 June 1917: A Battlefield Tour Guide* (Dublin, 2007).

Canadian Battlefield Memorials Commission, *Canadian Battlefield Memorials* (Ottawa, 1929).

Canadian War Records Office, *Canada in Khaki: A Tribute to the Officers and Men Now Serving in the Canadian Expeditionary Force* (London, 1917).

Canadian War Records Office, *Art & War: Canadian War Memorials*, introd. P. G. Konody (London, [1919]).

Clark, Alan, *The Donkeys* (London, 1961).

Coleman, Frederic, *From Mons to Ypres with French: A Personal Narrative* (London, 1916).

Cook's Tourists' Handbook for Belgium, Including the Ardennes: With Map and Plan (London, 1896).

Coombs, Rose E. B., *Before Endeavours Fade: A Guide to the Battlefields of the First World War* (13th edn., Old Harlow, 2010).

The Cyclists' Continental Companion: A Road Book of Belgium, Germany, France, Holland, Switzerland, Italy (London, 1899).

Dreysse, Wilhelm, *Langemarck 1914: Der heldische Opfergang der Deutschen Jugend. Mit einer Kunstbeilage nach einem Aquarell von Adolf Hitler* (Minden, [1934]).

Edmonds, J[ames] E. et al., *Military Operations: France and Belgium*, 14 vols. (History of the Great War; London, 1922–49).

Edwards, George Wharton, *Some Old Flemish Towns* (London, 1913).

Edwards, George Wharton, *Vanished Towers and Chimes of Flanders* (Philadelphia, 1916).

Falkenhayn, Erich von, *Die Oberste Heeresleitung 1914–1916 in ihren wichtigsten Entschließungen* (Berlin, 1920).

Farrar-Hockley, Anthony, *Ypres 1914: Death of an Army* (1967; London, 1970).

Fitzgerald, Percy, *A Day's Tour: A Journey through France and Belgium* (London, 1887).

Flandern nach 50 Jahren: Erinnerungsfahrt. 'Grünes Korps' Langemarck 1914/1964 (Düsseldorf, 1964).

Fox, Frank, *The King's Pilgrimage* (London, 1922).

Frichet, Henry, *La Bataille de l'Yser: Dixmude—la maison du passeur* (Paris, 1918).

The Gate of Eternal Memories: 'Menin Gate at Midnight' (or 'The Ghosts of Menin Gate'). The Story of Captain Will Longstaff's Great Allegorical Painting (Melbourne, [c.1929]).

Gmelin, Ulrich (ed.), *Das Langemarck-Studium der Reichsstudentenführung* (Großenhain, 1939).

Goebbels, Joseph, *Die Tagebücher von Joseph Goebbels*, ed. Elke Fröhlich, pt. I. *Aufzeichnungen 1923–1941*, vol. viii. *April–November 1940* (Munich, 1998).

Le Goffic, Charles, *Dixmude: Un chapitre de l'histoire des fusiliers marins (7 Octobre – 10 Novembre 1914)* (Paris, 1915).

Grand Quartier général, *Aux champs de gloire: Le Front belge de l'Yser*, illustr. Urbain Wernaers (Brussels, 1921).

Gruchmann, Lothar, and Weber, Reinhard (eds.), *Der Hitler-Prozess 1924: Wortlaut der Hauptverhandlung vor dem Volksgericht München I*, iv. *19.–25. Verhandlungstag* (Munich, 1999).

Hamilton, Ernest W., *The First Seven Divisions: Being a Detailed Account of the Fighting from Mons to Ypres* (London, 1916).

Heidegger, Martin, 'Universität Freiburg: Feierliche Imatrikulation, verbunden mit Langemarckgedächtnis', in Guido Schneeberger (ed.), *Nachlese zu Heidegger: Dokumente zu seinem Leben und Denken* (Bern, 1962), 156–8.

Heinemann, Olaf, *Der Tag von Langemarck: Geschichten von draußen und daheim* (Leipzig, 1915).

Heins, Armand, and Meunier, Georges, *En pays flamand: Croquis et notes* (Ghent, 1892).

Hindenburg, [Paul] von, *Out of My Life*, trans. F. A. Holt (London, 1920).

Hitler, Adolf, *Mein Kampf: Unexpurgated Edition*, trans. James Murphy (London, 1939).

Hitler, Adolf, *Mein Kampf*, trans. Ralph Manheim, introd. D. C. Watt (London, 1972).

Hitler, Adolf, *Mein Kampf: Eine kritische Edition*, ed. Christian Hartmann et al., 2 vols. (3rd edn., Munich, 2016).

Hoffmann, Heinrich (ed.), *Mit Hitler im Westen* (Berlin, 1940).

D'Ideville, Henry, *Lettres flamandes: Cassel, Bergues Saint Winoc, Dunkerque, Ypres, Oxelaere* (Paris, 1876).

Jünger, Ernst, *Der Arbeiter: Herrschaft und Gestalt* (Hamburg, 1932).

Jünger, Ernst, *Kriegstagebuch 1914–1918*, ed. Helmuth Kiesel (Stuttgart, 2010).

Jünger, Ernst, *In Stahlgewittern: Historisch-kritische Ausgabe*, ed. Helmuth Kiesel, 2 vols. (Stuttgart, 2013).

Kaufmann, Günter (ed.), *Langemarck: Das Opfer der Jugend an allen Fronten* (Stuttgart, 1938).

Kempowski, Walter, *Das Echolot: Ein kollektives Tagebuch. Januar und Februar 1943*, ii. *18. bis 31. Januar 1943* (4th edn., Munich, 1993).

Kennedy, Alexander B. W., *Ypres to Verdun: A Collection of Photographs of the War Areas in France & Flanders* (London, 1921).

Kindt, Werner (ed.), *Grundschriften der deutschen Jugendbewegung* (Düsseldorf, 1963).

Kollwitz, Hans (ed.), *The Diary and Letters of Kaethe [sic] Kollwitz*, trans. Richard and Clara Winston (Evanston, IL, 1988).

Kopetzky, Helmut, *In den Tod—Hurra! Deutsche Jugend-Regimenter im Ersten Weltkrieg: Ein historischer Tatsachenbericht über Langemarck* (Cologne, 1981).

Kretzschmar, W., *Deutsche Heldenfriedhöfe in Belgien und Frankreich* (2nd edn., Pößneck, 1928).

Kriegslieder des XV. Korps 1914–1915 von den Vogesen bis Ypern (Berlin, 1915).

Langemarck-Ausschuß (Hochschule und Heer) (ed.), *Langemarck-Gedanken* (Berlin, 1932).

Langemarck lebt: Wiedergabe der auf der Langemarck-Gedenkstunde d. Hannoverschen Studentschaften am 19. November 1941 gehaltenen Ansprachen (Hanover, 1941).

Liddell Hart, [Basil], *A History of the World War 1914–1918* (London, 1934).

Ludendorff, Erich, *My War Memories 1914–1918*, 2 vols. (London, 1919).

Luks, H. T., *Belgien und Holland: Praktisches Handbuch für Reisende* (Grieben Reise-Bibliothek 22; Berlin, 1891).

Macdonald, Lyn, *They Called it Passchendaele: The Story of the Third Battle of Ypres and of the Men Who Fought in It* (London, 1978).

McNair, Wilson, *Blood & Iron: Impressions from the Front in France & Flanders* (London, 1916).

Magrath, C. J., *Ypres–Yper: A Few Notes on Its History before the War* (London, [1918]).

Magrath, C. J., 'Life in Ypres, 1914–1918', in *The Pilgrim's Guide to the Ypres Salient* (London, [1920]), 1–4.

Mann, Thomas, *Der Zauberberg: Roman*, ed. Michael Neumann (Große kommentierte Frankfurter Ausgabe 5; Frankfurt am Main, 2002).

Mann, Thomas, *The Magic Mountain*, trans. H. T. Lowe-Porter (London, 1927).

Morris, Joseph E., *Belgium* (Beautiful Europe; London, 1915).

Mottram, R[alph] H[ale], *The Spanish Farm Trilogy 1914–1918* (London, 1927).

Mottram, R[alph] H[ale], *Ten Years Ago: Armistice & Other Memories. Forming a Pendant to 'The Spanish Farm Trilogy'*, foreword W. E. Bates (London, 1928).

Mottram, R[alph] H[ale], *Through the Menin Gate* (London, 1932).

Mottram, R[alph] H[ale], *Journey to the Western Front: Twenty Years After* (London, 1936).

Nolan, Patrick, *The Irish Dames of Ypres: Being a History of the Royal Irish Abbey of Ypres* (Dublin, 1908).

Oberkommando der Wehrmacht (ed.), *Sieg über Frankreich: Berichte und Bilder* (Berlin, 1940).

O'Brien, R[ichard] Barry (ed.), *The Irish Nuns of Ypres: An Episode of the War*, introd. John Redmond (London, 1915).

Office du Tourisme de Comines-Warneton, *14–18 Remembrance* (Comines, [2014]).

Omond, G. W. T., and Forestier, A., *Bruges and West Flanders: Painted by A. Forestier; Described by G. W. T. Omond* (London, 1906).

Oxenham, John, *High Altars: The Battle-Fields of France and Flanders as I Saw Them* (London, 1918).

Pinguet, J[ean], *Trois étapes de la Brigade des Marins: La Marne–Gand–Dixmude* (Paris, 1918).

Pollard, Hugh B. C., *The Story of Ypres* (London, 1917).

Pollard, Hugh B. C., *Ypern und sein Untergang* (Bern, 1917).

Pollard, Hugh B. C., *Ypres: En stads hjältesaga* (Stockholm, 1917).

Pulteney, William, and Brice, Beatrix, *The Immortal Salient: An Historical Record and Complete Guide for Pilgrims to Ypres* (4th edn., London, 1926).

Reed, Henry, 'Lessons of War', in Jon Stallworthy (ed.), *The Oxford Book of War Poetry* (Oxford, 1984), 254–7.

Reed, Paul, *Walking the Salient: A Walkers [sic] Guide to the Ypres Salient* (Battleground Europe; Barnsley, 1999).

Reichsarchiv/Kriegsgeschichtliche Forschungsanstalt des Heeres (ed.), *Der Weltkrieg 1914–1918: Die militärischen Operationen zu Lande*, 14 + 2 vols. (Berlin, 1925–56).

Renn, Ludwig, 'Deutschland, Deutschland über alles', in Kurt Kläber (ed.), *Der Krieg: Das erste Volksbuch vom großen Krieg* (Berlin, 1929), 34–6.

Rice, Stanley, *Neuve Chapelle: India's Memorial in France 1914–1918* (London, [1927]).

Rijksstudentenverbond (ed.), *Het Langemarck-Studium in Vlaanderen* (Brussels, [1941]).

Roberts, F. J. (ed.), *The Wipers Times: Including for the First Time in One Volume a Facsimile Reproduction of the Complete Series of the Famous Wartime Trench Magazine*, foreword Lord Plumer (London, 1930).

Robida, A[lbert], *Les Villes martyres: Lithographies originales* (Paris, 1914).

Ronarc'h, [Pierre-Alexis], *Souvenirs de la guerre (août 1914–septembre 1915)* (Paris, 1921).

Schauwecker, Franz, *So war der Krieg: 230 Kampfaufnahmen aus der Front* ([7th edn.,] Berlin, 1928).

Schreiner, Wilhelm, *Der Tod von Ypern: Schicksal in Flandern* (7th edn., Herborn, [1927]).

Schumann, Harry, *Geist von Langemarck: Das Erlebnis von 1914* (Dresden, 1934).

Schwäbische Kunde aus dem großen Krieg, ii, ed. Hauptmann d. Res. Schmückle im Auftrag des Königl. Württ. Kriegsministeriums (Stuttgart, 1918).

Schwarz, Hans, *Die Wiedergeburt des heroischen Menschen: Eine Langemarck Rede vor der Greifswalder Studentenschaft am 11. November 1928* (Berlin, 1930).

[Schwink, Otto], *Ypres, 1914: An Official Account Published by Order of the German General Staff* (London, 1919).

Sedgwick, S[idney] N[ewman], *At the Menin Gate: A Melodrama, and a Parable, Written for the League of Nations Union* (London, [1929]).
Seton Hutchison, Graham, *Pilgrimage* (London, 1935).
Soldan, George, *Der Mensch und die Schlacht der Zukunft* (Oldenburg, 1925).
Stad Ieper (ed.), *50 jaar Toerisme Ieper: Catalogus tentoonstelling 26 oktober tot 9 november 2008* (Ypres, 2008).
Swettenham, John, *To Seize Victory: The Canadian Corps in World War I* (Toronto, 1965).
Swinton, Ernest (ed.), *Twenty Years After: The Battlefields of 1914–1918 Then and Now* (London, 1936).
Taylor, A. J. P., *The First World War: An Illustrated History* (London, 1963).
Taylor, H[enry] A[rchibald], *Good-Bye to the Battlefields: To-Day and Yesterday on the Western Front* (London, 1928).
Terraine, John, *The Road to Passchendaele: The Flanders Offensive of 1917. A Study in Inevitability* (London, 1977).
Toc H, *Over There: A Little Guide for Pilgrims to Ypres, the Salient, and Talbot House, Poperinghe* (London, 1935).
Unruh, Karl, *Langemarck: Legende und Wirklichkeit* (Koblenz, 1986).
Vidal de La Blache, Paul, *États et nations de l'Europe: Autour de la France* (Paris, 1891).
Volkmann, Erich Otto, *Der Große Krieg 1914–1918: Kurzgefaßte Darstellung auf Grund der amtlichen Quellen des Reichsarchivs* (5th edn., Berlin [1924]).
Waidelich, W., *10 Jahre Langemarck-Studium Königsberg (Pr.): Kriegsrundbrief des Langemarck-Studiums Königsberg (Pr) aus Anlaß seines 10jährigen Bestehens* (Königsberg, 1944).
Walther, Karl August (ed.), *Das Langemarckbuch der deutschen Studentenschaft* (Leipzig, 1933).
Ward, Lock and Co.'s Guide to Belgium, Including the Ardennes and Luxemburg (5th edn., London, 1906).
Ward, Lock and Co.'s Handbook to Belgium and the Battlefields (7th edn., London, 1921).
Waugh, Evelyn, *Put Out More Flags* (London, 1943).
[Wehner, Josef Magnus], *Langemarck: Ein Vermächtnis* (Munich, 1932).
Der Weltkrieg im Bild: Frontaufnahmen aus den Archiven der Entente, introd. Werner Beumelburg (Munich, [*c*.1926]).
The Western Front: Drawings by Muirhead Bone (London, 1917).
Williams, G. Valentine, *With Our Army in France and Flanders* (London, 1915).
Williamson, Henry, *The Wet Flanders Plain* (London, 1929).
Wolff, Leon, *In Flanders Fields: The 1917 Campaign* (1958; London, 1960).
Wyndham Lewis, [Percy], *Blasting and Bombardiering* (London, 1937).
Ypres: Guide illustré du touriste à Ypres et aux environs ([2nd edn.,] Ypres, 1909).
Ypres and the Battles of Ypres (Illustrated Michelin Guides to the Battle-Fields 1914–1918; Clermont-Ferrand, 1919).
Zerkaulen, Heinrich, *Jugend von Langemarck: Ein Schauspiel in drei Akten und einem Nachspiel* (5th edn., Leipzig, 1935).

Ziese, Maxim, and Ziese-Beringer, Hermann, *Das unsichtbare Denkmal: Heute an der Westfront* (Berlin, [1930]).

Zuckmayer, Carl, *A Part of Myself* (London, 1970).

Newsreels

Pathé Gazette

Films

Ypres, dir. Walter Summers (GB, 1925).

Passchendaele, dir. Paul Gross (CA, 2008).

Audio Recordings

F&M, *Every Light Must Fade* (CA, 2008).

Websites

'Dire Heroes: Beyond Ypres' <https://boardgamegeek.com/blogger/715> [accessed 29 November 2016]

'Het IJzerpanorama' <http://www.wereldoorlog1418.nl/ijzerpanorama/index.html> [accessed 25 September 2015]

Secondary Literature

Abenheim, Donald, *Reforging the Iron Cross: The Search for Tradition in the West German Armed Forces* (Princeton, 1988).

Afflerbach, Holger, *Falkenhayn: Politisches Denken und Handeln im Kaiserreich* (Munich, 1994).

Ashplant, T[imothy] G., Dawson, Graham, and Roper, Michael (eds.), *The Politics of War Memory and Commemoration* (London, 2000).

Badsey, Stephen, and Taylor, Philip, 'Images of Battle: The Press, Propaganda and Passchendaele', in Peter H. Liddle (ed.), *Passchendaele in Perspective: The Third Battle of Ypres* (London, 1997), 371–89.

Baird, Jay W., *To Die for Germany: Heroes in the Nazi Pantheon* (Bloomington, IN, 1990).

Baird, Jay W., *Hitler's War Poets: Literature and Politics in the Third Reich* (Cambridge, 2008).

Barthes, Roland, *Mythologies*, trans. Annette Lavers and Richard Howard (New York, 2012).

Becker, Annette, *War and Faith: The Religious Imagination in France, 1914–1930*, trans. Helen McPhail (Oxford, 1998).

Beckett, Ian F. W., *Ypres: The First Battle, 1914* (Harlow, 2004).

Behrenbeck, Sabine, *Der Kult um die toten Helden: Nationalsozialistische Mythen, Rituale und Symbole 1923 bis 1945* (2nd edn., Cologne, 2011).

Berghoff, Hartmut, Korte, Barbara, Schneider, Ralf, and Harvie, Christopher (eds.), *The Making of Modern Tourism: The Cultural History of the British Experience, 1600–2000* (Basingstoke, 2002).

Bessel, Richard, and Schumann, Dirk, 'Introduction: Violence, Normality, and the Construction of Postwar Europe', in Bessel and Schumann (eds.), *Life after Death: Approaches to a Cultural and Social History of Europe during the 1940s and 1950s* (Cambridge, 2003), 1–13.

Bostyn, Frank, et al., *Passchendaele 1917: The Story of the Fallen and Tyne Cot Cemetery* (Barnsley, 2007).

Brandt, Susanne, *Vom Kriegsschauplatz zum Gedächtnisraum: Die Westfront 1914–1940* (Baden-Baden, 2000).

Brandt, Susanne, 'Das "In Flanders Fields Museum" in Ypern', *Geschichte in Wissenschaft und Unterricht* 67 (2016), 471–6.

Brown, Mary, and Massey, Carolyn, 'Teaching "the Lessons of Satire": Using *The Wipers Times* to Build an Enquiry on the First World War', *Teaching History* 155 (2014), 20–8.

Burke, Peter, Grange, William, Kessel, Martina, and Waterlow, Jonathan, 'Forum: Humour', *German History* 33 (2015), 609–23.

Buschmann, Nikolaus, and Reimann, Aribert, 'Die Konstruktion historischer Erfahrung: Neue Wege zu einer Erfahrungsgeschichte des Krieges', in Buschmann and Horst Carl (eds.), *Die Erfahrung des Krieges: Erfahrungsgeschichtliche Perspektiven von der Französischen Revolution bis zum Zweiten Weltkrieg* (Paderborn, 2001), 261–71.

Carmichael, Jane, *First World War Photographers* (London, 1989).

Chickering, Roger, *Imperial Germany and the Great War, 1914–1918* (3rd edn., Cambridge, 2014).

Conboy, Martin, and Steel, John (eds.), *The Routledge Companion to British Media History* (London, 2015).

Connelly, Mark, *We Can Take It! Britain and the Memory of the Second World War* (Harlow, 2004).

Connelly, Mark, *Steady the Buffs! A Regiment, a Region, and the Great War* (Oxford, 2006).

Connelly, Mark, 'The Ypres League and the Commemoration of the Ypres Salient, 1914–1940', *War in History* 16 (2009), 51–76.

Connelly, Mark, *Celluloid War Memorials: The British Instructional Films Company and the Memory of the Great War* (Exeter, 2016).

Constandt, Marc, *Een eeuw vakantie: 100 jaar toerisme in West-Vlaanderen* (Tielt, 1986).

Conway, Martin, *The Sorrows of Belgium: Liberation and Political Reconstruction, 1944–1947* (Oxford, 2012).

Cook, Tim, *Clio's Warriors: Canadian Historians and the Writing of the World Wars* (Vancouver, 2006).

Cork, Richard, *A Bitter Truth: Avant-Garde Art and the Great War* (New Haven, 1994).

Das, Santanu (ed.), *Race, Empire and First World War Writing* (Cambridge, 2011).

De Schaepdrijver, Sophie, 'Occupation, Propaganda and the Idea of Belgium', in Aviel Roshwald and Richard Stites (eds.), *European Culture in the Great War: The Arts, Entertainment, and Propaganda, 1914–1918* (Cambridge, 1999), 267–94.

De Schaepdrijver, Sophie, 'Death is Elsewhere: The Shifting Locus of Tragedy in Belgian Great War Literature', *Yale French Studies* 102 (2002), 94–114.

De Schaepdrijver, Sophie, *La Belgique et la Première Guerre mondiale* (Brussels, 2004).

De Schaepdrijver, Sophie, *Gabrielle Petit: The Death and Life of a Female Spy in the First World War* (London, 2015).

De Schaepdrijver, Sophie, 'Making Loss Legible: Käthe Kollwitz and Jane Catulle-Mendès', in Sarah Posman, Cedric Van Dijck, and Marysa Demoor (eds.), *The Intellectual Response to the First World War: How the Conflict Impacted on Ideas, Methods and Fields of Enquiry* (Brighton, 2017), 145–59.

Demm, Eberhard, *Censorship and Propaganda in World War I: A Complete History* (London, forthcoming 2019).

Dendooven, Dominiek, *The Menin Gate and the Last Post: Ypres as Holy Ground* (Koksijde, 2001).

Dendooven, Dominiek, 'The Journey Back: On the Nature of Donations to the "In Flanders Fields Museum"', in Nicholas J. Saunders and Paul Cornish (eds.), *Contested Objects: Material Memories of the Great War* (London, 2009), 60–72.

Dendooven, Dominiek, 'Asia in Flanders Fields: A Transnational History of Indians and Chinese on the Western Front, 1914–1920', PhD thesis, Universities of Antwerp and Kent, 2018.

Dendooven, Dominiek, and Chielens, Piet (eds.), *World War I: Five Continents in Flanders* (Tielt, 2008).

Derez, Mark, 'A Belgian Salient for Reconstruction: People and *Patrie*, Landscape and Memory', in Peter H. Liddle (ed.), *Passchendaele in Perspective: The Third Battle of Ypres* (London, 1997), 437–58.

De Wever, Bruno, '"Rebellen" an der Ostfront: Die flämischen Freiwilligen der Legion "Flandern" und der Waffen-SS', *Vierteljahreshefte für Zeitgeschichte* 39 (1991), 589–610.

De Wever, Bruno, 'Diksmuide: de Ijzertoren. Strijd om de helden von de Oorlog', in Jo Tollebeek, Geert Buelens, Gita Deneckere, Chantal Kesteloot, and Sophie De Schaepdrijver (eds.), *België: Een parcours van herinnering*, ii. *Plaatsen van tweedracht, crisis en nostalgie* (Amsterdam, 2008), 60–71.

Dithmar, Reinhard (ed.), *Der Langemarck-Mythos in Dichtung und Unterricht* (Berlin, 1992).

Dixon, Thomas, *Weeping Britannia: Portrait of a Nation in Tears* (Oxford, 2015).

Dyer, Geoff, *The Missing of the Somme* (London, 1994).

Echternkamp, Jörg, *Soldaten im Nachkrieg: Historische Deutungskonflikte und westdeutsche Demokratisierung 1945–1955* (Munich, 2014).

Edwards, John Peter, 'A War Remembered: Commemoration, Battlefield Tourism and British Collective Memory of the Great War', DPhil thesis, University of Sussex, 2005.

Elliott, Sue, and Fox, James, *The Children Who Fought Hitler: A British Outpost in Europe* (London, 2009).

Ernst, Wolfgang, *Im Namen von Geschichte: Sammeln—Speichern—Er/Zählen: Infrastrukturelle Konfigurationen des deutschen Gedächtnisses* (Munich, 2003).

Evans, Suzanne, *Mothers of Heroes, Mothers of Martyrs: World War I and the Politics of Grief* (Montreal, 2007).

Fischer, Hannelore (ed.), *Käthe Kollwitz: Die Trauernden Eltern. Ein Mahnmal für den Frieden* (Cologne, 1999).

Fox, Colin, 'The Myths of Langemarck', *Imperial War Museum Review* 10 (1995), 13–25.

Freytag, Anette, and Van Driessche, Thomas, 'Die Deutschen Soldatenfriedhöfe des Ersten Weltkriegs in Flandern', *Relicta* 7 (2011), 163–228.

Fuhrmeister, Christian, 'Klatschmohn und Ochsenbult: Zur Ikonographie der Kriegsgräberstätten des Volksbundes Deutsche Kriegsgräberfürsorge', in Gert Gröning and Uwe Schneider (eds.), *Gartenkultur und nationale Identität: Strategien nationaler und regionaler Identitätsstiftung in der deutschen Gartenkultur* (Worms, 2001), 119–34.

Fussell, Paul, *The Great War and Modern Memory* (London, 1975).

Gerwarth, Robert, and Horne, John (eds.), *War in Peace: Paramilitary Violence in Europe after the Great War* (Oxford, 2013).

Gerwarth, Robert, and Manela, Erez (eds.), *Empires at War 1911–1923* (Oxford, 2014).

Geyer, Michael, 'The Place of the Second World War in German Memory and History', *New German Critique* 71 (1997), 5–40.

Goebel, Stefan, *The Great War and Medieval Memory: War, Remembrance and Medievalism in Britain and Germany, 1914–1940* (Cambridge, 2007).

Goebel, Stefan, 'Exhibitions', in Jay Winter and Jean-Louis Robert (eds.), *Capital Cities at War: Paris, London, Berlin 1914–1919*, ii. *A Cultural History* (Cambridge, 2007), 143–87.

Goebel, Stefan, 'Commemorative Cosmopolis: Transnational Networks of Remembrance in Post-War Coventry', in Goebel and Derek Keene (eds.), *Cities into Battlefields: Metropolitan Scenarios, Experiences and Commemorations of Total War* (Farnham, 2011), 163–83.

Goebel, Stefan, 'Cities', in Jay Winter (ed.), *The Cambridge History of the First World War*, ii. *The State* (Cambridge, 2014), 358–81.

Gough, Paul, 'Sites in the Imagination: The Beaumont Hamel Newfoundland Memorial on the Somme', *Cultural Geographies* 11 (2004), 235–58.

Grayzel, Susan R., *Women's Identities at War: Gender, Motherhood, and Politics in Britain and France during the First World War* (Chapel Hill, NC, 1999).

Green, Andrew, *Writing the Great War: Sir James Edmonds and the Official Histories 1915–1948* (London, 2003).

Gregory, Adrian, *The Silence of Memory: Armistice Day 1919–1946* (Oxford, 1994).

Gregory, Adrian, *The Last Great War: British Society and the First World War* (Cambridge, 2008).

Haas, Stefan, 'Die kommunikationstheoretische Wende und die Geschichtswissenschaft', in Andreas Schulz and Andreas Wirsching (eds.), *Parlamentarische Kulturen in Europa: Das Parlament als Kommunikationsraum* (Düsseldorf, 2012), 29–43.

Hammond, Michael, and Williams, Michael (eds.), *British Silent Cinema and the Great War* (Basingstoke, 2011).

Hanna, Emma, *The Great War on the Small Screen: Representing the First World War in Contemporary Britain* (Edinburgh, 2009).

Harris, J. P., *Douglas Haig and the First World War* (Cambridge, 2008).

Haultain-Gall, Matthew, 'Bean, the Third Battle of Ypres and the Australian Narrative of the First World War', *Australian Historical Studies* 47 (2016), 135–51.

Herf, Jeffrey, *Reactionary Modernism: Technology, Culture, and Politics in Weimar and the Third Reich* (Cambridge, 1984).

Hettling, Manfred, and Echternkamp, Jörg (eds.), *Gefallenendenken im globalen Vergleich: Nationale Tradition, politische Legitimation und Individualisierung der Erinnerung* (Munich, 2013).

Heyvaert, Bert, '"A Little Sprig of the Empire": De Britse kolonie in Ieper tijdens het interbellum (1919–1940)', Licentiate dissertation, University of Leuven, 2002.

Hinrichsen, Alex W., *Baedeker's Reisehandbücher 1832–1990: Bibliographie 1832–1944; Verzeichnis 1948–1990. Verlagsgeschichte mit Abbildungen und zusätzlichen Übersichten* (2nd edn., Bevern, 1991).

Holmes, Richard, 'Sir John French and Lord Kitchener', in Brian Bond (ed.), *The First World War and British Military History* (Oxford, 1991), 113–39.

Horne, John, and Kramer, Alan, *German Atrocities, 1914: A History of Denial* (New Haven, 2001).

Howe, Horst, Missinne, Robert, and Verbeke, Roger, *De Duitse begraafplaats in Langemark* (Bruges, 2011).

Hubrechtsen, F[reddy], *Het Panorama van de IJzerslag, 1921* (Brussels, 1993).

Hüppauf, Bernd, 'Langemarck, Verdun and the Myth of a *New Man* in Germany after the First World War', *War & Society* 6/2 (1988), 70–103.

Hüppauf, Bernd, 'Langemarck-Mythos', in Gerhard Hirschfeld, Gerd Krumeich, and Irina Renz (eds.), *Enzyklopädie Erster Weltkrieg* (2nd edn., Padernborn, 2004), 671–2.

Hynes, Samuel, *A War Imagined: The First World War and English Culture* (London, 1990).

Iles, Jennifer, 'Recalling the Ghosts of War: Performing Tourism on the Battlefields of the Western Front', *Text and Performance Quarterly* 26 (2006), 162–80.

Ilgen, Volker, '"Ein sichtbares Zeichen zum Gedächtnis der Helden errichten": Krieg in Straßennamen', in Christian Geinitz et al. (eds.), *Kriegsgedenken in Freiburg: Trauer—Kult—Verdrängung* (Freiburg, 1995), 131–69.

Inglis, K[en] S., *Sacred Places: War Memorials in the Australian Landscape* (Melbourne, 1998).

Jakob, Volker, and Sagurna, Stephan (eds.), *Front 14/18: The Great War in 3D* (Steinfurt, 2014).

Ketelsen, Uwe-K., '"Die Jugend von Langemarck": Ein poetisch-politisches Motiv der Zwischenkriegszeit', in Thomas Koebner, Rolf-Peter Janz, and Frank Trommler (eds.), *'Mit uns zieht die neue Zeit': Der Mythos der Jugend* (Frankfurt am Main, 1985), 68–96.

King, Alex, *Memorials of the Great War in Britain: The Symbolism and Politics of Remembrance* (Oxford, 1998).

Kinsbergen, Marjolein, 'Memory Wars? Nationalisme en de herdenking van de Eerste Wereldoorlog in Duitse, Britse en Franse reisgidsen tijdens het interbellum', *Handelingen van het Genootschap vor Geschiedenis to Brugge* 151 (2014), 195–222.

Köster, Markus, '"Eine Burg des Glaubens": Ideologie, Architektur und Praxis nationalsozialistischer Jugendbauten am Beispiel der westfälischen HJ-Führerschule Haldem', in Edeltraut Klueting (ed.), *Denkmalpflege und Architektur in Westfalen 1933–1945* (Münster, 1995), 91–110.

Kolbe, Wiebke, 'Trauer und Tourismus: Reisen des Volksbundes Deutsche Kriegsgräberfürsorge 1950–2010', *Zeithistorische Forschungen* 14 (2017), 68–92.

Koselleck, Reinhart, and Jeismann, Michael (eds.), *Der politische Totenkult: Kriegerdenkmäler in der Moderne* (Munich, 1994).

Koshar, Rudy, '"What Ought to be Seen": Tourists' Guidebooks and National Identities in Modern Germany and Europe', *Journal of Contemporary History* 33 (1998), 323–40.

Koshar, Rudy, *From Monuments to Traces: Artifacts of German Memory, 1870–1990* (Berkeley and Los Angeles, 2000).

Kramer, Alan, *Dynamic of Destruction: Culture and Mass Killing in the First World War* (Oxford, 2007).

Krumeich, Gerd, 'Langemarck', in Étienne François and Hagen Schulze (eds.), *Deutsche Erinnerungsorte*, iii (Munich, 2001), 292–309.

Krumeich, Gerd, 'Zwischen soldatischem Nationalismus und NS-Ideologie: Werner Beumelburg und die Erzählung des Ersten Weltkriegs', in Wolfram Pyta and Carsten Kretschmann (eds.), *Burgfrieden und Union sacrée: Literarische Deutungen und politische Ordnungsvorstellungen in Deutschland und Frankreich 1914–1933* (Munich, 2011), 295–312.

Kühne, Thomas, *Belonging and Genocide: Hitler's Community, 1918–1945* (New Haven, 2010).

Lagrou, Pieter, *The Legacy of Nazi Occupation: Patriotic Memory and Nazi Recovery in Western Europe, 1945–1965* (Cambridge, 2000).

Lamb, Robert J., *James Kerr-Lawson: A Canadian Abroad* (Windsor, WO, 1983).

Laqueur, Thomas W., *The Work of the Dead: A Cultural History of Mortal Remains* (Princeton, 2015).

Larabee, Mark D., 'Baedekers as Casualty: Great War Nationalism and the Fate of Travel Writing', *Journal of the History of Ideas* 71 (2010), 457–80.

Lauwers, Delphine, 'Le Saillant d'Ypres entre reconstruction et construction d'un lieu de mémoire: Un long precessus de négociations mémoirelles, de 1914 à nos jours', PhD thesis, European University Institute, 2014.

Lefebvre, Henri, *The Production of Space*, trans. Donald Nicholson-Smith (Malden, MA, 1991).

Lehnert, Herbert, 'Langemarck—historisch und symbolisch', *Orbis Litterarum* 42 (1987), 271–90.

Lloyd, David W., *Battlefield Tourism: Pilgrimage and the Commemoration of the Great War in Britain, Australia and Canada, 1919–1939* (Oxford, 1998).

Löhr, Wolfgang, 'Langemar(c)k und der Kartellverband katholischer deutscher Studentenvereine', in Marc Zirlewagen (ed.), *'Wir siegen oder fallen': Deutsche Studenten im Ersten Weltkrieg* (Cologne, 2008), 397–406.

Longworth, Philip, *The Unending Vigil: A History of the Commonwealth War Graves Commission 1917–1984* (London, 1985).

Lowenthal, David, *The Past is a Foreign Country—Revisited* (Cambridge, 2015).

McCarthy, Helen, 'The League of Nations, Public Ritual and National Identity in Britain, *c.*1919–1956', *History Workshop Journal* 70 (2010), 108–32.

Macfarlane, Robert, *The Old Ways: A Journey on Foot* (London, 2012).

Malvern, Sue, 'War Tourisms: "Englishness", Art, and the First World War', *Oxford Art Journal* 24 (2001), 45–66.

Malvern, Sue, *Modern Art, Britain and the Great War: Witnessing, Testimony and Remembrance* (New Haven, 2004).

Meire, Johan, *De stilte van de Salient: De herinnering aan de Eerste Wereldoorlog rond Ieper* (Tielt, 2003).

Mitter, Rana, 'War and Memory since 1945', in Roger Chickering, Dennis Showalter, and Hans van de Ven (eds.), *The Cambridge History of War*, iv. *War and the Modern World* (Cambridge, 2012), 542–65.

Moeller, Robert G., *War Stories: The Search for a Usable Past in the Federal Republic of Germany* (Berkeley and Los Angeles, 2001).

Mosse, George L., 'National Cemeteries and National Revival: The Cult of the Fallen Soldiers in Germany', *Journal of Contemporary History* 14 (1979), 1–20.

Mosse, George L., *Fallen Soldiers: Reshaping the Memory of the World Wars* (Oxford, 1990).

Moyd, Michelle, 'Centring a Sideshow: Local Experiences of the First World War in Africa', *First World War Studies* 7 (2016), 111–30.

Myers, Jason, *The Great War and Memory in Irish Culture, 1918–2010* (Palo Alto, CA, 2013).

Nelson, Robert L., *German Soldier Newspapers of the First World War* (Cambridge, 2011).

Nipperdey, Thomas, *Deutsche Geschichte 1866–1918*, i. *Arbeitswelt und Bürgergeist* (Munich, 1990).

Nora, Pierre, 'Between Memory and History: *Les Lieux de Mémoire*', *Representations* 26 (1989), 7–24.

Nübel, Christoph, *Durchhalten und Überleben an der Westfront: Raum und Körper im Ersten Weltkrieg* (Paderborn, 2014).

Pennell, Catriona, 'Learning Lessons from War? Inclusions and Exclusions in Teaching First World War History in English Secondary Schools', *History & Memory* 28/1 (2016), 36–70.

Peukert, Detlev J. K., *The Weimar Republic: The Crisis of Classical Modernity* (London, 1993).

Pöhlmann, Markus, *Kriegsgeschichte und Geschichtspolitik: Der Erste Weltkrieg. Die amtliche deutsche Militärgeschichtsschreibung 1914–1956* (Paderborn, 2002).

Prior, Robin, and Wilson, Trevor, *Passchendaele: The Untold Story* (2nd edn., New Haven, 2002).

Prost, Antoine, *In the Wake of War: 'Les Anciens Combattants' and French Society*, trans. Helen McPhail (Providence, RI, 1992).

Prost, Antoine, 'Verdun', in Pierre Nora (ed.), *Realms of Memory: The Construction of the French Past*, iii. *Symbols*, trans. Arthur Goldhammer (New York, 1998), 376–401.

Prost, Antoine, 'The Dead', in Jay Winter (ed.), *The Cambridge History of the First World War*, iii. *Civil Society* (Cambridge, 2014), 561–91.

Pyta, Wolfram, *Hindenburg: Herrschaft zwischen Hohenzollern und Hitler* (Munich, 2009).

Reichherzer, Frank, *'Alles ist Front!': Wehrwissenschaften in Deutschland und die Bellifizierung der Gesellschaft vom Ersten Weltkrieg bis in den Kalten Krieg* (Paderborn, 2012).

Reimann, Aribert, *Der große Krieg der Sprachen: Untersuchungen zur historischen Semantik in Deutschland und England zur Zeit des Ersten Weltkriegs* (Essen, 2000).

Rogan, Eugene, *The Fall of the Ottomans: The Great War in the Middle East, 1914–1920* (London, 2015).

Roper, Michael, *The Secret Battle: Emotional Survival in the Great War* (Manchester, 2009).

Rother, Rainer (ed.), *Geschichtsort Olympiagelände 1909–1936–2006* (Berlin, 2006).

Sabol, Steven, 'A Brief Note from the Editor', *First World War Studies* 1 (2010), 1–2.

Saunders, Nicholas J., *Killing Time: Archaeology and the First World War* ([2nd edn.,] Stroud, 2010).

Saunders, Nicholas J., and Cornish, Paul (eds.), *Contested Objects: Material Memories of the Great War* (London, 2009).

Scates, Bruce, *Return to Gallipoli: Walking the Battlefields of the Great War* (Cambridge, 2006).

Schmidt, Siegfried J., 'Medien, Kultur: Medienkultur. Ein konstruktivistisches Gesprächsangebot', in Siegfried J. Schmidt (ed.), *Kognition und Gesellschaft: Der Diskurs des Radikalen Konstruktivismus*, ii. (Frankfurt am Main, 1992), 425–50.

Schmidt, Ulf, *Secret Science: A Century of Poison Warfare and Human Experiments* (Oxford, 2015).

Schneider, Gerhard, *'... nicht umsonst gefallen'? Kriegerdenkmäler und Kriegstotenkult in Hannover* (Hanover, 1991).

Schulte, Regina, 'Käthe Kollwitz's Sacrifice', *History Workshop Journal* 41 (1996), 193–221.

Schwarz, Bill, *Memories of Empire*, i. *The White Man's World* (Oxford, 2011).

Seal, Graham, *The Soldiers' Press: Trench Journals in the First World War* (Basingstoke, 2013).

Searle, Muriel V., *Down the Line to Dover: A Pictorial History of Kent's Boat Train Line* (Tunbridge Wells, 1984).

Shelby, Karen D., *Flemish Nationalism and the Great War: The Politics of Memory, Visual Culture and Commemoration* (Basingstoke, 2014).

Sherman, Daniel J., *The Construction of Memory in Interwar France* (Chicago, 1999).

Siebrecht, Claudia, *The Aesthetics of Loss: German Women's Art of the First World War* (Oxford, 2013).

Simmons, Jack, 'Railways, Hotels, and Tourism in Great Britain, 1839–1914', *Journal of Contemporary History* 19 (1984), 201–22.

Smets, Marcel (ed.), *Resurgam: La Reconstruction en Belgique après 1914* (Brussels, 1985).

Steinle, Matthias, 'La Grande Guerre dans la série télévisée *Trente ans d'histoire* (1964): Un projet de réconciliation franco-allemand au sein d'une commémoration gaulliste', in Christian Delporte, Denis Maréchal, Caroline Moine, and Isabelle Veyrat-Masson (eds.), *La Guerre après la guerre: Images et construction des imaginaires de guerre dans l'Europe du XXème siècle* (Paris, 2010), 343–65.

Stichelbaut, Birger, and Chielens, Piet, *The Great War Seen from the Air: In Flanders Fields, 1914–1918* (New Haven, 2014).

Strachan, Hew, *The First World War in Africa* (Oxford, 2004).

Süss, Dietmar, *Death from the Skies: How the British and Germans Survived Bombing in World War II*, trans. Lesley Sharpe and Jeremy Noakes (Oxford, 2014).

Thomson, Alistair, *Anzac Memories: Living with the Legend* (Melbourne, 1994).

Tippett, Maria, *Art at the Service of War: Canada, Art, and the Great War* (Toronto, 1984).

Todman, Dan, *The Great War: Myth and Memory* (London, 2005).

Ulrich, Bernd, *Die Augenzeugen: Deutsche Feldpostbriefe in Kriegs- und Nachkriegszeit 1914–1933* (Essen, 1997).

Vance, Jonathan F., *Death So Noble: Memory, Meaning, and the First World War* (Vancouver, 1997).

Verhey, Jeffrey, *The Spirit of 1914: Militarism, Myth, and Mobilization in Germany* (Cambridge, 2000).

Watson, Alexander, *Enduring the Great War: Combat, Morale and Collapse in the German and British Armies, 1914–1918* (Cambridge, 2008).

Weber, Thomas, *Hitler's First World War: Adolf Hitler, the Men of the List Regiment, and the First World War* (Oxford, 2010).

Welch, David, *Germany and Propaganda in World War I: Pacifism, Mobilization and Total War* (London, 2014).

Weidner, Marcus, '"Wir beantragen...unverzüglich umzubenennen": Die Straßenbenennungspraxis in Westfalen und Lippe im Nationalsozialismus', in Matthias Frese (ed.), *Fragwürdige Ehrungen!? Straßennamen als Instrument von Geschichtspolitik und Erinnerungskultur* (Münster, 2012), 41–98.

Weinrich, Arndt, *Der Weltkrieg als Erzieher: Jugend zwischen Weimarer Republik und Nationalsozialismus* (Essen, 2013).

Williams, Michael, *Ivor Novello: Screen Idol* (London, 2003).

Wills, Clair, *Dublin 1916: The Siege of the GPO* (London, 2009).

Wilson, Ross J., *Landscapes of the Western Front: Materiality during the Great War* (New York, 2012).

Winter, Jay, *Remembering War: The Great War between Memory and History in the Twentieth Century* (New Haven, 2006).

Winter, Jay, 'Commemorating War, 1914–1945', in Roger Chickering, Dennis Showalter, and Hans van de Ven (eds.), *The Cambridge History of War*, iv. *War and the Modern World* (Cambridge, 2012), 310–26.

Winter, Jay, and Prost, Antoine, *The Great War in History: Debates and Controversies, 1914 to the Present* (Cambridge, 2005).

Winter, Jay, and Sivan, Emmanuel (eds.), *War and Remembrance in the Twentieth Century* (Cambridge, 1999).

Wohl, Robert, *The Generation of 1914* (London, 1980).

Ypersele, Laurence van, 'The Great War in Belgian Memories: From Unanimity to Divergence', in Shanti Sumartojo and Ben Wellings (eds.), *Nation, Memory and Great War Commemoration: Mobilizing the Past in Europe, Australia and New Zealand* (Oxford, 2014), 133–47.

Ziemann, Benjamin, *Contested Commemorations: Republican War Veterans and Weimar Political Culture* (Cambridge, 2013).

Ziino, Bart, *A Distant Grief: Australians, War Graves and the Great War* (Crawley, WA, 2007).

PICTURE ACKNOWLEDGEMENTS

Figure 1: from Laurence Binyon and William Strang, *Western Flanders: A Medley of Things Seen, Considered and Imagined* (London, 1899), 6–7.

Figures 2, 5–6, 8–17, 22, and 26–8: from the authors' private collections.

Figures 3, 19, 20, and 21: from In Flanders Field Museum.

Figure 4: from Hugh B. C. Pollard, *Ypern und sein Untergang* (Bern, 1917).

Figures 7, 23, 24, and 29–30: from photographs by the authors.

Figure 18: from Günter Kaufmann (ed.), *Langemarck: Das Opfer der Jugend an allen Fronten* (Stuttgart, 1938), 27.

Figure 25: from Bayerische Staatsbibliothek Munich, Bildarchiv.

Map 2: from C.A.T.A. Tours, Brussels.

INDEX